Exploring Boarding School Challenges for Women and Third Culture Kids

Worlds Away from Home

Edited by Nicky Moxey and Linda Devereux

Routledge
Taylor & Francis Group

LONDON AND NEW YORK

Designed cover image: © Getty Images

First published 2025
by Routledge
4 Park Square, Milton Park, Abingdon, Oxon OX14 4RN

and by Routledge
605 Third Avenue, New York, NY 10158

Routledge is an imprint of the Taylor & Francis Group, an informa business

British Library Cataloguing-in-Publication Data
A catalogue record for this book is available from the British Library

Library of Congress Cataloging-in-Publication Data
Names: Moxey, Nicky, editor. | Devereux, Linda, editor.
Title: Exploring boarding school challenges for women and third culture kids : worlds away from home / edited by Nicky Moxey, Linda Devereux.
Description: Abingdon, Oxon ; New York, NY : Routledge, 2025. | Includes bibliographical references and index. |
Identifiers: LCCN 2024044403 (print) | LCCN 2024044404 (ebook) | ISBN 9781032876313 (paperback) | ISBN 9781032876399 (hardback) | ISBN 9781003533665 (ebook)
Subjects: LCSH: Boarding school students--Psychology. | Boarding schools. | Women--Education. | Girls--Education.
Classification: LCC LC47 .E97 2025 (print) | LCC LC47 (ebook) | DDC 373.1801/9--dc23/eng/20250117
LC record available at https://lccn.loc.gov/2024044403
LC ebook record available at https://lccn.loc.gov/2024044404

ISBN: 9781032876399 (hbk)
ISBN: 9781032876313 (pbk)
ISBN: 9781003533665 (ebk)

DOI: 10.4324/9781003533665

Typeset in Times New Roman
by KnowledgeWorks Global Ltd.

"This well-researched book forms a welcome addition to the growing literature on the psychological fall-out from the British boarding habit. It focusses on those sent away from the warmth of overseas childhoods to abide in schools in an unknown country called 'home'. At an incomprehensible distance from their families, their losses are equally incomprehensible."

Nick Duffell, *psychohistorian and author of* The Making of Them

"In a rich combination of theory and moving personal testimony Moxey and Devereux have assembled narrative accounts by those sent to British boarding schools as very young children. The plight of third culture kids, whose parents were employed in military, mercantile and missionary occupations is central. This important contribution to the literature on boarding school syndrome conveys yet another psychological tragedy of the British Empire and the multiple losses, cruelty and abuse endured. A compelling read, it will be of interest to therapists, historians and those who have suffered a similar childhood."

Joy Schaverien PhD, *Jungian analyst, psychotherapist and author of* Boarding School Syndrome: The Psychological Trauma of the 'Privileged' Child

"This book offers a departure from the literature to date about boarding school survivors. The latest phase of boarding school populations increasingly includes students from overseas and with this, brings its own set of challenges. It is a very welcome addition to the boarding school literature to hear from these third culture survivors and to have their narratives assessed by qualified professionals."

Allison Paech-Ujejski, *Chair and Director of Boarding School Survivors – Support*

"This is a substantial book, combining lived experience accounts with a research-based approach in examining both the cultural and psychological impact of boarding school. The focus on girls' experiences is very welcome. Highly recommended."

Thurstine Basset, *Mental Health Training Consultant, Author, Social Worker, Formerly Director at Boarding Concern*

"What a brave, heart-felt and groundbreaking book. I love that light is being shone on the experiences of female boarding school survivors who lived in another country (third culture kids (TCKs)). In this new collection of personal testimonies interlinked with psychology, Nicky Moxey and Linda Devereux share a compelling look at the impacts of being a TCK. Thank you."

Piers Cross, *author of* How To Survive & Thrive in Challenging Times, *film producer of* Boarding On Insanity, *and podcast host of* An Evolving Man

Exploring Boarding School Challenges for Women and Third Culture Kids

Through personal testimonies, this book offers insights into the boarding school experiences of women and third culture kids (TCKs), examining the particular challenges for those who are sent away from their families and all that is familiar to board in a country that feels worlds away from home.

The stereotype of expatriate families is of glamorous lives lived in exotic locations with access to wealth and privilege. However, many of these families feel pressure to send their children 'home' to boarding school in their passport country without understanding the long-term implications of this choice. This book explores such long-term effects, starting with laying an accessible theoretical framework for the reader by drawing on scholarship from the fields of psychology, the study of TCKs, and the growing understanding of adverse childhood experiences (ACEs). The text then moves into the personal testimonies of 16 individuals, most of whom are TCKs or cross-cultural boarders, shedding light on the particular challenges they've faced. The book ends by offering hope and help with chapters providing insights and practical strategies for supporting those affected by boarding school.

This user-friendly, accessible volume will appeal to professionals working with transcultural boarders, ex-boarders, or those who are considering sending their own children to boarding school.

Nicky Moxey, an ex-boarder, originally spent 33 years as a project manager and Agile coach. She is retraining as an integrative counsellor and intends to work with boarding school survivors after she qualifies.

Linda Devereux is a third culture kid with more than 40 years of teaching experience in schools and universities. Linda is an Adjunct Research Fellow at Charles Sturt University, Australia, where she researches and publishes in the fields of transcultural childhoods, life narrative, boarding school, and the transition to university.

Dedication

Linda: For Max and our children. Your love has kept me writing, and with gratitude to Mum (1934–2024) and Dad (1931–2024) who did not want to send me away.

Nicky: For people like me, who have spent decades knowing that there is something missing, and for the partners of ex-boarders whose emotional needs are not being met; there is hope.

Contents

5 Insights from the personal testimonies: Gendered experiences of childhood boarding   112

LINDA DEVEREUX

5.1 *Abandoned 112*
5.2 *Bereaved 114*
5.3 *Captive in an institution 116*
5.4 *Consequences – dissociation, strategic survival strategies, and mental health problems 120*
5.5 *Mental health challenges – at school and in adult life 122*
5.6 *Boarding schools and gender 122*

6 Insights from personal testimonies: Third culture kids and boarding school   128

LINDA DEVEREUX

6.1 *Multiple losses and unacknowledged grief of TCKs 129*
6.2 *Loss of place and belonging 131*
6.3 *Travel 134*
6.4 *Multiple sources of trauma for TCKs and their families 134*
6.5 *Peer relationships 136*
6.6 *Conclusion 139*

7 Coming home (a therapist's view)   144

ROE WOODROFFE

8 A safe haven   161

ULRIKA ERNVIK

Index   *166*

List of contributors

Linda Devereux is an Adjunct Research Fellow at Charles Sturt University, Australia, where she researches and publishes in the fields of transcultural childhoods, life writing, boarding school, and the transition to university. She is a TCK who grew up in Congo, Scotland, and Australia. Linda has many decades of experience teaching in schools and universities. Her doctoral thesis, an examination of transcultural childhood, resulted from a passion to understand the long-term effects of mobile childhoods and boarding school on children.

Ulrika Ernvik holds a master's in social work qualification and is a licensed psychotherapist and author of the book *Third Culture Kids: A Gift to Care For* (2019). she grew up in Congo and lived in Thailand with her family. Ulrika believes parents ideally should be present for their children, physically and emotionally. She suggests, from her personal and professional experience, how parents who must consider boarding school can ensure that their children are safe and nurtured.

Roe Woodroffe trained first in a psychodynamic and then in an integrative psychosynthesis therapy modality. She retired in 2021 after a 37-year career in private practice, including a decade-long period where she was a tutor at the Re-Vision Centre in London. Many of her clients were ex-boarders. Roe writes about how the patriarchal nature of the boarding school experience impacts our *anima*, our feminine soul, and the importance and urgency of reconnecting with the 'wild' child in us all in order to heal.

Suzanne Zeedyk is a research scientist and developmental psychologist specialising in infant attachment. Based for many years at the University of Dundee, Scotland, as an Honorary Fellow, she has stepped away from full-time academic work to set up an independent consultancy. She now lectures on the topics of relationships, brain development, stress regulation and trauma. Amongst her best-known publications are her book *Sabre Tooth Tigers & Teddy Bears* and her documentary film *The Connected Baby*.

Preface

Each story in this collection is a work of astonishing bravery. It takes a special kind of honesty to recognise early damage in oneself, and to explore that in one's own mind; but to then describe the events that caused that damage, and expose one's soul to the world – and, perhaps, to parents, partners, children – is a work of outstanding courage. Why would anyone want to do that? The short answer is that it is important for people whose boarding school experience has left a wound to tell our stories, to be seen and heard. There is also the wish to alert parents contemplating sending their children to boarding school about the hidden dangers.

If you read with a sensitive ear, you will find common themes; patriarchy – giving girls little or no say in their fate – combined with misogyny, sexism, homophobia, heteronormativity, transphobia, ableism, classism, and racism. Some of these issues explored in the stories show up as an artefact of the historical and cultural context of the contributor's lives; and all are still prevalent today within British culture, particularly perhaps within the magnifying-glass atmosphere of a boarding school, where there is no escape from the lens of being different.

The core of the stories came together at a workshop for boarding school survivors – a double handful of women sharing experiences amongst ourselves, exploring with a group therapist and her assistant some of the contours of damage caused by our time at boarding school. This core was joined by others who also wanted – no, needed – to tell their stories.

We are a very mixed bunch; some people from families with a tradition of sending both boys and girls to boarding school. Other families were doing so for the first time, often mystified by the strange terminology, rules, and traditions. Some of us were sent as young as six, others at 11 or 12. Many of us were sent to the UK from overseas – from Africa, Asia, and the Middle East; classic third culture kids. Others had barely left the British Isles.

A child needs safety and love in the same way that they need air, food, and water. It is almost impossible for an institution to provide that. Instead, we were brought up by our peers; by similarly abandoned children suffering from broken attachments. There is no hierarchy in pain. We all suffered from the need to shape ourselves to the new realities we found ourselves in. Eminent anthropologist Dr Judith Okely summarises the process thus:

> Eventually the imitating child becomes the part. To survive in a place which beats down diversity, the victim has to believe in the rightness of his or her controller. Children and adolescents are most vulnerable, their minds and bodies may be permanently shaped.
>
> (J. Okely, 1996, *Own or Other Culture*, Routledge)

We range in age from early 30s to mid-70s. People often do not fully realise the life-changing effects of boarding school on their systems until later in life, when the defences erected at school to enable us to survive the experience have crumbled under the influence of time and lived experience.

Some of us went from school to prestigious universities, some held down demanding careers, and some drifted from job to job. Three of the contributors are trainees or practising psychotherapists. The necessity of finding your equilibrium with the support of a therapist can often lead to the desire to support others suffering from similar wounds, as well as a need to challenge the broader, often normalised, structures (such as early boarding) that led to such wounding.

This is a book about the experiences of individuals who attended boarding school and the perspectives given are from people who are predominantly, but by no means exclusively, white, cisgender, and able-bodied. All the personal stories are true accounts, although many of the contributors have chosen to write anonymously, to protect themselves or relatives. Details such as dates, schools, or names of teachers, have largely been excluded to preserve anonymity. Please be aware that recollections in this book cover themes of the dark side of privilege and the verbal, emotional, and physical abuse of children. Many are from a colonial context. The recollections can be disturbing and include references to suicide. If you choose to read ahead, please ensure you are resourced to receive stories of this nature.

We owe a debt of gratitude to Nick Duffell, on several counts. He founded his Boarding School Survivors' organisation in 1990, going on to document, over the course of the next 30+ years, that particular range of pathologies that commonly occur in children who have been wounded by boarding school. The four-day workshop that many of us attended was revelatory, and life-changing in the most positive way. All royalties from this book will go to Nick's organisation, to help subsidise workshop places for people unable to meet the cost.

Nick has also been extraordinarily generous in allowing us to quote extensively from those works which he published himself, *The Making of Them* and *Wounded Leaders*. We feel that interspersing each individual's story with a quote from these works takes each person's story from the particular to the generally applicable – and shows how the generally applicable relates to an individual's pain.

As well as the personal stories, we have been able to include several academics and authors among our number. Their chapters form the supporting pillars of the book's arch, with the personal stories being the keystone.

Suzanne Zeedyk writes powerfully about attachment theory and the possible detrimental effects of the boarding school's aim of 'building character'. Dr Zeedyk is a research scientist and developmental psychologist, with a specialty in infant attachment. Based for nearly 20 years at the University of Dundee, Scotland, she stepped away from full-time academic work in 2011 to set up an independent consultancy.

Linda Devereux is an educator and an Adjunct Research Fellow at Charles Sturt University in Australia. Dr Devereux highlights the challenges of transcultural childhoods, particularly when young children are sent away to boarding schools a long way from where their parents live. This rupture may intensify that felt by those sent to board within a familiar cultural setting. Third culture kids are forever pulled between the culture in which they grow up and the culture their parents call home. They may find it hard to say where 'home' is.

Roe Woodroffe trained first in a psychodynamic and then in an integrative psychosynthesis therapy modality. She retired in 2021 after a 37-year career in private practice, including a decade-long period where she was a tutor at the Re-Vision Centre in London. Many of her clients were ex-boarders, and she trained alongside Nick Duffell and worked with him as a supervisee for the last ten years of her career. Roe writes about how the patriarchal nature of the boarding school experience impacts our anima, our feminine soul, and the importance and urgency of reconnecting with the 'wild' child in us all in order to heal.

Ulrika Ernvik is a Master of Social Work, a psychotherapist, and the author of the book *Third Culture Kids: A Gift to Care For*. If you have reached the end of the book and still feel that boarding is an option you must consider for your children, Ulrika offers suggestions for reducing the potential damage to the family. She explains how to prepare the child for school, building resilience with the hope of avoiding the worst effects.

Finally, huge thanks to those who have given so much of their time and attention to the editing of this book, especially Sophie Yates, who put much effort into content and copy editing, and Jane Pooler who also edited content and researched and shared ideas.

The book would have foundered without Linda's clear-eyed view of the themes and motifs expressed in the stories, and where the gaps were in supporting the book's arguments. Her ability to draw hypotheses from the data, and back them up through comparison with the existing literature, has been indispensable.

My role has been that of project manager and commissioning editor. I have greatly appreciated being able to share the work of editing and, more importantly, learning from the ideas and expertise of those who have contributed to this project.

We hope you enjoy this book. Well, 'enjoy' is perhaps not the right word. We hope you read these brave stories and use them as a data feed into your own decision-making. If you have been damaged by boarding school, there is hope; especially if you can reconnect to the wild child who lives in all of us. If you have no option but to send a child away, either within your country of residence or from halfway across the world, please read the final chapter on resilience and do what you can to prepare yourself and your child. If you are contemplating sending a child to board for the advantages such an education can provide before that psychologically important age of 16 or so – the last two years of a British high school education, when an adolescent is naturally drawn towards peer support, and parental influence becomes less hands-on – please, think again. Boarding school can cause damage that no aware parent could possibly wish to inflict on their child.

With warm wishes,
Nicky (June 2024)

Acknowledgements

A great many people have contributed to this book. Without them, it would simply not have been possible to write it.

First and foremost of these are the brave women who have chosen to share their stories with the world, and the authors of longer pieces who describe so well the theory behind the pain.

There were many people who wanted to have their story included, but life prevented them in some way. Thank you to each one for the supportive vibes and an occasional shoulder to cry on!

Nick Duffell has been extraordinarily generous with allowing us to use excerpts from his published works, and we greatly appreciate his support, encouragement, and general advice.

Margaret Laughton and Allison Paech-Ujejski, editors of *Men's Accounts of Boarding School: Sent Away*, and Nikki Simpson, editor of *Finding Our Way Home: Women's Accounts of Being Sent to Boarding School* were lavish with their time and support.

We (Linda and Nicky) owe a debt of gratitude to Simon Partridge for introducing us!

Thank you also to Ruth Tudor and Sarah Heydon for holding space for many of us.

Lastly, we would like to acknowledge the support of friends, families, partners, and personal therapists, who must all have felt fed up hearing about *The Book* at times!

Chapter 1

Introduction

Linda Devereux and Nicky Moxey

Boarding schools have been part of the British education system for hundreds of years. However, it is only in recent decades that the long-term psychological effects of living in a school for nine months out of every twelve has come under sustained psychological and academic scrutiny. Although others had written about boarding schools before them, the ground-breaking work of Nick Duffell and Joy Schaverien highlighted the long-term negative effects of early boarding for many individuals and brought the topic into the public consciousness. Bowlby (1982), Schaverien, and Duffell argue that breaking the attachment bonds between children and their families, and the subsequent emotional losses that early boarders experience, can lead to long-term psychological distress (Duffell, 2000, 2014; Duffell & Bassett, 2016; Schaverien, 2011, 2015, 2021). Listening to clients in her psychotherapy work, Schaverien noticed that those who boarded from a young age exhibit a cluster of behaviours and emotional states that she called 'boarding school syndrome'. Boarding school syndrome results from the unacknowledged grief a child experiences as a result of being separated from their parents and home, kept captive in an institution, and subjected to its rules and regulations. The child is, essentially, taken from all that is familiar and 'fostered with strangers' who do not love them (Schaverien, 2015: 7).

Duffell's work developed from workshops which he ran for adults who had attended boarding schools. These 'boarding school survivors', he argues, endure emotional deprivation in boarding school without familial love and comfort. In order to survive, children learn to hide their vulnerability and supress their emotions. They develop a 'strategic survival personality', based on fitting in and appearing independent and self-reliant. The strategic survival patterns may help the child to survive in school, but when carried over into adulthood these, often unconscious, behaviours can damage emotional well-being and close relationships with others.

Others have contributed to the growing body of knowledge about the effects of early boarding. For instance, Alex Renton, a journalist and the eighth generation from his family to attend boarding school, writes movingly about his experience as a child who attended boarding school in response to a long-term family tradition. Renton drew public attention to the abuses and cruelty he and many others experienced at boarding school and he continues to be active in seeking justice for

DOI: 10.4324/9781003533665-1

those who were damaged by adults in authority who misused the trust afforded to them (Renton, 2017). Mark Stibbe writes about the addictions that he developed as a result of the loss and grief he experienced at boarding school and his need for a spiritual, as well as a psychological, dimension to healing and recovery (Stibbe, 2016), and Simon Partridge has drawn attention to the fact that many children of the British upper class may have their attachments to parents damaged even before school as a result of being raised by nannies or governesses (Partridge, 2021). Partridge argues that children brought up in this environment may already feel abandoned by their parents. They may have already learned to mask their feelings of distress and so they may seem to adjust more easily to the separation from home when they go to boarding school. Such deeply held and early instilled hurts may not easily be acknowledged or identified by individuals themselves. In fact, as Duffell argues, the particular traits adopted by men at boarding school may set them up for a life of power enhanced by the old boy's networks of the elite boarding establishments (Duffell, 2014). This theme is further developed in Richard Beard's book, *Sad Little Men*. Beard, like Duffell, highlights the long-term negative consequences of boarding on men who then become the leaders of the country (Beard, 2021).

Not everyone who attends an elite boarding school may be rewarded with the same access to the country's powerful institutions. For instance, children sent to board in the UK from overseas generally expect to return to their passport country once their education is complete. These young children can experience particular kinds of bullying and racism at boarding school. In his cross-cultural narrative, *A Black Boy at Eton*, Dillibe Onyeama details the overt racism he experienced from peers and staff (Onyeama, 2022). His experience lends weight to an argument that boarding school is not a safe place for anyone who stands out as 'different'. Safety at boarding school comes from aligning with the dominant culture. Those who do not fit in are targeted (James, 2023: 8).

Another book which examines the experience of cross-cultural children sent to board in the UK, *The Boarding School Girls*, is based on the experiences of its authors, Roya Ferdows and Soosan Latham and interviews they conducted with other girls who were sent from Iran to board in the UK (Latham & Ferdows, 2018). The girls report varying responses to their experiences; generally, those who were older when they were sent to board were better able to cope. Most experienced some traumatic adjustments to living in such a different culture so far from their parents without sufficient English language skills. Many also struggled with the complexities of developing a bi-cultural identity and dealing with their long-term feelings of abandonment.

Others who have written autobiographically about women's experiences of boarding school include anthropologist Judith Okely, who analysed her own unhappy boarding school experience (Okely, 1996), and Christine Jack, who recounts her experience of attending a Catholic boarding school in rural Australia (Jack, 2020). Nikki Simpson extends the understanding of women's experiences of boarding school through her edited collection of narratives (Simpson, 2019).

These narratives highlight the particular ways in which shame, public humiliation, and cruelty are often used to control girls in boarding school. Girls are taught to be polite and to serve others through curbing their own appetites and desires.

As others who have conducted literature reviews have noted, reflecting wider patriarchal stereotypes, women's autobiographical writing about boarding school seems to have generated less attention in the popular press than books written by men; there is a 'disproportionate emphasis on boys' boarding experiences' (James, 2023: 3). Based on her work with both men and women who have been sent to boarding school as children, Joy Schaverien argues that there are significant differences in men's and women's experiences. For instance, women are trained in selflessness at boarding school. They must curb their own desires and be neither needy nor greedy, and while men are prepared to 'serve their country', women are taught to 'serve men' (Schaverien, 2015: 43). Many of the women Schaverien worked with experienced significant body shaming. Some developed disturbed relationships with food. Schaverien argues that more research is needed to understand further the long-term impacts of these gendered experiences of boarding school on women.

Another area which Schaverien suggests is under-researched is the experience of children who are sent to board in a different country to where their parents live. These exiles, as Schaverien calls them, may experience an additional layer of grief and loss because if their parents live abroad, they are in a sense 'homeless' (Schaverien, 2015: 151). Others have called these children who spend a significant part of their childhood living overseas because of their parents' work, global nomads (McCaig, 2002) or third culture kids (TCKs) (Pollock & Van Reken, 2009, Van Reken, 2011).

Once we began examining the testimonies of the contributors to this book in depth, we realised that the majority of them, all but four, are TCKs. This surprised and intrigued us. In addition, once we examined the backgrounds of contributors to many of the books mentioned above, we discovered that TCKs appear to be overrepresented in books that emerge from therapeutic practice.

The Independent Schools Council (ISC) publishes some useful statistics on the demographics of the UK boarding school population. For instance, Table 3 from their 2023 census (this and other references from this publication are reproduced with permission) shows that the total number of boarders is 66,325 or 12% of the independent school population. From Fig. 19 of this publication we learn that 25,469 of these children have parents who live overseas, approximately 38% of the boarding population. The majority of the children who attend UK boarding schools from overseas are from China, which abandoned its One Child policy in 2016. Children today are therefore 'beneficiaries' of this policy and they may well have six earning adults – parents and two sets of grandparents – financially supporting each child. Table 13 of the ISC census (reproduced below) allows us to see the numbers of British children whose parents are working abroad and who are boarding, helpfully divided into those people in the Armed Forces and others who live abroad.

Table 1.1 Reproduced from the ISC Census 2023, Table 13: Numbers of British pupils with parents living overseas divided into type of school attended

British pupils whose parents:	Senior	Mixed-age	Junior	Single-sex: boys'	Single-sex: girls'	Co-ed	Schools with boarders	Day schools	Total
Live abroad	2,264	1,001	177	266	469	2,707	3,298	144	3,442
Serve in HM forces	1,418	1,850	1,302	126	267	4,177	3,995	575	4,570
New British pupils whose parents:									
Live abroad	661	316	78	41	118	896	1,017	38	1,055
Serve in HM forces	235	245	275	18	35	702	653	102	755

Tellingly, the percentage of these TCKs children in the boarding community (5%) is much lower than the percentage of such children who contribute to the boarding school literature (see below). Something happens to these children that, for many, makes them want to share their experiences either through testimonies resulting from therapeutic settings (Simpson, 2019, Laughton et al., 2021) or by contributing to other research on boarding schools (Priestner et al., 2023).

The first three books in Table 1.2 are, unsurprisingly given that they emerge from therapeutic settings, focused on people who feel that they were damaged by their experience of boarding school. We were able to identify the TCKs from most of the narratives, and where we were unsure, the editors of the books were able to help us with this data.

The book *The Psychological Effect of Boarding School: The Trunk in the Hall* (Cavenagh et al, 2023) is more sympathetic towards boarding, although many of the chapters recount challenging, if not traumatic, experiences of adult ex-boarders. The authors argue that those children who do not cope well at boarding school come from families where there are already problems. An example is intergenerational boarding school families, perhaps where these children have damaged childhoods with parents who lack warmth as a result of their own boarding school experiences and are emotionally unavailable to their children. We have attempted to estimate the number of TCKs whose experiences are reflected in this book. However, our estimate is only a 'best guess' as the different chapters in the book rely on different sources of evidence. The book appears to bundle cross-culture kids

Table 1.2 Comparison of categorisation of respondents in publications about boarding school

Category/Book	Worlds Away From Home	Men's Accounts of Boarding Schools	Finding Our Way Home	The Trunk in the Hall
Third Culture Kids	75%	32%	63%	12.70%[a]
Family tradition	6%	16%	13%	27.50%
Cross culture	6%			13.70%[b]
Parent ambition/ convenience	6%			8.80%
Mental illness	6%			2.90%
Quality of local schools		11%		10.80%
Unsure/Other	0%	42%	25%	23.50%
Total respondents	16	19	16	186

Notes
[a] Enumerates TCK military respondents only
[b] TCK mercantile and missionary respondents bundled in this category alongside cross-cultural ones.

and third culture/mercantile kids in its demographic breakdown, and the editors were not able to help us clarify which participants were TCKs. We have, therefore, probably missed some. However, it appears TCKs are over-represented in each of these texts.

Another striking feature of the stories in Nikki Simpson's book, and those that you will read in the following chapters, is that many of the individuals in each collection experienced significant challenges in their early lives *before* being sent to boarding school far away from where their parents lived and worked. These early challenges, some of which are described as adverse childhood experiences (ACEs), have been shown to have long-term physical and psychological consequences (Felitti, 2002, 2019). TCK Training, an organisation committed to supporting TCKs and their families, has released three reports based on their research into the lives of those who raise families overseas because of work commitments (Crossman et al., 2022, 2023; Crossman & Wells, 2022). Crossman et al. collected data from just over 1,900 adult TCKs who completed a survey based on Felitti's ACE questionnaire. The authors used this approach so that they could compare the experiences of adult TCKs with those of adults from other developed and developing countries. They found that the demonstrated level of adversity facing TCKs growing up was higher than in studies of individuals living in single countries. This was particularly true for the families living overseas who moved often. The survey respondents reported very high levels of childhood emotional abuse, emotional neglect and household mental illness leading the authors to conclude that '[t]he privileges of finance and/or world travel do not make children and families immune from concerns of emotional health. They do, however, lessen their access to support networks – both family/community ties and welfare services' (Crossman et al., 2022: 2).

Another challenge for a child who faces many physical relocations is the loss of the landscape and the environment to which they are attached. There is a sheep-farming term, 'heft', that describes how a lamb running on open moorland knows that a particular valley is home, safety, and the next one along is not. There is a growing body of evidence which suggests that humans can respond to place in similar ways (Bartos, 2013; Grimshaw & Mates, 2022). Casey (2001) describes the relationship thus:

> The relationship between self and place is not just one of reciprocal influence . . .each is essential to the being of the other. In effect, *there is no place without self and no self without place.*
>
> (Casey, 2001: 684, emphasis in original)

For TCKs, the loss of family, the disruption to friendships, and the loss of place, combined with being sent to boarding school, alone, in an alien environment, may well contribute to an existing ACE load, rendering the child less able to cope with the vicissitudes of boarding school life before they enter its doors. Our testimonies give ample examples of these challenges and we discuss them in detail in chapters following the personal testimonies.

As suggested above, there are gaps in our knowledge about boarding school and its long-term effects. Women's experiences of boarding and TCK's experiences of being sent to boarding school are under-researched. Perhaps the time has now come to look at specific groups of adults who have attended boarding school as children in more detail. It is time to move beyond generalised understandings of boarding school trauma and boarding school syndrome, which offer an overarching theoretical framework, to look at the specific experiences of particular groups. Teasing out the differences between the experiences of different groups will help those who were sent to boarding school to understand their own unique position better. In addition, this information will be useful to families and schools to help them support children from diverse backgrounds. Those working therapeutically with boarding school survivors will also benefit from a deeper awareness of the nuanced experiences of particular client groups.

In this book, we bring together expertise from multiple fields of study to deepen our understandings of the boarding school experiences of 16 individuals, 15 of whom identify as women and 1 who identifies as non-binary. We draw on scholarship on boarding school, TCKs, ACEs, and gender. We argue, based on the expert chapters, the personal stories – our testimonies to our lived experiences of boarding school – and our analysis of the key themes which emerge from these narratives, that there are a number of challenges particular to TCKs who attend boarding school. These include frequent moves due to the nature of expatriate work, which contribute to multiple goodbyes and unresolved grief, including the loss of loved overseas homelands. These challenges are compounded by the fact that some TCKs grow up in countries where they are exposed to violence and political instability, which in turn may expose them to ACEs and other trauma. In addition, TCKs at boarding school live at a greater distance from their parents and they may feel that they do not fully 'belong' in their passport country. If these children are then bullied at boarding school for their perceived 'difference', it is not surprising that they may seek therapeutic help as adults in greater numbers than their monocultural peers.

Nick Duffell describes the need for a child to develop a 'strategic survival personality', a projected front that hides their vulnerabilities, in order to get through school. It is often not for years – perhaps decades – that this front wears thin, and it becomes unbearably obvious to the adult that they need therapeutic help. The testimonies presented here illustrate the challenges we faced, but they may fail to address the needs of each wounded soul. Roe Woodroffe's chapter provides some direction, a focus on the *anima* in all of us, and a way for that fettered, wounded child to mature and live freely once more.

There is hope.

Linda and Nicky

Bibliography

Bartos, A. E. 2013. *Children sensing place.* Emotion Space and Society, 9, 89–98.

Beard, R. 2021. *Sad Little Men. Private Schools and the Ruin of England.* London, Penguin Random House.

Bowlby, J. 1982. *Attachment and loss: Retrospect and prospect.* American Journal of Orthopsychiatry, 52, 664–678.

Casey, E. S. 2001. *Body, self and landscape.* In: Adams, P., Hielscher, S. & Till, K. (eds.) *Textures of Place. Exploring Humanist Geographies.* Minneapolis, MN: University of Minnesota Press.

Cavenagh, P. et al. 2023. *The Psychological Impact of Boarding School: The Trunk in the Hall.* Abingdon, UK, Routledge.

Crossman, T., Smith, E. V. & Wells, L. 2022. *TCKs at Risk. Risk Factors for Globally Mobile Families.* Georgia, USA: TCK Training.

Crossman, T. & Wells, L. 2022. *Caution and Hope. The Prevalence of Adverse Childhood Experiences in Globally Mobile Third Culture Kids.* Georgia, USA: TCK Training.

Crossman, T., Wells, L., Vahey Smith, E. & McCall, L. 2023. *Sources of Trauma in International Childhoods: Providing Individualised Support to Increase Positive Outcomes for Higher Risk Families.* Georgia, USA, TCK Training.

Duffell, N. 2000. *The Making of Them.* London, Lone Arrow Press.

Duffell, N. 2014. *Wounded Leaders. British Elitism and the Entitlement Illusion – A Psychohistory.* UK, Lone Arrow Press.

Duffell, N. & Bassett, T. 2016. *Trauma, Abandonment and Privilege: A Guide to Therapeutic Work with Boarding School Survivors.* UK, Routledge.

Dunlea, M. 2019. *Bodydreaming in the Treatment of Developmental Trauma: An Embodied Approach.* Abingdon, UK, Routledge.

Felitti, V. 2002. *The relationship between adverse childhood experiences and adult health: Turning Gold into Lead.* The Permanente Journal Winter 6(1), 44–47.

Felitti, V. 2019. *Origins of the A.C.E. Study.* American Journal of Preventative Medicine, 56(6), 787–789.

Grimshaw, L. & Mates, L. 2022. *'It's part of our community, where we live': Urban heritage and children's sense of place.* Urban Studies 59, 1334–1352.

Independent Schools Council *Annual Report 2023.* https://www.isc.co.uk/media/9316/isc_census_2023_final.pdf

Jack, C. 2020. *Recovering Boarding School Trauma Narratives: Christopher Robin Milne as a Psychological Companion on the Journey to Healing.* Abingdon, UK, Routledge.

James, G. 2023. *The psychological impact of sending children away to boarding schools in Britain: Is there cause for concern?* British Journal of Psychotherapy, 39, 592–610.

Latham, S. & Ferdows, R. 2018. *The Boarding School Girls. Developmental and Cultural Narratives.* Abingdon, UK, Routledge.

Laughton, M., Paech-Ujejski, A, & Patterson, A. (ed.). 2021. *Men's Accounts of Boarding School: Sent Away.* Abingdon, UK, Routledge.

McCaig, N. 2002. *Raised in the margin of the mosaic: Global nomads balance worlds within.* International Educator, Spring, 10–17.

Okely, J. 1996. *Own or Other Culture.* Abingdon, UK, Routledge.

Onyeama, D. 2022. *A Black Boy at Eton.* London, UK, Penguin.

Partridge, S. 2021. *Boarding school syndrome: Reconsidered in social context and through the lens of attachment theory.* Attachment, 15, 269–278. https://www.londonaceshub. org/_files/ugd/3f7b5b_d7b739d918f241bcbb4cad5effebb611.pdf

Pollock, D. & Van Reken, R. 2009. *Third Culture Kids: Growing up among Worlds.* Boston, Nicholas Brealey Publishing.

Priestner, A., Oden, J., Cavenagh, P. & Mcogersib, S. (eds.). 2023. *The Psychological Impact of Boarding School: The Trunk in the Hall.* Abingdon, UK.

Renton, A. 2017. *Stiff Upper Lip. Secrets, Crimes and the Schooling of a Ruling Class.* Great Britain, Weidenfeld and Nicolson.

Schaverien, J. 2011. *Boarding school syndrome: Broken attachments a hidden trauma.* British Journal of Psychotherapy, 27, 138–155.

Schaverien, J. 2015. *Boarding School Syndrome. The Psychological Trauma of the 'Privileged' Child.* Hove, UK, Routledge.

Schaverien, J. 2021. *Revisiting boarding school syndrome: The anatomy of psychological traumas and sexual abuse.* British Journal of Psychotherapy, 37, 606–622.

Simpson, N. (ed.) 2019. *Finding our Way Home: Women's Accounts of Being Sent to Boarding School.* Abingdon, UK, Routledge.

Stibbe, M. 2016. *Home at Last: Freedom from Boarding School Pain.* UK, Malcolm Down Publishing.

Van Reken, R. 2011. *Cross Cultural Kids: The new prototype.* In: Bell-Villada, G., Sichel, N., Eidse, F., Schellenberg, C. & Orr, E. (eds.) *Writing Out of Limbo. International Childhoods, Global Nomads and Third Culture Kids.* Newcastle upon Tyne, Cambridge Scholars Publications.

Wharton, N. & Marcano-Olivier, M. 2023. *An exploration of ex-boarding school adults' attachment styles and substance use behaviours.* Attachment & Human Development, DOI: 10.1080/14616734.2023.2228761

Chapter 2

Stepping from denial into curiosity

Boarding school through an attachment-trauma lens

Suzanne Zeedyk

The elite British boarding school system has been in existence for several centuries. A key aim of such education has always been to instil 'character'. Are there risks to building that character? That's the question we'll be exploring in this chapter.

It is easy to find explicit examples of this goal. Eton College emphasised in 2020 its intention to 'nurture the character, skills and dispositions' that are most central to their community (Glennon & Hinton, 2020). In 1848, when Rev Nathaniel Woodard was founding the first of the Woodard Schools, he stated pointedly that they would be based in 'sound principle and sound knowledge', which would be achieved in part by 'removing the child from the noxious influence of home and home comforts' (Partridge, 2013). Boys have more regularly been the focus of such character-building efforts, given that they have been resident in boarding schools for longer, but in today's gender-inclusive environment, character for girls also becomes important. A marketing survey produced in 2021 by Study International identified schools for boys and for girls that 'equip students not only with 21st century skills, but also with character and heart' (Study International, 2021).

Over the past three decades, a chorus of voices has highlighted risks associated with the kind of character typically nurtured in elite boarding school environments. Autobiographies have been published detailing the heartache suffered by children who attend them (Renton, 2017). Podcast series and films have been recorded, conveying stories of fear, shame, and confusion. Theoretical explanations of the mechanisms by which boarding experiences generate harm have been developed (Duffell, 2000). Facebook groups and social gatherings have been created to connect individuals seeking to make sense of their time at boarding school.

And yet, even with all these voices, many people still find it surprising to contemplate the idea that boarding schools could cause lasting emotional damage. It is surprising not only for those who attended as students, but also for the parents who sent their children to such establishments and for the staff who work there. Members of the wider public, too, continue to be surprised by media stories of the dynamics at play in such institutions.

DOI: 10.4324/9781003533665-2

Perhaps 'surprised' is not quite the right word. Maybe something stronger is needed, such as 'shocked' or 'askance'? Contemplating the idea that elite boarding schools, which earn significant sums of money in fees and underpin networks of power, could cause traumatic experiences for children is unsettling. It is a possibility that requires courage to consider.

For many people, that courage is too hard. The idea that you sent your child to a school where they suffered harm is tough for a parent. The idea that you yourself might have been traumatised by experiences that were entirely normal at your school, or in your family, is confusing. The idea that you are employed in a setting where you frequently see children distressed, but you cannot change the culture, is guilt-inducing. If an idea proves too uncomfortable to contemplate, then there is a perfectly good solution available: denial. That's how we human beings protect ourselves from unresolvable discomfort. We reach for denial. What if denial is a core element of character-building within the boarding school system?

Some commentators would argue that even this question is confusing. The blogger Maria points out that 'many people think their damage is a strength' (Maria, 2019). Cultural messages abound about the necessity for business leaders to operate with tough efficiency or for the Royal Family to display dignity during public funerals via emotional reserve. How can you be said to be in denial over something that you recognise – but see as valuable, rather than problematic?

As a developmental psychologist who has studied attachment relationships for three decades, I find these questions fascinating. In this chapter, I aim to do two things. First, I want to explore ways in which boarding school experience might be associated with trauma. Some of these links are already recognised within the literature on boarding school syndrome, but others are only now emerging as considerations. Second, I want to reflect on what can be done to help people step out of denial and into curiosity.

2.1   Attachment and trauma

Let's begin with attachment. This is the biological need for connection with which all babies are born.

Human infants are remarkably vulnerable and immature, much more so than other mammals, due in part to our large brains. We are born earlier in the gestation period than other mammals, when our skulls are still small enough to fit through birth canals. This evolutionary adaptation has left us as a highly social species, with babies extremely dependent on attention from adults for their survival. Even as newborns, we have a sophisticated capacity to tune into and make meaning of the facial expressions, bodily movements, and communicative gestures of other people. Social engagement is wired deeply into our brains and stress regulatory systems.

The attachment system is one consequence of that dependence. When infants experience warm, attuned responses to their emotional and physiological states, then they develop a sense of trust in relationships and in themselves. They learn that someone will come to help when they are overwhelmed. They learn it is not shameful to ask for help or comfort when they need it. They learn to be in touch with the bodily states we call 'emotions', and over time, that self-awareness will enable them to develop empathy and other-awareness. All of these processes are unconscious. They are in place and functioning long before infants have the language or representational abilities that are needed to allow them to reflect consciously on their experiences.

The attachment system leads human beings to seek belonging. In order to thrive emotionally and physically, we need to feel confident that we are connected to others, that others care about us, that we matter. The possibility that we (and our needs) might not matter to others is deeply threatening. It is not too strong to describe it as existential, because if a vulnerable human infant does not have someone looking out for him or her, then the stark reality is they will die. The evolutionary processes that have shaped us have built existential anxiety about relationships into our very biology.

The study of attachment began in the 1930s, with the work of psychiatrist John Bowlby. It now overlaps with the study of trauma and emotional regulation, led by researchers such as Allan Schore, Judith Herman, Bessel van der Kolk, Gabor Maté, and others. The fundamental discovery they have made is that childhood distress, when endured without help, alters the way that a child's biology develops. Those alterations occur in the systems of the body that govern hormones, heart rate, breathing, digestion, and all the others that keep us physically healthy, as well as in the development of neural pathways in the brain. These discoveries have become more accessible to the public over the past two decades.

That leaves us well placed to ask: can the sciences of attachment and trauma help to explain how boarding school experiences might be damaging?

2.2   Boarding school damage

There are at least five primary processes by which boarding school might shape children's development in harmful ways. Not all children will experience all five, of course – and that variance is an important point to which we will return shortly.

2.2.1   Attachment rift

A key way in which boarding school can cause emotional damage is by creating distance and distrust in a child's relationship with his or her parents. This 'attachment rift' has been emphasised by the leading theorists of boarding school survivor syndrome (Duffell, 2000; Schaverien, 2015). When a parent sends a child away, the child learns that love is risky. You can't trust it, and you can't depend on people who say they love you. Sustaining relationships becomes based in performance, rather than emotional authenticity. Emotions must be controlled, rather than embraced. Duffell describes the terrible 'double-bind' that is created for children sent to boarding school. Their parents have effectively said to them: 'I sent you away because I love you'. There is no way out of this trap. Ironically, even children who are removed by strangers into the care system do not face a bind so strangulating as this. Schaverein skilfully tracks the impact of this double-bind during adulthood. The impulse to abandon someone you love before they can abandon you becomes wired into your stress system. In essence, an attachment rifts transforms love from a state of safety to a state of terror. It is not surprising, then, that boarders' sense of belonging comes to reside in institutional membership rather than in family connection. An attachment rift can be formed at any age, including in adolescence, but the earlier in life a child is sent away to learn these lessons of fear, the greater the damage, because the stress system of a young child is so immature and fragile.

2.2.2 Lack of repair following rupture

Attachment rifts become embedded within a child's psyche because their feelings cannot be spoken aloud to the people who caused them. It is one thing to feel abandoned, angry, lonely, or confused. It is another to be prevented from talking about those feelings. A large component of the emotional damage created by boarding school occurs because children's uncomfortable feelings are denied by parents. This is an example of the rupture-repair cycle, emphasised within contemporary attachment theory (Gold & Tronick, 2020). Ruptures are a normal part of all human relationships. They range from small mismatches, such as being distracted by a mobile phone, to major fights that include slamming doors and name calling. The damage to relationships occurs not because of the presence of ruptures, but because of the failure to repair the rupture. Children sent away to boarding school typically live in permanent rupture. It becomes simply a way of life for them. They learn that love is inherently risky, fundamentally untrustworthy. The prohibition against speaking about feelings was highlighted by Bateson (1956) in his classic publication on double-bind traps. He said that a child's inability to reconcile two (or more) deeply conflicting existential messages leads to an internal split, where the conflict is hidden away, left unacknowledged, and unresolved. These are intolerable lessons for a child to learn early in life. It alters their psychology and their biology. It makes any emotionally intimate relationship scary, daunting, perhaps impossible.

2.2.3 Adverse childhood experiences

In addition to a basic attachment rift, many children at boarding school encounter additional adverse experiences. These include sexual, physical, or emotional abuse, such as bullying, shaming, humiliation, violence, rape, grooming, or living in fear of any of these. Children can also be neglected, for example by being given inadequate food, warmth, or comfort. These are all examples of events now known as adverse childhood experiences (ACEs). Although it was the founder of attachment theory John Bowlby who first used this phrase (in 1981),[1] it was the 1998 publication by medical doctors Felitti and Anda (1998) that finally gave it public attention. Their seminal study revealed a measurable link between traumatic events in childhood and poor health outcomes in adulthood, such as heart disease, liver disease, depression, and substance use. Trauma is essentially a stressor, and stress changes the body. The language of ACEs is, as yet, rarely used in relation to boarding school, but that is likely due to timing. The ACEs framework emerged within public awareness after Boarding School Syndrome. Moreover, ACEs tend to be associated with families rather than institutions, even though there is no conceptual requirement for this. The opportunity now exists to examine useful links between ACEs and institutions.

2.2.4   Lack of companionship for sharing discomfort

It might be argued that the greatest damage derives not from what children experience but from whether they have to bear it alone. If a child has no one with whom they are able to share their distress – no friend, no sibling, no staff member, no parent – then they are forced to carry it alone. Their feelings go unspoken, unacknowledged, unprocessed. Children learn that it is not only parents who are emotionally untrustworthy, but that everyone is untrustworthy. This is an impossible emotional ask. Human beings are biologically wired for connection. Without companionship, our stress systems are pushed into overdrive. That is why the ACEs framework distinguishes between 'stress' and 'toxic stress'. It is when stress reaches toxic levels that the risk of long-term damage is exacerbated. An attachment perspective brings an additional layer of insight to this account of stress. Having to cope with big, overwhelming feelings on your own generates shame. If what you are experiencing is too dark, too silly, too disgusting to be openly acknowledged by others, then the unspoken message is that the feelings you have about that experience are shameful. You yourself are shameful for having such feelings. It begins to be clear just how easily boarding school culture breeds shame.

2.2.5   Relational experiences prior to boarding

A proportion of children will arrive at boarding school already carrying high degrees of distress, either consciously or unconsciously. For example, the style of parenting they encountered at home, from infancy onwards, may have been based in emotional distance, lack of affection or touch, language devoid of emotional references, high performance pressure, or care delivered by an employee such as a nanny (who may have been suddenly discharged when their service was no longer required). This is the kind of psycho-sociological perspective offered by Partridge (2021), who observes that an emotionally reserved style of parenting is normative within the British elite class who expect to send their children away to board from an early age. He argues that it is unhelpful to view boarding trauma only through an individualistic lens. He believes a collective perspective must also be brought to this subject. Essentially, Partridge is pointing out that just because a group (i.e., a class, a society) considers a way of relating to be perfectly ordinary and normal does not mean it is emotionally healthy. This insight is applicable to any country and any class group. If a child is born into a family that relates in an emotionally cold fashion, they will arrive at school already carrying toxic levels of stress, even if that stress is now familiar and unconscious. Such normalised emotional repression may be behaviourally functional, in that it makes it looks like you are 'coping' just fine, even though external behaviour does not mean that one's internal state is emotionally healthy. From this perspective, it becomes clear that any theoretical framework designed to make sense of boarding schools' impacts should begin long before the child arrives at the school gates.

In summary, the damage of boarding school can derive from a multitude of sources. It is simultaneously disconcerting and illuminating to see the logic laid out so clearly. There will be other sources we should consider in addition to the five I have explored here. We can only begin to do that, though, if we are alert to the possibility that multiple sources will contribute. That awareness is not yet well grounded in discussion of boarding school impacts, and I hope it will strengthen as public conversation continues.

2.3   Dose-response relationship

Not all children will be subject to all of the primary processes just discussed. Paying attention to that variance can help in making sense of differences in the long-term emotional impacts of boarding school. Some children are deeply damaged by their boarding school experiences and others less so. Some children find boarding school to be a respite from dysfunctional family interactions or frequently disrupted friendships, while other children never lose their sense of grief over the losses incurred. There are many children who never find any sense of ease in the routines of boarding school, yet others seem to adjust quickly. Amongst the numerous questions to be asked is whether we can get better at understanding these differences, thereby helping adults to heal and preventing harm for children in the future.

The concept of the 'dose-response relationship' is one framework that might help. This is a key concept within the literature on ACEs, utilised to predict differential impacts of traumatic childhood events. It shows that as a person's exposure to stressors increases (dose), so also does the extent of the consequences (response). The fact that the ACEs framework measures exposure to stress via a numeric scoring system (ranging from 0 to 10) makes it easy to perceive this relation.

A multitude of studies using the ACEs framework have now shown that as ACE scores increase (dose), so too do poor adult outcomes (response). Felitti's 2002 review provides a sobering summary. For example, an ACE score of four or more greatly increases a person's risk of depression, as compared to a score of zero. The risk of heart disease increases by 390% and the risk of attempted suicide by 1,220%. With an ACE score of six, the likelihood of using intravenous drugs is increased by an astounding 4,600%. Although the ACEs framework remains controversial, with critics arguing that quantitative scoring is not a suitable approach to relational trauma, its advocates insist that it has been seminal in helping to understand trauma. They point to the thousands of ACEs studies conducted since the original 1998 publication as support for their view.

I believe that the dose-response relationship can be a helpful framework for making sense of differential impacts of boarding school. I am not advocating a scoring system, but rather a conceptual shift, in which we conceive of children's (possible) experiences of boarding school as doses of stress. While this shift will not account for all aspects of their experiences, it provides a novel means of thinking about variation in impact. If we are to extend the discussion of boarding school syndrome so that it reaches a wider audience, we will need multiple routes that enable people to see what currently tends to go unseen. In British society, boarding school has been normalised as an esteemed and desirable form of education (even if available only to the extremely rarefied 1% of the population who can afford it), which renders this conversation culturally challenging.

When we apply a dose-response lens to boarding school, it becomes obvious that variation in children's experiences will be considerable. Some children will have arrived at school with attachment systems woven of emotional distance and insecurity. Their experience with emotional repression may lead them to appear to cope well with separation. Other children, raised in warmer parenting environments, may display agonised partings from their parents. Renton (2017), for example, recounts the stories of children left hysterically pleading in the school drive as their parents speed away after parting, ignoring their cries. How might partings at airports, for children from cultures outside Britain, unfold? Most importantly, were parents able (and willing) to talk with children about their feelings of anxiety, anger, or abandonment? Many children sent to boarding school gain the sense that it is shameful to speak those aloud, leaving the ruptures to remain forever unrepaired. This is certainly the experience of Joanna Brittan (2021), whose fierce advocacy for the Boarding School Survivors (BSS)'s movement derives in part from the fact that her mother was resolutely opposed to listening to any of Joanna's childhood distress, even many years later in adulthood. A valuable (if still appalling) contrast exists in the circumstances of children who have been forcibly removed to residential schools against parental wishes, as happened in Native North American communities (Pember, 2019). Under these circumstances, repair between parent and child would not have presented the same resistance. These children had not been sent away but were taken away.

Once they arrived at school, some children will have experienced extreme bullying in school, such as that described by Elon Musk in his South African boarding school when he was thrown down a set of stairs and hospitalised (Blystone, 2022). Daniel Paul describes, in a conversation on social media (2022), how the new boarders at his school were 'welcomed' by other students with a ritual of locking them in their own suitcase, rolling them down several flights of stairs and then leaving them. The 'screams of the youngest' have never left him, 30 years on. Other children will have encountered less severe or even no bullying. (Or is it possible that bullying is an inherent aspect of boarding school as an institution?) Some children will have found little respite from distress when they returned home, while for others the short summer months offered a kind of haven. We now know how prevalent sexual violation is in boarding school cultures. Many children experience this directly, from either adults or fellow pupils, while the remainder experience it indirectly, alert to the messages of a sexualised environment and the presence of threatening individuals. The documentary film 'Chosen' was produced in 2008 to make exactly those points (Rees, 2009). When boarding is international, children risk additional losses, such as the familiar foods, traditions, music, and language that make up one's daily sense of self and belonging. Some children will have had available someone whom they trusted enough to talk with about these stressors (e.g., a friend, a sibling, a staff member). Many other children, though, will have handled these fearful feelings and events entirely on their own, without any support or companionship.

The descriptions I have just given are in no way novel. They are all situations that have been copiously described in the literature on boarding school syndrome and in biographical accounts of boarding. My point in collecting them together is to illuminate the variance amongst them. If we are to make sense of the diverse impacts of boarding school, we need to get better at considering that variance. The ACEs dose-response framework is one means of assisting with that.

Once we pay attention to that variance, it becomes ironically easier to identify stressors that have, largely, been omitted from considerations. For example, girls in boarding school may be subjected to forms of shaming and psychological abuse that differ substantially from that typically enacted on boys. The stories in this book point to that possibility. We can begin to ask: what other primary processes of stress should be added to the five I have explored in this chapter?

The language of stress has not often been used in the boarding school literature. Perhaps now is the time to begin doing so? It provides a new scaffold for making sense of children's experiences, and it ties the literature on boarding school more closely to the contemporary science of trauma. The two fields have much to offer one another.

2.4   Denial

The ideas I have been discussing are likely to engender strong feelings. For some people, these will be relief and affirmation, because they recognise their own experiences in my descriptions. For others, the feelings will be surprise, anger, and even affront. Such discomfort is exactly why denial is so common within the boarding school world. I wish we could talk more often about that denial.

Parents do not (usually) send their children to boarding school with the intention of damaging them. Founders do not (usually) establish schools with the aim of harming children. Staff do not (usually) seek employment at them with the goal of undermining development. And many adults who negotiated the boarding school journey as children would argue they did not suffer any lasting negative consequences. So how do we make sense of the growing number of voices who claim that harm is often done?

It is hard for any of us to consider the possibility that we have harmed someone else. It conflicts with our sense of our self as a 'good person'. We feel ashamed or criticised or maligned to hear otherwise. We naturally resist that discomfort. It is also hard to consider that we were harmed or mistreated as children. Were we not 'worthy enough' to be loved, heard, listened to, comforted? Have we ended up, in some sense, as 'broken' or as 'damaged goods'? It makes complete sense to me that, rather than consider any of these deeply uncomfortable possibilities, people reach for denial to protect their sense of self. We humans hang on to beliefs about ourselves (and our intentions) at the expense of confronting reality. Feeling better often seems preferable to knowing the truth. That's the temptation of denial. It soothes us.

The stultifying impact of denial has recently been discussed in another important area: tackling the climate crisis. Historian Naomi Oreskes has said in Greta Thunberg's new collection on this topic (Oreskes, 2022) that 'no one wants to admit to being duped by disinformation or blinded by a myth, and people in positions of privilege rarely examine the basis for that privilege'. Perhaps the time has come for those of us seeking change in regard to boarding schools to focus more directly on how denial functions, both individually and institutionally. How powerfully does denial operate in preventing us from acknowledging and addressing the emotional distress carried by so many current and ex-boarders?

2.5   Stepping out of denial

Let me end, therefore, by asking a practical question. What can be done to encourage individuals, organisations, and society to step out of denial about the harms of boarding school? There is already a heartening groundswell of change underway – or this book would not exist. What can be done to expand its reach and impact? Here are some ideas. Every single one of them requires courage.

Tell your story. If you are a boarding school survivor who has realised that the experience left you with wounds, keep telling your story. First and foremost, tell it to yourself. You are the most important audience. Then, as long as it feels safe to do so, tell it to your family, your friends, your colleagues, previous boarders, and others who have never thought much about boarding. Your story deserves to be told if you wish it to be. Peter Forbes, known for his views on photography as a tool of culture change, believes that 'stories create community, which opens us up to the claims of others'. Every time you share your story, you create a path on which others can choose to follow. You normalise the telling of uncomfortable stories.

Become knowledgeable about the science of attachment and childhood trauma. There is now a massive amount of information publicly available about childhood trauma. The more knowledgeable you are, the better you will understand your own story and be able to articulate it to others, if you so choose. The literature on childhood trauma too easily implies that traumatic experiences mostly occur in chaotic (usually poor) families where there is active abuse or neglect. The idea that institutions could create adverse childhood experiences is still a new one.

I recall the occasion on which an older man said to me: 'I have worked out that my ACEs are the result of a lengthy stay I had in a children's hospital ward in the 1950s. I have never seen that listed amongst ACEs, but it is absolutely where I suffered, not only because of forced separation from my mother but also at the hands of impatient nurses. I have never really recovered from those experiences'. If hospitals dedicated to caring for children can foster lasting emotional injury, then so can elite educational institutions.

Get curious about your institutional policies and practice. If you are a member of staff at a boarding school, it is imperative that you and your colleagues find the courage for reflection. Is there any possibility that your institution could be causing emotional harm to children or young people? Harm can be caused without awareness or intention and can hide in plain sight, amongst ordinary, everyday routines. Most institutions still resist undertaking such contemplation precisely because they are nervous, even ashamed, about what they might discover. That resistance is denial in action. A therapist who works with boarding school survivors wrote recently to me to say: 'Nothing is going to change until boarding schools (and the government) recognise attachment theory, as only then will they change their policies. Meanwhile, we have thousands of children in these schools, with no access to trauma-informed support'. Change starts because someone is willing to go first. Your institution can set courageous new standards for how children are treated and how they mature. It can set the example for helping adult survivors to recover from historic harm enacted perhaps in the very classroom you teach in. If you are not part of the change, then you are part of the resistance. While that may sound stark, it is the kind of uncomfortable truth this book seeks to tell.

Ban early boarding. Many critics have called for a prohibition against early boarding. Given what we now know about the long-term impacts of childhood distress, it is incumbent upon us to ask difficult questions about whether early boarding remains acceptable. Institutional practices that were once common, such as corporal punishment and poor food, are no longer tolerated. Might we be moving towards a time in which early boarding is similarly regarded? If so, the question arises: what age is suitable for boarding? Many residential schools still advertise for children from the age of seven. Is that an acceptable norm? If not, what should the minimum norm be? On what grounds do you choose between 8 or 9 or 11 or 16? Coalitions such as Boarding School Action have been campaigning on this very question (McVeigh, 2014), but there is a long way yet to go. Their arguments are underpinned by the United Nations Convention on the Rights of the Child (1989), to which the United Kingdom is a signatory. It promises children that they have a legal right to a family life. It is indeed a challenge to think of boarding schools, which are so culturally esteemed, as contravening children's rights. I believe that major progress on this shift can begin only when institutions finally become willing to engage with the discomforting idea that the 'service' they offer (and from which they make money) can cause children emotional harm. Once you stop denying the risk, you get much better at safeguarding children.

Ensure that parents consider attachment needs. There are 65,000 children in British boarding schools today, approximately 40% of whom are from overseas (Independent Schools Council, 2021). Their parents have made the choice to send them for a variety of reasons. One thing that can be done to reduce denial about the issues discussed in this chapter is to ensure that parents are informed about children's attachment needs, even when those insights are uncomfortable. The advice that would then follow might include:

Do not send children to boarding school at an early age, and do not send them against their will.

Ensure that parents talk with their children about this decision and that they listen to all of children's feelings, especially uncomfortable ones.

Listen closely to what children tell you. Don't try to talk them out of any difficult feelings, but instead discuss together what a parent can do to support them when they feel this way. This support helps children to develop self-awareness about what they need during times of distress. That self-awareness will serve them not only in the present, but also in the future.

Send the child to school with familiar objects that will help them feel connected to home. These might be stuffed animals, clothing, jewellery, photographs, or a bottle of Mum's perfume. These all fall into the category of 'transitional objects',[2] which serve as a bridge to home when a child is missing someone they love. The sensory nature of the object has a physiological impact on the child's stress system, comforting the agitation caused by the grief of longing.

Absolutely ensure that children are not subjected to bullying or other forms of neglect and abuse. If there is any possibility of such threat, children need to be able to trust parents enough to tell them about it.

If the school does not have a safeguarding policy that the parents believe will facilitate emotional and physical safety, then they should not send their child to that school.

We have learned a tremendous amount in the past decades about the long-term, biological importance of steady, attuned relationships. We have become aware of the realities of children living in residential institutions. There is no longer any reason that children should have to suffer to be at school. It is our responsibility as the adults to ensure that they don't.

2.6   Conclusion

I have learned much about our common humanity by working with the boarding school community. I began my career as a developmental psychologist more than 30 years ago, studying babies. I have never lost my fascination with the idea that we are born already able to connect with others, already active participants in relationships. Understanding the harm suffered by so many children who were sent to boarding school by parents who wanted, for the best of reasons or the most conventional of reasons, to strengthen their 'character' has only bolstered my fascination. Human beings have a biological need for belonging. It is up to us whether the 'belonging environments' we create are grounded in emotional thriving or emotional dysfunction. This is as true for educational establishments as it is for our wider society. Let's keep finding the courage to be curious.

Notes

1 Bowlby, J. (1981). *Attachment and Loss: Retrospect and Prospect. American Journal of Orthopsychiatry*, 52[4], 664–678. This forgotten link is discussed in: Partridge, S. (2019). *The origins of the adverse childhood experiences movement and child sexual abuse: A brief history*. Attachment, 13(1), 113–116.
2 The term 'transitional object' was first introduced by paediatrician Donald Winnicott in 1950s. Alper (2011) provides an excellent overview of his ideas and how they extend from infancy into later childhood.

Bibliography

Alper, M. 2011. *Transitional objects and other companions of childhood*. Blog Series. https://merylalper.com/2011/06/28/transitional-objects/]

Bateson, G. 1956. *Toward a theory of schizophrenia*. Behavioural Science, 1(4), 251–256.

Beard, R. 2021. *Sad Little Men: How Public Schools Failed Britain*. Vintage Digital Publishers.

Blystone, D. 2022. *Who Is Elon Musk?* Investopedia website. https://www.investopedia.com/articles/personal-finance/061015/how-elon-musk-became-elon-musk.asp

Boarding School Survivors Annual Conference. https://www.boardingschoolsurvivors.co.uk/

Boarding School Survivors. Closed Facebook Group. https://www.facebook.com/groups/143749179546597/

Bowlby, J. 1981. *Attachment and loss: Retrospect and prospect*. American Journal of Orthopsychiatry, 52(4), 664–678.

Brittan, J. 2021. *The female perspective of boarding school*. Podcast series 'An Evolving Man', led by Piers Cross. https://www.piers-cross.com/aem-podcast-18-joanna-brittan-the-female-perspective-of-boarding-school-child-sexual-abuse-csa

Cross, P. An Evolving Man Podcast Series. https://www.piers-cross.com/an-evolving-man-podcast

Duffell, N. 2000. *The Making of Them: The British Attitude to Children and the Boarding School System*. Lone Arrow Press.

Felitti, V. 2002. *The relation between adverse childhood experiences and adult health: turning gold into lead*. The Permanente Journal, 6(1): 44–47. https://www.ncbi.nlm.nih.gov/pmc/articles/PMC6220625/

Felitti, V. J., Anda, R.F., et al. 1998. *Relationship of childhood abuse and household dysfunction to many of the leading causes of death in adults: The Adverse Childhood Experiences (ACE) study*. American Journal of Preventative Medicine, 14(4), 245–58.

Forbes, P. *Biography*. Website. https://peterforbes.org/biography

Gammidge, T. Norton *Grim and Me*. https://www.tonygammidge.com/norton-grim-and-me

Glennon, C. & Hinton, C. 2020. *Character Education at Eton*. Report published by Research Schools International. Quote from page 29. https://www.etoncollege.com/wp-content/uploads/2020/06/Character-Education-at-Eton-final.pdf

Gold, C. M. & Tronick, E. 2020. *The Power of Discord: Why the Ups and Downs of Relationships are the Secret to Building Intimacy, Resilience and Trust.* Little, Brown & Spark Publishers.

Independent Schools Council. 2021. *Census and Annual Report.* London. https://www.isc.co.uk/media/7496/isc_census_2021_final.pdf

Maria. 2019. *England's ruling pathology: Boarding school syndrome.* Contribution to blog series: 'Out of the Crooked Timber of Humanity'. https://crookedtimber.org/2019/11/07/englands-ruling-pathology-boarding-school-syndrome/

McVeigh, T. 2014. *Campaign urges boarding schools to stop taking young children.* The Observer, 10 May 2014. https://www.theguardian.com/education/2014/may/10/campaign-boarding-schools-young-children

Oreskes, N. 2022. *Why didn't they act?* In Thunberg, G. (Ed.), *The Climate Book.* Penguin Random House: New York. Quote pg. 31.

Partridge, S. 2013. *Review of TV series: 'Stiff upper lip'.* Attachment: New Directions in Psychotherapy and Relational Psychoanalysis, 7, 111–116.

Partridge, S. 2019. *The origins of the adverse childhood experiences movement and child sexual abuse: A brief history.* Attachment, 13(1), 113–116.

Partridge, S. 2021. *Boarding school syndrome: Reconsidered in social context and through the lens of attachment theory.* Attachment, 15, 269–278. https://www.londonaceshub.org/_files/ugd/3f7b5b_d7b739d918f241bcbb4cad5effebb611.pdf

Paul, D. 2022. Twitter conversation. 19 November. https://twitter.com/TeacherTailor/status/1593972449489682433?s=20&t=f9-5L3CqT2izJnPa8iab0A

Pember, M.A. 2019. *Death by civilisation.* The Atlantic, 8 March. https://www.theatlantic.com/education/archive/2019/03/traumatic-legacy-indian-boarding-schools/584293/

Rees, G. 2009. *'Chosen' Confronts Abuse with Candour.* Website: Dart Centre for Journalism & Trauma. https://dartcenter.org/content/chosen-confronts-abuse-with-candor

Renton, A. 2017. *Stiff Upper Lip: Secrets, Crimes and the School of a Ruling Class.* Weidenfield Nicolson Publishers.

Schaverien, J. 2015. *Boarding School Syndrome: The Psychological Trauma of the Privileged Child.* Routledge.

Study International. 2021. *International schools in the UK: Building character through education.* Study International website. https://www.studyinternational.com/news/international-schools-in-the-uk-building-character-through-education/

United Nations Convention on the Rights of the Child. Ratified 1989. https://www.unicef.org/child-rights-convention/convention-text

Chapter 3

Transcultural childhoods, third culture kids, and boarding school

Linda Devereux

In an increasingly globalised and mobile world, many societies are becoming more multicultural and growing numbers of adults and children now live in complex cultural situations. The contributors to this book reflect this cultural diversity. Almost all of the individuals who have shared their stories here could be classified as third culture kids (TCKs) (Useem et al., 1963; Van Reken, 2011). That means that they spent a significant part of their developmental years living overseas because of their parents' work or education (Van Reken, 2011: 33). Although their unique life circumstances have been recognised as significant to understanding the challenges of boarding school before (Schaverien, 2015; Schaverien, 2019; Trimingham Jack & Devereux, 2019), in this chapter insights from psychology, the study of TCKs and the growing understanding of the long-term negative effects of adverse childhood experiences (ACEs) are used to examine the particular challenges for those who are sent away from their families and all that is familiar to board in a country which does not feel like home.

3.1 What is a TCK?

Ruth Hill Useem first used the term third culture kid (TCK). A sociologist studying the lives of American families living and working overseas, she labelled the country the TCK's parents grew up in as the 'first culture'. This culture strongly influences the home the TCK is raised in. For example, it usually determines the language(s) spoken in the family home and the family's cultural values and traditions. TCKs grow up with stories about 'home' – their passport country – and they may visit this country regularly and have ongoing contact with extended family living there. The 'second culture' is the name Useem gives to the culture of the country where the parents move to live and work. This is the country in which the TCK grows up. TCKs do not belong completely to either the first or second cultures. They are not fully *of* their passport country because they do not grow up within its culture, and they may be 'woefully ignorant' of the nuances of its social customs (Van Reken, 2011: 26). However, neither are they completely of their second culture, because they and their parents are guests in that country.

DOI: 10.4324/9781003533665-3

These globally mobile families see themselves as outsiders in their adopted homeland and they generally plan to return to their passport country at some stage. TCKs inhabit what has been described as a third cultural space which is influenced both by their parents' culture and by the culture of the country in which the child grows up, but this third culture is not a blend of two cultures (Van Reken, 2011). Instead, it is a relational culture created at the 'intersections of societies' by people who mediate or bridge cultures (Cottrell, 2011: 61). TCKs tend to develop their own life patterns which are different to those of individuals who are born and raised in one culture, and their sense of belonging may come from their relationships with others with similar backgrounds rather than from a particular country (Pollock & Van Reken, 2009).

Another important influence on the TCK identity is that these children's parents are frequently overseas in representational roles. They do the work of their sponsoring organisation whether it be the armed forces, a church or volunteer society, an international business, or an organisation such as the UN. These expatriates neither work for the host country's institutions nor independently. They work for their sponsoring organisation and, as the stories in this book demonstrate, these organisations can have a significant impact on the lives of TCKs and their families. For instance, there may be pressure on TCKs to behave in particular ways which reflect the representational role of their parents (Cottrell, 2011). They may find that they are expected to be 'little missionaries' or 'little ambassadors' (Pollock & Van Reken, 2010: 15) or to behave in ways 'fitting' to the military rank of their father which is stencilled onto the door of the family home in a military compound (Musil, 2011: 455). The sponsor organisation's policies can also dictate many different aspects of family life, such as when, where, and how often the family moves, which house they live in, and where and how children will be educated. This may include decisions about boarding school.

Many TCKs, myself included, have felt anger and/or resentment towards the sponsor organisation because of the decisions and lifestyles that were forced upon our families. In my case, some of the organisational decisions caused significant challenges, exposure to danger, and long separations from my parents and other loved ones (Devereux, 2010, 2012, 2015; Trimingham Jack & Devereux, 2019). I am not the first TCK to have felt that I was less important than my parents' work (Marshall et al., 2013; Van Reken, 1988). Donna Musil, the child of a military family, describes a similar reaction to the 'militarisation' of her childhood. Living with absentee parents, constant mobility, and constant losses, she led a 'highly structured life in chaotic countries' (Musil, 2011: 459). Musil argues that such a degree of control by a powerful organisation can mean that the TCK grows up learning that their practical and emotional needs are 'secondary to something else' and they may come to believe that their own needs have no value (Musil, 2011: 459).

However, the loss of the sponsor community which has created that overarching structure and its connection to all that has been 'home' can also be keenly felt. Military kids may feel cast adrift when they lose their military ID and can no longer visit military bases without an escort (Musil, 2011). Missionary and diplomatic kids may feel that they have lost status or their sense of purpose when they are no longer 'on the field', and mercantile kids may lose privileged lifestyles and the close communities of company compounds when they return to their passport countries. Anne Baker Cottrell argues that many TCKs grieve the loss of the 'third culture' resulting from the *community* created by the sponsor organisation when they return to their 'home' countries – often to go to school or university (Cottrell, 2011). The TCK loses a group of people which understands them in a unique way and to which they have had daily access. This loss can shake or shatter their sense of who they are and where they belong, and the TCK may struggle to find another space where they can create an identity which reflects their complex social history (Cottrell, 2011: 75).

There is considerable variety in how strongly each individual TCK identifies with the culture of their passport country and the adopted country in which they live as a child. For example, if they attend a local language primary school and make close friendships with children from their adopted culture, the TCK may be more likely to feel that culture represents a strong part of who they are. Some may even see themselves as primarily of this culture and they may reject the culture of their passport country (Palmer, 1999). In contrast, children who live in expatriate compounds with other families from their passport country and attend a school run by members of this community with classes conducted in the language of their passport country, may feel strong ties with their passport country, or, as described above, with their sponsor community. These children may be less likely to feel that their adopted cultural home, the second culture, forms a significant part of who they are.

One thing that almost all TCKs have in common is that at some point they will return to their passport country and this transition can be difficult. Because of their 'third cultureness', the child may feel that they do not belong in a country that is supposed to be home. The transition can be particularly hard if the TCK moves to a region with little population movement. They may find, for example, that at school everyone else knows one another and nobody understands or cares about their transcultural life experiences. The TCK experience may not be valued by their monocultural peers and teachers, and the child may feel they are regarded as odd, different, or even deficient in some way (Tanu, 2015: 22).

Those who have studied TCK suggest that there are many advantages which come from transcultural childhoods (see, for instance, Ernvik, 2019; Pollock & Van Reken, 2009; Pollock & Van Reken, 2010; Van Reken, 2011). For example, TCKs are often thought of as: flexible; culturally aware; adventurous and comfortable travellers; multilingual; and, at ease with people from a wide variety of backgrounds and in a range of social settings. The TCK contributors to this book valued their transcultural childhood experiences as the narratives in the chapters that follow demonstrate.

Nevertheless, there are also challenges which come from living the life of a TCK. In addition to those discussed earlier, many TCKs experience: multiple life changes and many goodbyes; grief and loss of friends, pets, homes, and environments; a sense of rootlessness and restlessness; feelings of belonging everywhere, but nowhere; and, a lack of access to extended family (Pollock & Van Reken, 2009). More recently, a number of researchers have also pointed out that TCKs may grow up in situations where they can be exposed to violence. For instance, military kids, by the nature of their parents' work, are exposed to the realities of war, violence, and death and they may worry about the safety of their parents (Musil, 2011). A number of TCKs grow up in countries with poor healthcare and infrastructure. Poor roads correspond with greater numbers of motor vehicle accidents and struggling health care systems mean people die from preventable diseases. My own transcultural childhood was punctuated by violence because I lived in a country struggling with the transition to independent government following an exploitative colonial past. The political instability and meddling by foreign powers led to civil unrest. Before I turned seven, I was evacuated from my adopted country twice, held under house arrest for four months, witnessed a violent attack on my mother, and learned that my closest school friend from boarding school was murdered along with her family (Devereux, 2010, 2012, 2015, 2017). My experiences are not uncommon in certain groups of TCKs.

3.2   TCKs and adverse childhood experiences (ACEs)

As a result of greater understanding about the long-term physical and psychological effects of exposure to unresolved grief, violence, and trauma, a number of researchers have questioned whether the challenges described above translate into ACEs (see Chapter 2) in the lives of TCKs. In a large survey of 1,904 adult TCKs, the TCK Training organisation used a slightly modified version of Vincent Felitti's (Felitti, 2002, 2019) ACE questionnaire to gain insights into the lives of TCKs (Crossman et al., 2022; Crossman & Wells, 2022; Crossman et al., 2023). The researchers chose this approach so that they could compare the TCK ACE scores with other ACE studies which have been conducted in developed and developing countries. They found that the level of adversity facing TCKs was 'higher than in studies of individuals living in single countries' (Crossman et al., 2022: 2). Moreover, the ACE scores for individuals in the study sample were 'higher than those seen in studies of monocultural populations both in the developed and in the developing world' (Crossman & Wells, 2022: 45). Comparative studies demonstrate that most countries have fewer than 15% of respondents with ACE scores of four or more. In the TCK study, 21% of TCKs reported ACEs of four or more, and they reported very high levels of emotional abuse, emotional neglect, and household mental illness.

Individuals with ACEs of four or more are: 32 times more likely to have learning or behavioural issues; twice as likely to develop heart disease or cancer; seven times more likely to develop alcohol dependence; have a 400% greater risk of emphysema or chronic bronchitis; are four times more likely to suffer from depression;

and, 12 times more likely to attempt suicide (Crossman & Wells, 2022: 9). The stereotype of internationally mobile families may be that they are wealthy and privileged and therefore at less risk of ACEs, PTSD, or other mental health struggles. However, Crossman, Wells, and Vahey Smith's study 'suggests the opposite' is true (Crossman & Wells, 2022: 46).

3.3   TCKs and parental support

A number of studies demonstrate that the presence of supportive, reliable adults is crucial for children who experience stressful situations. (See, for instance, Devereux, 2015, 2017, Ernvik, 2019.) Parents who are physically and emotionally available to their children can help them to negotiate changes, make friends, and develop a sense of purpose and belonging, either in a new country or when they return to their passport country. Parents can also help their children acknowledge their loss and grief. When parents acknowledge and validate the TCK's feelings as a normal reaction to change, it helps the child to know that they are not alone and that there is not something wrong with them. Crossman, Vahey Smith, and Wells take this argument further. They suggest that studies indicate that positive childhood experiences in the presence of supportive adults in a supportive environment can actually counteract the negative effects of children's ACE scores (Crossman et al., 2022; Crossman & Wells, 2022). Nevertheless, as the narratives which follow suggest, boarding school does not often offer this type of environment to an already vulnerable TCK. These institutions may, in fact, create an environment where the TCK is socially isolated, bullied, or emotionally abused and their ACE score may increase.

3.4   Third culture kids and boarding school

Another experience which those who have contributed to this book have in common is that each of us was sent to boarding school. Most of us were sent 'home' to boarding school in our passport country. For the majority of contributors, this was the UK.

Those who have studied the long-term effects of boarding school on young children agree that moving to boarding school is a difficult transition for any child because it breaks the attachment bond between the child and their parents and forces an immature child to become independent before they are developmentally ready for such a process (Duffell, 2000, 2014; Duffell & Bassett, 2016; Schaverien, 2011, 2015, 2019, 2021). However good the boarding school, the adults in charge are not the children's parents. They do not love the child as parents do.

Many children experience bullying at boarding school, and this seems to be a particular risk for those who stand out as being *different* in some way to the majority of children in the school. Boarding schools function by dealing with children in groups, and they aim to create a shared identity based on the ethos of the school. They have been recognised as 'people changing organisations' (James, 2023: 7, drawing on the work of Wakeford). This process relies on new children understanding how things work and 'fitting in' with the dominant culture and the school norms. If a child is seen as odd, or inferior in some way to those in the dominant group, they often become targets for peer victimisation (James, 2023). This victimisation can be through physical aggression, verbal abuse, humiliation, or social exclusion, and it can have a 'significant and lasting' impact on an individual's mental health in adulthood (James, 2023: 8). Of course, all children may be teased in a school setting if they stand out as being different in some way, but in boarding school the child cannot escape. They are captive to the institution (Schaverien, 2015). Day students can go home in the afternoon and talk to their parents or caregivers about what is happening. They can feel safe overnight and their parents may help them to develop strategies to cope at school. However, even the most dedicated boarding school staff are unable to supervise the children in their care 24 hours a day, seven days a week, and they usually have so many children in their care that it is not possible to give enough time and attention to students who are struggling (Cross, 2023; Franz, 2014).

Evidence from the Crossman et al. study supports the notion that TCKs may be particularly vulnerable at boarding school. 235 of the respondents in their survey sample attended boarding school. Physical neglect was reported by 15% of these individuals (compared with 7% for other TCKs in the survey). One-fifth of the TCKs who boarded reported physical abuse. Those who attended boarding schools also had the highest rate of child-to-child sexual abuse of any educational setting in the study – just under 30%. In addition, these students experienced the highest rates of grooming behaviour from adults or a person at least five years older than them. Overall, the rates of sexual harm were higher for those children who had attended boarding school (Crossman et al., 2022). The study report does not make it clear where these events took place – in the home or in the school. However, it is reasonable to assume that as these children spent nine out of every 12 months in an institution, at least some of the damage reported occurred in boarding schools.

TCKs who are sent to boarding school a long way from where their parents live do not have enough access to their parents and families. Living in a different country to their parents, the TCK boarder cannot easily spend the weekend, or mid-term breaks at home and they cannot go home if they are unwell. If their family lives in a very remote location overseas, it may only be possible for the child to visit them once a year for the long school holidays. These conditions contribute to a sense of isolation and rejection.

Adjusting to living in a new country is hard enough for children who have easy access to supportive and loving parents or caregivers. Adjusting to living in an institution – a boarding school – is very hard for most children. Doing both at once – moving country and moving to a new boarding school – is a 'double burden' for a child to bear. As the testimonies of the contributors to this book demonstrate, the double burden experience can cause negative effects which can last a lifetime.

Bibliography

Cottrell, A. B. 2011. *Explaining differences: TCKs and other CCKs, American and Japanese TCKs*. In: Bell-villada, G., Sichel, N., Eidse, F., Schellenberg, C. & Orr, E. (eds.) *Writing Out of Limbo: International Childhoods, Global Nomads and Third Culture Kids*. Newcastle upon Tyne: Cambridge Scholars Publishing.

Cross, P. 2023. *An Evolving Man* Podcast Series. https://www.youtube.com/watch?v=4cSthMeTEjQ Interview with Person Irresponsible. Podcast

Crossman, T., Smith, E. V. & Wells, L. 2022. *TCKs at Risk. Risk Factors for Globally Mobile Families*. Georgia, USA: TCK Training.

Crossman, T. & Wells, L. 2022. *Caution and Hope. The Prevalence of Adverse Childhood Experiences in Globally Mobile Third Culture Kids*. Georgia, USA: TCK Training.

Crossman, T., Wells, L., Vahey Smith, E. & Mccall, L. 2023. *Sources of Trauma in International Childhoods: Providing Individualised Support to Increase Positive Outcomes for Higher Risk Families*. Georgia, USA: TCK Training.

Devereux, L. 2010. *From Congo: Newspaper photographs, public images and personal memories*. Visual Studies, 25, 124–134.

Devereux, L. 2012. *Stuck Between Earth and Heaven: Memories Missionaries and Making Meaning from an African Childhood in a Post-colonial World*. Axon.

Devereux, L. 2015. *Narrating a Congo Missionary Childhood (1958–1964): Memory and Meaning Examined through a Creative Non-Fiction Text and Exegesis*. Doctor of Philosophy, Australian National University.

Devereux, L. 2017. *Overseas missionaries and their families: Can the homecomings for those affected by trauma be reimagined?* In: Jackson, D., Cornshaw, D. & Dewerse, R. (eds.) *Reimagining Home: Understanding, Reconciling and Engaging with God's Stories Together*. Macquarie Park, NSW: Morling Press.

Duffell, N. 2000. *The Making of Them*. London, Lone Arrow Press.

Duffell, N. 2014. *Wounded Leaders. British Elitism and the Entitlement Illusion – A Psycho-history*. UK: Lone Arrow Press.

Duffell, N. & Bassett, T. 2016. *Trauma, Abandonment and Privilege: A Guide to Therapeutic Work with Boarding School Survivors*. Abingdon, UK, Routledge.

Ernvik, U. 2019. *Third Culture Kids. A Gift to Care For*. Mariestad Sweden, Familjegadje.

Felitti, V. 2002. *The relationship between adverse childhood experiences and adult health: Turning gold into lead*. The Permanente Journal Winter 6, 44–47.

Felitti, V. 2019. *Origins of the A.C.E. Study*. American Journal of Preventative Medicine, 56, 787–789.

Franz, J. B. 2014. *The Mango Bloom. Managing a Missionary Children's Hostel in Zaire*. Denver Colorado, Ourskirts Press.

James, G. 2023. *The psychological impact of sending children away to boarding schools in Britain: Is there cause for concern?* British Journal of Psychotherapy, 39, 592–610.

Marshall, J., Taylor, M., Philips, H. & Browne, D. 2013. *Mission and Motherhood: The Hidden Sacrifice. A Snapshot of Yakusu Missionary Mothers*. San Bernardo CA, Jane Marshall.

Musil, D. 2011. *On making BRATS*. In: Bell-Villada, G., Sichel, N., Eidse, F., Schellenberg, C. & Orr, E. (eds.) *Writing Out of Limbo. International Childhoods, Global Nomads and Third Culture Kids*. Newcastle upon Tyne: Cambridge Scholars Publishing.

Palmer, A. 1999. *Issues facing returning missionaries and how spiritual direction can help*. Spiritual Growth Ministries, 1–8.

Pollock, D. & Van Reken, R. 2009. *Third Culture Kids: Growing up among Worlds*. Boston, Nicholas Brealey Publishing.

Pollock, D. & Van Reken, R. 2010. *Third Culture Kids. Families in Global Transition*. Boston: Nicholas Brealey Publishing.

Schaverien, J. 2011. *Boarding school syndrome: Broken attachments a hidden trauma.* British Journal of Psychotherapy, 27, 138–155.

Schaverien, J. 2015. *Boarding School Syndrome. The Psychological Trauma of the 'Privileged' Child.* Hove, UK, Routledge.

Schaverien, J. 2019. *Foreword.* In: Simpson, N. (ed.) *Finding Our Way Home. Women's Accounts of Being Sent to Boarding School.* Abingdon, UK: Routledge.

Schaverien, J. 2021. *Revisiting boarding school syndrome: The anatomy of psychological traumas and sexual abuse.* British Journal of Psychotherapy, 37.

Tanu, D. 2015. *Towards an interdisciplinary analysis of the diversity of 'Third Culture Kids'.* In: Benjamin, S. & Dervin, F. (eds.) *Migration, Diversity and Education. Beyond Third Culture Kids.* Bassingstoke, UK: Palgrave Macmillan.

Trimingham Jack, C. & Devereux, L. 2019. *Memory objects and boarding school trauma.* History of Education Review, 48, 214–226.

Useem, J., Donaghue, J. & Useem, R. 1963. *Men in the middle of third culture.* Human Organisation, 22, 169–179.

Van Reken, R. 1988. *Letters Never Sent.* USA, David C Cook.

Van Reken, R. 2011. *Cross cultural kids: The new prototype.* In: Bell-Villada, G., Sichel, N., Eidse, F., Schellenberg, C. & Orr, E. (eds.) *Writing Out of Limbo. International Childhoods, Global Nomads and Third Culture Kids.* Newcastle upon Tyne: Cambridge Scholars Publications.

Chapter 4

Personal stories

Linda Devereux, Nicky Moxey, and 14 others

4.1 Introduction to our personal stories: why we write

In the part of the book you are about to read we share our personal stories. These narratives, or testimonies, are written in different styles and they reflect our different experiences of being sent to boarding school. We have largely followed a structure which Nicky suggested, based on the approach used in the workshops organised for boarding school survivors (BSSs). Inevitably, this structure means we cannot cover everything about so many years of our lives, and there will be gaps and silences in our stories.

Most of us do not write for a living, and some of us found it a very difficult task. Several of us found it was cathartic to write about our experiences. As Deborah says in her poem – writing may help to 'cure pathology'. Linda finds writing helps to clarify her thoughts and putting the words *on a page* helps stop them swirling around continuously in her head (Devereux, 2023: 126). Writing can also bring unexpected results and reveal hidden secrets to ourselves and others. Writing may contradict deeply ingrained patterns of being silent and not making a fuss or upsetting others (Barclay, 2019: 125). It can feel hard to break these patterns, because it is counter to many boarding school rules about 'not telling'. For example, as our stories demonstrate, many of us are used to being censored. We were not allowed to tell our truths about boarding school in letters to our parents. Many of us felt that we were not permitted to have our own voice. Breaking these taboos can feel liberating, but it can also feel risky.

An additional challenge is that we have all written about experiences that were traumatic. We have written about events that were deeply distressing at the time and which may continue to haunt us. Creating and sharing a personal testimony can be a powerful act for a survivor of trauma. It can create a place to 'speak' and act against family silences (Devereux, 2010), powerlessness, and shame, and it can bear witness to injustice and suffering. However, giving a witness testimony is not without risks. Stories can be misinterpreted, rejected, or used by others for different purposes to those the author intended (Gilmore, 2002: 699). Breaking a long-held silence, putting personal, and/or previously private, experiences into the public domain can feel intimidating (Smith & Watson, 2001).

DOI: 10.4324/9781003533665-4

Reading the testimony of others can be life changing. It can help us to understand more about ourselves, others, and our world. It can also be hard. Holding the suffering of another is not easy, knowing how to respond may be difficult, and understanding the implications of a story when it is about a very different lived experience to our own can also be challenging. It is possible to miss things which are very significant to the writer because it is so far removed from our own understanding of the world.

Writing testimony – personal stories about our lives – serves different purposes to writing to entertain. This means that what you will read in the section that follows is not necessarily 'good' writing in a literary sense. As editors, we have not 'crafted' the stories that each person shared. We chose to leave the original words and voices of each contributor with minimal intervention. Some of those who have contributed found it was impossible to write a tightly structured narrative, and the words have tumbled out more as a stream of consciousness. Others dictated an oral version of their stories to Nicky which they then later read and adapted. Traumatic experiences can affect memory in a variety of ways. Some people experience amnesia about certain events (Duffell & Bassett, 2016: 78; Schaverien, 2015: 32), while others recall excessive detail (Pederson, 2014: 339). You will find evidence of each in our narratives.

Most of us are third culture kids (TCKs). That is, we grew up overseas because of where our parents lived and worked. We have grouped the TCK narratives into three broad categories. We have used the terms mercantile, missionary, and military to describe the families of our contributors. One thing that the three groups have in common is that the majority of families were working overseas for a sponsor organisation – a large corporation or international company, a missionary group, or the armed forces. These communities, as our narratives illustrate, shaped each TCK experience and the decisions and policies of the sending organisation affected our lives in a variety of ways.

The other stories are contributed by women from a variety of backgrounds. One is a cross-cultural kid (CCK). She was sent to study in the UK from her passport country and home. Another was sent to boarding school because she was being bullied in her day school and a third writes about the shame and confusion of having a parent who had a mental illness. Deborah, who comes from a long family tradition of boarding, chose to write a poem. What we have in common is that we were each, in one way or another, positioned as 'different' at boarding school. We each experienced or witnessed bullying and/or exclusion from staff and/or students. In the two chapters which follow our stories, we have teased out some of the additional commonalities and differences in our experiences.

We have each sought to understand more about our past experiences of boarding school and how the behaviours we learnt as young children might continue to influence our lives as adults. We believe that, although there is a growing body of knowledge about the long-term consequences of early boarding, there is more to learn, particularly about the experiences of women, TCKs, and others who are somehow seen as 'different' in an institutional environment where conformity is safest.

We each hope that the risks we have taken in sharing our experiences will help others.

Bibliography

Barclay, J. 2019. *Afterword*. In: Simpson, N. (ed.) *Finding Our Way Home. Women's Accounts of Being Sent to Boarding School*. Abingdon, UK, Routledge.

Devereux, L. 2010. *From Congo: Newspaper photographs, public images and personal memories*. Visual Studies, 25, 124–134.

Devereux, L. 2023. *On a plane from Canberra to Melbourne*. Survive & Thrive: A Journal for Medical Humanities and Narrative as Medicine, 8.

Duffell, N. & Bassett, T. 2016. *Trauma, Abandonment and Privilege: A Guide to Therapeutic Work with Boarding School Survivors*. Abingdon, UK Routledge.

Gilmore, L. 2002. *Jurisdictions: I, Rigoberta Menchu, The kiss, and scandalous self-representation in the age of memoir and trauma*. Signs: Journal of Women, Culture and Society, 28, 695–718.

Pederson, J. 2014. *Speak, trauma: Towards a revised understanding of literary trauma theory*. Narrative, 22, 333–353.

Schaverien, J. 2015. *Boarding School Syndrome. The Psychological Trauma of the 'Privileged' Child*. Hove, UK Routledge.

Smith, S. & Watson, J. 2001. *Reading Autobiography: A Guide for Interpreting Life Narratives*. Minneapolis, University of Minnesota Press.

4.2   Third culture kids groupings

There is a concept in sheep farming called 'hefting'. Farmers who run herds of sheep across the wide open, unfenced spaces of the North York Moors, or Dartmoor, for example, rarely need to rescue a lamb that has wandered off the particular patch of moor that this farmer has grazing rights on; because the lamb rapidly becomes rooted to this little valley, this patch of woodland, and if it strays, hurries home again. Nevil Shute describes the same phenomenon in *A Town Like Alice*, talking about young calves in the Australian outback. A child who grows up outside the UK might know in their bones that it rains only in November, say; that the correct colour for soil is red; and they are steeped in the vibrant colours, smells, and heat of the local market. Now transport them to a boarding school in grey, cold, rainy England. There is little doubt that these children have an extra layer of bereavement to deal with.

Then, too, the particular culture of the child's family may play into the stresses of boarding school. These are inevitably broad brush, but are confirmed anecdotally by the adults these children grew into.

Might it be more difficult for the child of missionaries to complain about a boarding school paid for by the mission, so that their parents can do their vital work for God? If the child were to be so ungrateful, they would literally be putting souls at risk. Does this perspective make the child feel less worthy?

Similarly, the home culture of a parent in the Armed Forces, living a life of service – potentially a life-threatening role – might have been one of a stiff upper lip, fitting in to a situation however difficult for the good of all. These children may move home frequently, from one armed forces home to another; each time, the furniture, cutlery, linen that came with the home must be checked off against an inventory. Does this rigidity, this expectation of correct behaviour, make it almost impossible for an unhappy child to protest?

On the face of it, the mercantile child might have an easier ride. However, like the missionary child, they might live in more exotic locations; and like the military one, frequent moves might be the norm. This often has the effect of the family becoming the most constant thing in a world of changes, underlining the force of abandonment when the child is sent away.

4.3   Mercantile

4.3.1   Nicky M

My father was an honorary game warden when I was a kid in Africa (Kenya, then Zambia), and my lifestyle was idyllic. The weather was great, of course; I went barefoot 99% of the time. School attendance was often negotiable with my father; I was always at the top of the class, so my dad figured that a few days out now and then getting a different kind of education wouldn't hurt. We frequently went camping in a game reserve, and some of my happiest childhood memories are of listening to elephants' tummies rumbling as they sailed past ignoring us, surprisingly quietly, filling the sky as we crouched low; watching a giraffe stand on tippy-toe to nibble an acacia tree; seeing a family of warthogs trot down a red murram path, tails held as high as could be.

My mother didn't appreciate camping, so excursions were usually just my father and me. I have wonderful memories of sleeping in the bush, watching stars rise from the horizon, and the sky being so bright with stars that they threw a shadow. We sometimes visited Maasai villages, where Dad would be whisked off to talk to the men, and I would be ritually polite to the women before being released to play with the kids; knowing myself to be utterly incompetent as they stalked game, or made their own spears and bows and arrows, or even when they told stories.

School itself was a bit of a pain. My father's paid job was as a petrochemical engineer working for one of the big oil companies, and for some reason I don't understand that meant that we moved house a lot; usually every eight or nine months or so. And every time we moved house I changed schools, even if all we'd done was move from one side of town to another. I had attended nine primary schools by the time I was 11.

The process of going to a new school was always the same. I'd turn up, in whatever scratchy new uniform was required, generally after the start of term and always after the start of the school day, because change never seemed to happen with any regard to any timescale other than my dad's. I'd be led into the classroom appropriate for my age, be found a desk, be given an assessment; and then as soon as the teacher had seen the assessment, I'd be moved up a year group or two.

The shortest time I spent in an age-appropriate classroom was 10 minutes, before I'd even taken my satchel off my shoulder, because the teacher asked me to solve the equation he'd written on the board; the longest was a full morning.

I have a Mensa-level IQ, am good at maths, and was a voracious reader from a very early age. I remember coming home from my first day at school, a few days after my fourth birthday, and throwing a tantrum because 'they' hadn't taught me to write, as Mum and Dad had promised they would; I already knew how to read. So schoolwork was always easy, whatever age group I was in; and if I hadn't figured out how to join whatever looked fun in the playground, I could always curl up in the corner and read. The only school I remember actively disliking was my last in Kenya, something which was trying to mimic the British prep school system, with a straw boater as part of the uniform. I had to catch the school bus for that, and it was my first experience of bullying; my boater went out of the window, and my shiny new red Thermos flask was deliberately dropped and smashed. Luckily that only lasted a term before we moved country. I remember no interaction with a child at that school apart from that incident – I assume I read a lot.

The school day lasted from 7.30am to 1pm, so of equal importance were the afternoons. In Kenya my parents mostly played tennis; there were always kids at the sports grounds to play with, or we might go swimming. My sister is 12 years older than me, and sometimes got dumped with the job of looking after the lot of us – which she shared with the rest of her gang; care was sometimes a bit sketchy, but no-one got hurt! The Nairobi Club had a kiosk at the entrance to the swimming pool, which would dispense drinks and ice-creams, paid for on your parents' 'chit'; I remember my father being rather cross one time after I'd 'bought' ice-creams for everyone!

Then if we didn't go to the club, I was perfectly happy to amuse myself at home. My favourite of our houses was right on the edge of Nairobi, on a hill, with endless horizons. On the plain below was a train line, and occasionally a toy train would silently move across. Next to the house was a little patch of woodland, which I was sternly forbidden to go into, so of course it was irresistible to explore; and on the other side was a pair of children who were considered undesirable to play with, who of course made the best playmates. I still have a scar on my scalp caused by wriggling under the barbed wire fence to go and play with them!

The house's garden was also a wonderful playground, if I was alone. At the bottom there might be hedgehogs to find. Then the bank behind the house was clay, a perfect consistency for making endless dolls' tea sets, which would bake satisfactorily hard in the sun. And if all else failed, there was always sister-tormenting; she had discovered boys, or rather boys had discovered her, and there was often some lank-haired dreamer sitting waiting for a glimpse of her on the wall outside the house, or even allowed into the lounge, where I would wriggle myself between them on the settee until bribed to GO AWAY with a lollipop or similar. Horrid child :)

Both my mother and father worked, and so my grandmother had uprooted herself from England to come out to this foreign country to look after my sister and me.

She must have been in her late 70s when I was born, and I ran rings around her, physically – I don't recall a lot of actual supervision. She was, however, the person I'd go to and tell all about my day. Dad was for play and adventures, Mum was for hugs, and Gran was for stories. My sister went back to England to start nursing training when I was five, and in any case was at boarding school in Eldoret for chunks of the year, so didn't really feature in my early childhood. I was happy, and had all the company I wanted. I have a lovely memory of a time Gran and I went fishing – I think just before I started school – in the local dam. We caught a boot! When we moved to Zambia she went back to England for a while, and I missed her enormously.

Zambia was much less fun than Kenya. For a start, we flew on my tenth birthday, so I didn't get a party, and Mum had made me give away almost all my toys and books. I'm not sure why, but we spent months and months in a hotel when we got to Zambia before we moved into a house.

The hotel was BORING. There was nothing to do; Dad was off working, and Mum didn't feel confident enough to go out on the streets of this strange country, so we were locked inside the walls. No exercise; I never found the stairs, so even moving around the hotel was done via the lifts. Meals were a highlight. I put on a lot of weight – to the point where I failed a glucose tolerance test; I had diabetes. Probably Type 2, but not necessarily – half a century later I'm still not on the typical medication for it.

Finally, we escaped from the hotel into a proper house. And the house came with a dog! I'm not sure what happened to our Kenyan dogs, we always had some – but my own dog, a black Labrador pup, had been run over shortly before we left, so I didn't miss them. Mostly they loved my father, and tolerated me … There had been one extra-special dog, an Alsatian stray that adopted us when I was perhaps five or six, who was absolutely mine. To the point where he pined if we were apart for any length of time. He'd escape from whatever restraint or locked room he was kept in, and would appear in my school classroom, causing all kinds of consternation. Rex was a BIG dog, and didn't like people except for me. I miss him still…

Anyway, the house in Lusaka came with Tosca, a wonderful Rhodesian Ridgeback, who also looked as fierce as could be, but was really a sweetheart who was fine with being dressed in doll's bonnets and sitting in a row with the teddies when I played school. We once had a man selling something appear unexpectedly on the veranda, and this fierce guard dog leaped up and hid behind my five-foot-nothing mother! I got a bike and learned to ride it by cycling round and round the garden, 'helped' by the dog.

We moved house again, up to the Copperbelt and Kitwe, and a new school. I was actually kept in the right age group there, and was soon made Head Girl and Head of Sport. (I'm still not sure why on earth anyone thought I was suitable to be Head of Sport. Maybe because I was tall! I did quite enjoy organising people into doing house chants and the like at sports days.) One day I got called into the Head's office and told I was going to sit some exams that day, which turned out to be the 11 Plus exam for the UK. I passed, even though I was supposed to write an essay on the elm tree; I wrote that I'd never seen one, and explained that I was going to write about the baobab tree in the playground instead, where we played marbles among the roots, and ate our mid-morning snacks leaning against its warm bark.

Then boarding school brochures began to appear on the dining room table. There was no suitable secondary school near to home, apparently; I was 11, what did I know. I was given the choice, South Africa or England. England was exotic, a place I'd visited only a few times, and there was one school that played lacrosse; I'd never heard of it, but it sounded cool, so I picked that one.

\#

We took a long holiday in England to settle me in to school. I remember hugging Tosca the day we left and running my hand along the short wiry hair down the centre of his back. Neither of us appreciated the extent of the parting. I started school late, of course; my Dad was not one for turning up on time for anything. About three weeks late, plenty of time for everyone else to have settled into friendship groups. I have a clear memory of being driven up the drive to the boarding house and the housemistress greeting us in the hall. I looked up, tilting my head back higher than usual because I had to wear this beret thing, and seeing dozens of girls leaning over the balcony, silently watching me.

Mum hugged me and nearly knocked the beret off. I remember feeling embarrassed because the hug went on so long... Dad just play-punched me in the shoulder and told me to be good. Then they were gone, the sound of tires on gravel fading.

The only bed left was the bottom bunk, below a tall, sporty-looking girl who didn't look happy to see me. I crawled in, then sat up too soon when someone spoke to me, and ripped a bit of hair out on the bedsprings too close above. It might have been an omen...

Sleeping in a bunk bed turned out to be a nightmare. She could feel any movement. I learned to cry silently, rigid, missing home, Mum, my dogs, and the simple freedom to run outside in the warmth, knowing that all these were an impossible distance away. The only safe movement was to turn my head softly from time to time to pour out the pools of water gathered in my eye sockets, sleepless. Going to the loo at night was unthinkable; how to wriggle out of tight-tucked regulation sheets and blanket without disturbing her? I was cold enough anyway, how could I bear the run to the toilet cubicles half-way down the length of the house, risking being caught and punished for being out of bed? I knew there was a floorboard that thumped as you walked on it, but exactly where was it in the dark?

After about a week of this, the housemistress came up to the dorm to talk to me. I remember watching a game that some of the others were playing, trying to work out the rules so I could ask to join in. She informed me that she'd had a letter from my father, authorising her to use physical punishment, including the cane. I didn't believe her – discipline at home was the occasional spanking, and I hadn't received one for years. She went and got the letter; every activity in the dorm stopped, watching the drama play out. I read it; it was without question my father's handwriting, and his instruction. I knew I was utterly on my own then, no possibility of safety or support anywhere. I told the housemistress that if she ever tried to hurt me, I would hurt her back; and we left it at that. I crawled into my bed-cave and turned my head to the wall.

That turned out to be the last straw, beyond the point my 11-year-old self could cope with. I started wetting my knickers in the daytime, desperately ashamed, and with no way of dealing with either the problem or its product. I got a urine infection. I stank.

There were 80 girls in my house, and three baths. No showers. The hot water tank allowed for maybe ten regulation-depth baths before it went cold. The baths went to the first comers; those girls who had lessons in the classrooms close to the door in the main school, a quarter of a mile away, and who were faster than me. I gave up trying to compete. At home I had showers two or three times a day, in privacy, as long and hot as I wanted. I could not bring myself to try and wash in freezing water in those bath cubicles, with their walls only a little higher than head height. It was guaranteed that someone in the next cubicle would stand on the edge of their bath and peer in, maybe bring their friends to look too at the stinky girl who sat crying on the floor fully clothed instead of being in the bath. The loss of privacy was a constant assault on my soul, scraping it raw.

After a couple of weeks my dorm-mates had had enough. Tall-and-sporty from the top bunk leaped down, reached into my cave in the bottom bunk, and hauled me out, dumping me on the floor. I lay there whilst they decided to give me a cold bath, then four of them grabbed an arm and a leg each and tried to pick me up. We got to the dorm door before I was able to wriggle free and crawl back into my bunk. I picked up my book and pretended nothing had happened. The routine was repeated. Again. And again. And again. Each time I tried to go back to 'safety', feeling more and more miserable and ashamed, and each time more people joined in the 'fun'.

Somewhere around the fifth repetition something changed in my mind, with an almost audible note. I stopped being part of the group. I can remember with perfect clarity deciding on my course of action, and warning my tormentors that I was going to fight them in earnest; that I was going to save my strength until I could make most impact, but that I was then going to go all out, and someone might get hurt. The next time they picked me up I waited until we were in the broad landing at the top of the stairs, and kicked and pulled and punched until they let go. One of them was lying at the bottom of the stairs, very still. I stood up and started to walk back to my bed again.

It was at this point that the housemistress came running up the stairs and asked me what the hell I thought I was doing, the first time she'd spoken to me since the letter incident. I noted that the girl at the bottom of the stairs was sitting up.

I can't remember what was said, but I ended up in the sanatorium, and with a doctor's appointment the next day. He diagnosed the urine infection, which by this time needed pills and a course of medicinal baths twice daily. The baths were wonderful! As deep as I wanted, as hot as I wanted, and I could stay in that warmth and comfort for as long as I pleased. I even had a lock on the door, once Matron realised that I was eager for them.

I slept in the san for the rest of that first half term, going downstairs for lessons, having food brought up, bathing at leisure. I don't recall any contact at all with my dorm mates. Or with anyone else, for that matter. I was like a ghost, the only child in the building after school. I read a lot.

I quite liked this ghost-like existence; being alone was better than being despised. I spent most exeat weekends for the next seven years as a ghost, one or two other overseas girls wandering around too, rarely encountering each other. Half terms were usually spent at the home of one of my mother's brothers or sisters; at my favourite aunt's, whose own girls were grown, I was left alone all day but could get a hug when she came home from work. At my uncle's, my cousins were closest in age but I could never fit in. I remember going shopping with my younger girl cousin once. I'd never been on a bus, and had no idea how to do it; and in any case, I had no money for either bus fare or shopping – no-one at school had thought to issue me with some of the cash my father gave me each term, which was immediately confiscated. My cousin probably thought me slow, rather than being a lost child far away from home…

After that first half term I was sent back to the dorm. I was mostly invisible, unless someone wanted something. Most conversations for the next seven years were transactional, at the 'pass the salt' level – with the salt being dropped into my hand because no-one wanted to touch me; skirts held aside if we passed in a corridor to avoid contamination. I have a few clear memories of feeling grateful for being spoken to as a human being. The day girls were rather more communicative, but of course they were a subspecies; I had absorbed enough of the school culture to know that.

At least I had caused the bath nightmare to be changed. The sixth form got their own bath, forbidden to the younger girls; but every form below them had its own bath night. There were 12 of us third formers, and I was able to sprint faster than some of them; so I got a warm bath most Mondays.

You learn to be grateful for the smallest of mercies.

I went back to Africa twice a year, to whatever house my parents were calling home; it was rarely the same house. I remember being excited once because it WAS going to be the same; and then they had painted my bedroom as a surprise, and that loss of expected continuity was a blow to the gut. Those few short weeks of holiday were just enough to get a taster of feeling loved and safe; then it was time to go back to school. Airport departures felt like a ragged, blunted knife going in; and as the distance to school narrowed over the hours to come, it slowly twisted until the pain was white noise, and dissociation shut me down for another term. I have perhaps half a dozen memories from the seven years I spent at boarding school, other than the dorm events described above (which are engraved in minute, painstaking detail, down to the wood grain pattern on the landing floor). There is nothing wrong with my memory; I have plenty before, and after, boarding school. I can only conclude that mini-me was mentally somewhere else for the whole boarding school experience. It was safer.

#

4.3.2 *In loco parentis*

IF BOARDING SCHOOLS ACCEPT THAT CHILDREN ARE LEFT WITH THEM *IN LOCO PARENTIS* [WITH PARENTAL RESPONSIBILITY] ON A CONTRACTUAL BASIS, HOW CAN THEY POSSIBLY SUCCEED? THE RATIO OF 30 OR 40 CHILDREN TO ONE HOUSEMASTER IS FAR TOO HIGH. ANYONE WHO HAS BEEN A PARENT KNOWS THAT TWO CHILDREN TEST YOU TO THE LIMIT. THIS IS AS TRUE TODAY AS IT WAS 30 OR 50 YEARS AGO. BOARDING SCHOOLS COMPEN- SATE FOR THE SCARCITY OF PARENTS BY DELEGATING AUTHORITY ROLES TO OLDER CHIL- DREN. IT IS SAID TO ENCOURAGE SOCIAL RESPONSIBILITY, BUT THERE IS NO GUARANTEE. GOVERNMENT BY DIVIDE AND RULE MAY BE POWERFULLY EFFECTIVE IN SCHOOLS AS IN NATIONS, BUT IT IS NOT A RECIPE FOR HEALTH OR LONG-TERM STABILITY. BESIDES, THERE IS, I BELIEVE, A NATURAL LAW THAT STATES THAT CHILDREN SHOULD NOT BE BROUGHT UP BY OTHER CHILDREN. WILLIAM GOLDING'S *LORD OF THE FLIES*, IRONICALLY DEEMED IMPORTANT ENOUGH TO STUDY WHEN I WAS AT SCHOOL IN THE EARLY SIXTIES, IS A TES- TIMONY TO THIS. THE CHILDREN END UP SCAPEGOATING AND KILLING A FAT CHILD, WHO BECOMES THE SACRIFICIAL VICTIM, SYMBOLISING THEIR OWN LOSTNESS.

PUBLIC SCHOOLS HAVE LONG MADE LOUD CLAIM FOR THE VALUE OF THEIR COM- MUNITY LIFE. BUT A COMMUNITY LIFE BUILT AT THE EXPENSE OF INDIVIDUALS WHO HAVE TO SACRIFICE THEIR OWN NEEDS FOR CARE AND BELONGING IS HARDLY LIKELY TO BE WHOLESOME.

THE MAKING OF THEM, NICK DUFFELL, LONE ARROW PRESS, 3RD ED., P.156

4.3.3 Marysa

Aged just eight years old, I'd been coerced into excitement about coming to the UK to boarding school by my older brother, who himself had been forced to promise me that there would be unlimited sweets and fun times ahead.

Having taken off in bright, yet thundery, rainy-season skies at Lagos airport, the four of us – my mother Elisabeth, father Clive, and brother Chris – were whisked off in a British American Tobacco company car to our destination; boarding school!

The first thing I remember was the utterly grey, depressing sky and the endless rain, not like the dramatic downpours of Africa, but unrelenting and damp, which resulted in me feeling chilled to the bone. I was cold all the time!

We drove down a long winding driveway and came to a halt in front of a large Victorian country house, which had been re-purposed into a Catholic boarding school in the middle of the Somerset countryside. The headmaster, aged 50 some- thing, was awaiting our arrival with, as it later became apparent, that special, reas- suring demeanour reserved for anxious parents dropping off their children for the first time. 'Don't worry, they'll be absolutely fine!' he said, as he ushered us off into the large draughty mansion to be introduced to our fellow 'inmates'.

My father and mother left us to our fate and it soon became apparent that we had been abandoned. We pleaded in all of our infrequent communications home to be allowed to come back, but to no avail. The school had letter-writing evenings. These letters were all censored, so that if any child was to write about how they really felt, that child would be forced to re-write their letter, saying what the school would like the parents to read.

I was in shock and to compound matters, I felt so traumatised that I retreated into a shell of myself and didn't properly come out of that shell for two years. Starting life as a precocious, inquisitive, and chatty child, at that school I lost my voice, my confidence, and my ability to focus my mind on the educational aspect, which was after all the main reason I was there.

A month after our arrival we were called out of our lessons and taken to the headmaster's house, where his wife greeted us alongside him. They told us they had some sad news to announce – our parents had just split up. They also said that we'd no longer go back to Nigeria, because our father had been posted to Nairobi, and our mother would now be living in Holland with her parents! To be honest, the biggest shock was realising that we couldn't go back to our beloved Nigeria, which had been our home, or to our Nigerian family, who had nurtured us and cared for us as though we were born to them. I was in shock.

Soon after that, I, along with the others, were sat down in a large hall and made to do a 'test'. I didn't realise the significance of the test, so really wasn't concentrating and thought it too much of a brain-game to bother even trying to complete it, preferring to stare out of the window instead and dream of my African life that I had left behind. That test turned out to be an IQ test, the results of which led to the teachers concluding that I was 'retarded'. Wanting to learn Latin, I asked if that would be possible but was turned down on account of the IQ test results. This 'labelling' became synonymous with my name, Marysa Wicks – but this got shortened to 'thicky-wicky', or on the sports grounds to 'weedy-wicky', hardly the most flattering of nicknames!

I tried to hang out with my brother but was admonished by a very strict teacher with attitudes that belonged to the last century. She told me 'Little girls do not play with little boys'. 'So what do they do?' I asked. 'They sit on benches', she said, beckoning me to one nearby.

I had arrived with linguistically-perfect pigeon English, which was my mother-tongue at the time. After all Ibrahim, my father's cook, had essentially been the main caregiver, alongside his wife Mariama, for the formative years of our life, so we'd become part of his family, eating with them in their small house, surrounded by his children and enjoying the community spirit that was always so strongly a part of Ibrahim. This was not deemed to be the right accent so I was assigned an elocution teacher who, over the course of several sessions, worked on my pronunciation, through reading the Ladybird books, Jack and Jill. Now I have a 'posh' public school accent that for me hides my true roots.

Maths lessons were a particular chore, because the teacher would screech out mathematical questions, and if we got the answer wrong, we'd be sent to the end of the queue. And guess who got sent to the end, time and time again?

I asked to be relieved of having to eat scrambled eggs but was forced to eat them anyway. It feels to me that there was an element of satisfaction at inflicting suffering on young children. I was needle-phobic yet kept waiting at the end of a queue of pupils awaiting their jabs, as my surname was Wicks. Clinging to the banister and having worked myself up good and proper, the impatient, exasperated doctor made a point of jabbing me in a particular way so as to increase my stress and pain even further.

No, boarding school was not good in any sense of the word for me. It trapped me, limited me, curtailed the freedom that I had experienced bare-foot on the red, sandy earth of Zaria, Northern Nigeria, and it traumatised me.

Emotions at boarding school were to be hidden, so after a time I became adept at not showing them, or at least attempting to look more sassy than I actually felt. The shutting down of emotions is probably the single most negative influence of the experience of boarding school, because it has made healthy conflict-resolution extremely challenging in my adult life, as it did not equip me with the right emotional tools. From a starting point of disengagement and dissociation it has taken a life-time of learning to access my feelings again and be able to talk about them. This is a journey I am still on.

#

4.3.4   On toughening up

... WE CAN WELL IMAGINE THAT A LITTLE BOY WHO HAS EXPERIENCED HIS PARENTS' CARE EVERY DAY OF HIS LIFE SO FAR MAY GO INTO SHOCK WHEN BEING LEFT BY THEM IN THE CONFINES OF A HUGE, UNFAMILIAR INSTITUTION. THIS *THRESHOLD EXPERIENCE*, APTLY DESCRIBED BY SIMON PARTRIDGE, MEANS THAT THE LITTLE BOY SOON REALISES THAT HE CANNOT IN ANY WAY CONTROL HIS NEW ENVIRONMENT. THE NEXT LOGICAL STEP IS TO CONTROL HIMSELF. THE FIRST THING TO DEAL WITH IS HIS EVIDENT FEAR AT BEING ALONE AND HIS SAD FEELINGS THAT GO ALONG WITH IT, COMMONLY KNOWN AS HOMESICKNESS. HE HAS NO OTHER CHOICE BUT TO REPRESS THESE FEELINGS AND TO REFUSE TO IDENTIFY HIMSELF AS ONE WHO HAS SUCH EMOTIONS, BECAUSE TO BE SEEN FEELING THESE THINGS WOULD MAKE HIM VULNERABLE AMONGST THE OTHER LITTLE BOYS WHO ARE BUSY TOUGHENING UP.

WOUNDED LEADERS, NICK DUFFELL, LONE ARROW PRESS,
2ND ED., P. 79

4.3.5   Morag

I was born in The Hague, Holland and I had a brother called Ewan who was two years older than me. He had been born in Algeria and sometime between him and me we moved to Holland.

My father worked for Shell Oil Company as a geophysicist so he was finding the oil! My mother had been to college and qualified as a physiotherapist in Glasgow but left any possibility of working in that field behind when she married Dad and started life as a Shell wife. Women were not allowed to work as Shell wives.

Mum was left alone in Algiers when Ewan was born, and she had to get on with life – a 23-year-old Scottish girl never out of Scotland and deposited in a foreign land. The men would go to the Interior (desert) for six weeks at a time and come back for two weeks at home.

The Algerian war erupted whilst my parents were living there – their flat was bombed. My mother always had a very 'get on with it' attitude, and maybe this type of experience is where it all began for her.

When the family moved to The Hague life was a little different I think as Dad was home-based. My parents were a loving couple and we had a pretty balanced home life I think, not that I remember lots about it.

We moved to Bromley, London when I was about six months old and lived in a very suburban street. Again Dad went up to Shell Centre in London each day to work and Mum was at home with us. I don't remember anything about this time at all but I can imagine it was very isolating for my mother.

We moved to Brunei after this when I was about three years old and lived in the Shell Camp. These camps were quite colonial in style, very elegant houses, some on stilts, some low bungalows but all a little off the ground. The housing estate was always called 'The Camp'. My brother and I both went to the Shell school there and I think this was a very happy time for all of us. We had two servants, a household helper and a gardener, and a lovely house. I had no idea that this colonial lifestyle was in any way unusual, and how strange it is that these colonial terms were still in use. I think the ex-pat lifestyle was great for us all, but I can see the start of real impermanence setting in while I write this. There was a very vibrant social life for the adults in these places. Lots of parties, golf, beer, and gin and tonic, and pretty, long party dresses.

We then moved to Balikpapan in Indonesia when I must have been about five, about two weeks before Christmas. I know it was just before Christmas as my Mum tells the story of having to take down the Christmas decorations and pack up home to move to Balikpapan at the drop of a hat. This would never happen now and I can't think what the urgency must have been to uproot a family weeks before Christmas with no notice. En route to Balikpapan with two small children in tow, our parents were told to stop in Singapore. We lived in a hotel for about five months as the houses weren't ready for us to move in to!

I had very happy memories of tearing all over the Goodwood Park hotel, and staying up late at night with my brother to spy on the dinner guests and cocktail drinkers.

We lived in the Goodwood Park Hotel in Singapore and went to school in the Ladyhill Hotel where our classroom was in a hotel room. PE time was swimming in the pool outside our school room/hotel room, which I vaguely remember as great fun. But looking back now at this story so far, I can't imagine how stressful this must have been for a young mother with her two small children. Times and attitudes were very different then. However, they did seem to be having a thoroughly good time!

When we finally arrived, life in Balikpapan was hard and wild. We lived in a camp of five homes in the middle of the jungle and it was basic indeed. We always ran around with no shoes on and were all over the place. The ex-pat women really struggled here with no mod cons; but we did have servants and a gardener. And quicksand and snakes! There was a very small school and Ewan and I attended the school with I think five other children. I think we only stayed in Balikpapan for about 18 months.

From there we moved to Oman. I was just six years old, Ewan was eight. He was sent straight back to Perthshire in Scotland to school as he had already attended six or seven schools and his education was considered to be suffering as a result. I wonder if the writing was on the wall for him already in his life, as he was a very sensitive little boy and was terrified of going to boarding school and being separated from the family. I felt his loss from home hugely and was effectively an only child for most of the next five years.

I on the other hand was able to go to the local Shell school for nearly five years and stay at home, which I loved. Again, home life in Oman was happy and carefree, or so it seemed to us then. I wore cut down jeans to school, no shoes most of time and had bleached blonde hair. We had no uniform at school, we went to the beach every day, had servants who lived with us. We regularly camped under the desert stars on only a camp bed. We did our food shopping in a shop called The Commissary (comi for short). I had lots of friends who were British, Dutch, and Danish too; the mix in a Shell Camp and our school was split fairly evenly between the English and Dutch speakers. As far as I remember we were educated separately too, a Dutch corridor and an English corridor in the school.

My brother really missed out on this experience and for that I am so sad. He used to beg to come home and not return to the UK to school each holidays, but off he went each time to cold dark Scotland. We lived in a world of sunshine, light, and turquoise sea, and Scotland was so very different to that. He was miserable at school and God knows what happened to him there. Our stories are interwoven, we were very close siblings and I loved him very much and tried to protect him. I used to feel so sad when he had to leave at the end of each holiday but didn't really understand what it was all about. Tragically, he took his life many years later aged 27 after years of sadness. What a fuck up. He had succumbed to mental health issues and suffered from addiction problems.

So that was me up to the age of ten when I also went back to Scotland to St Leonards School in St Andrews. The junior school was called St Katherine's and it was a big, grey, imposing boarding house. I had been a very carefree and happy girl full of fun and mischief when I was small. I was already quite an independent little lady, often called bossy, who was quite capable of taking care of myself aged seven or so. I can see now how this personality may have been formed by having to be grown up about leaving, moving, loss, settling in to new places, and just generally coping with whatever was thrown at us.

By aged ten, I had lived in nine different homes in seven different countries. We went on to move to Sarawak in Malaysia when I was 12, before finally moving back to Bromley in Greater London, Kent; then my parents' last move was to Sussex when I was 14 years old.

So this sounds to me now like a long list of places which was my life, no wonder I can't remember much. I feel sad that I can't go back to that heat and dust which feels like home to me. But now my home is Thame and I am rooted here, not moving again – well, maybe!

#

Arriving at St Katherine's School, St Leonard's, Fife, Scotland
I clearly remember arriving at St K's with my parents on a dark, cold, and wet evening in what must have been early September, aged ten. The boarding house had a huge stone entrance way with a door, and we were met by a lady in a tweed two-piece suit much like my granny used to wear in those days. There was a huge stairway ahead of me, one which I was to run up and down hundreds of times over the next two years. I have strong memories of flying down the stairs swinging round the landings on the huge wooden circular stair posts. We used to run down as fast as we could and try to fly!

On arrival at the house I remember almost immediately being introduced to a cuddly sort of older girl aged 11, who was to be my owl. I was to be one of two owlets who this girl was assigned to look after – she had two wings and an owlet to put under each one. My owl then showed myself and my parents up to the second-floor dormitory which had about ten beds.

I was shown my bed and chest of drawers and I almost immediately told my parents they had better go as I had a lot to do!! Already in independence coping mode, this story is told over and over as an example of how capable I was as a young child. My mother has told me how upset and shocked she and my father were by my approach and obvious lack of attachment and any concern at saying goodbye to them. From my perspective these memories are very strong, but they are feelings as much as concrete memories, of bewilderment and panic, I think. I can just remember the atmosphere in myself of having to get on with things and be grown up. It sounds odd to use the word atmosphere but I can't accurately describe it as a memory, more a feeling or atmosphere, a smell, an energy, and a colour.

I had a massive trunk full of outlandish uniform made of brown Harris Tweed, the like of which I had never seen. We had a navy-blue heavy cloak with lined hood, tweed skirt, and brown jumper for everyday wear, a Sunday uniform, a Tweed coat, a brown Gaberdine Coat for rain and summer wear, and a red cord beret for wear on Sundays and high days. Oh my God, what a load of stuff to manage for a girl who'd worn cut down shorts and t shirts with no shoes for most of her life!

We had a piece of furniture by our beds called a Judy which we could hang things in and put shoes in the bottom of. It was like a wardrobe with a curtain in front of it. So of course, no private place to put anything away, no locked area at all and no privacy. I have never before or after heard or seen of such a piece of furniture, how strange. Were these unusual furnishings just invented for boarding schools? Our duvet was called a downy and I'd never slept with a downy before. We also had a travel rug to put on our beds and mine was a turquoise mohair one which I had at school until it was threadbare.

I had stopped sucking my thumb just before going to boarding school as I was told it was babyish and I remember this transition well. I remember feeling that I had to grow up a bit.

I think I took one teddy with me and it was a tiny koala bear with fur and a grey teddy. These sat on my bed next to my pajama case.

My memories of my first days at school are very sketchy. I remember atmospheres and light and sounds more. I can remember the darkness, the long corridors of the boarding house, walking in our heavy cloaks to the dining room which was a few minutes away and walking along the covered walkway between our house and school which were attached. On reflection our world was very small – we lived and schooled on a small plot, and never really left the school grounds. In fact, to cross the threshold onto the Pends, which was the road which went down to the harbour and North Sea beyond, was forbidden and seemed very dangerous and naughty.

I can't remember any days in particular, any particular happy occasions or events, but I did make friends and get on OK in general, I think. I found schoolwork hard, and maths in particular was a big struggle and stress for me, but I think I just tried to do my best to get by.

Although I hadn't ever heard of a transition moment or transition as a theory before I attended the boarding school workshop I can identify a moment when I did perhaps transition into a different character, the character which I have lived with ever since. I can now identify the sensations that this transition was based on and I think they were fear and self-preservation. I could not possibly have identified these emotions then but now I can see how I was shutting down a part of my personality and growing a different bit in order to protect myself and survive, although I didn't even know that was what I was doing then.

What happened to me was that one day when I was walking back from school to the boarding house I noticed things being thrown out of a high turret window and the things were falling to the garden and grass below. It was in the afternoon after school, and I think I had stayed on to do some extra work. I realised that they were my things, my clothes and maybe a silk scarf I had as a comforter. It didn't take me long to register what was happening and for me to go into warrior mode. I marched up three flights of stairs to the dorm to confront the girls and stood in the doorway and faced them down. I can bring back fear, sadness, tension, and that feeling in my chest which I have felt for many years when faced with a threat. I was like a little cornered animal, attacking for my dignity and sense of self and unconsciously fighting for my place in the pack. I remember steeling myself to face those three or four girls and striking as hard as I could with words and my presence.

That sense of self-preservation has served me well in my life, but I now wonder what life would have been like if I hadn't had to fend for myself from such a young age. That sense of self-preservation has also damaged me in my adult life as it has caused me to walk away and leave behind people and relationships at the first hint of harm to myself or threat. The girls who were throwing my stuff out of the window became friends later which is quite odd, but maybe because I stood up to them. I have had ongoing issues with leaving friends and groups behind without almost a backward glance if things go a bit wrong for me. I didn't recognise until quite recently that this was as a result of boarding school.

I did become a bit of a troublemaker at school after this, I think. I took no nonsense from my peers and adults alike. I was quick to break rules and would have no qualms about pointing out injustices to teachers and standing up for myself. I was one of the girls who was up for a laugh and we certainly pushed the boundaries. I'm still struggling with rules, and have a big problem with authority – I'm working on this! Another effect on my personality, from constantly having to pack up at the end of term, is that if I'm stressed, I will throw things away – sometimes even sentimental things. And I hate packing! These things have had a deep effect on my life and my family.

I can see how hard it must have been to keep 75 girls aged 10 to 12 in tow, and we were essentially left to bring ourselves up. Rules and discipline were large at school, any love or care came from other girls, and we were a gang of little urchins trying to get through. But I can now identify that none of the adults really cared about us, they were distant and strict and our only little comfort was to go to the dispensary where we hoped we would be given a spoonful of malt extract at bedtime. The queue of girls each evening waiting to see matron and hoping for malt was always long. Sometimes you got a teaspoon, sometimes not. Sometimes it was cough medicine we were given instead and that wasn't a win!

At age 12 we moved again up to St L's to another boarding house, another chapter, another dorm, another home, different rules, same strange institutional life of repetition and regulation but in a bigger setting. The little fish had been sent into the bigger pool. The rebel was firmly formed; the rebel still exists in every aspect of my personality, and I thank God for her. She kept me safe and now I recognise her for what she is and laud her, but also now realise how she was formed. I need to set her to peace and rest and try to find the other bits of me.

That tough little girl who survived, that tiny terror who spoke back, who grew tall and became a lioness in life, love, and motherhood and who eventually stumbled and fell.

4.3.6   On the pseudo adult

THE PSEUDO-ADULT IS ENCOURAGED IN THE NORMAL GROWING UP PROCESS BUT KICKED INTO OVER-DRIVE BY THE ETHOS OF SELF-RELIANCE ACTIVELY PROMOTED BY ALL PARTIES – BY THE SCHOOLS, OF COURSE, WHO ARE SELLING TRAINED MINDS AND INDEPENDENCE, AND BY THEIR CUSTOMERS, THE PARENTS, WHO DO NOT WANT TO FEEL GUILTY. WORSE STILL, IT IS WELCOMED BY THE CHILD HIMSELF, DEALING AS HE IS WITH THE PAINFUL DISTANT MEMORY OF HOME, NOW ASSOCIATED WITH ALL FORMS OF VULNERABILITY AND DEPENDENCE WHICH NEED TO BE DISOWNED, BEGINNING WITH HOMESICKNESS. THIS NEED TO KEEP THE TWO CONFLICTING POLES APART KEEPS THE SURVIVOR'S BRAVE FACE ON AT SCHOOL AND HELPS IT MORPH INTO A FUNCTIONING FALSE SELF IN LATER LIFE. THE FEAR OF NOT BEING ABLE TO DO SO GIVES THE BRITTLE QUALITY.

WOUNDED LEADERS, NICK DUFFELL, LONE ARROW PRESS, 2ND ED., P. 81

4.3.7 Kat

The Beginning of the End by Kat Kjellström Corbet

Dad dropped the bombshell on a fine summer's day at my aunt's cottage in Norfolk. I was happily playing the recorder in the garden when he ceremoniously stepped outside and demanded my attention because he had 'an important announcement' to make:

> You won't be going back to the local primary school next term. You'll be going to boarding school instead. Won't that be fun?

My heart sank. The boarding school in question was about an hour's drive north from where we were living in Scotland at the time. I'd attended their Sports Day a month earlier and felt completely out of place in what was to me a foreign environment. Coming from a state school, I wasn't used to rubbing shoulders with haughty aristocrats or their arrogant offspring who had clearly already been schooled in the art of knowing who was worth talking to and who wasn't.

I quickly got the impression that lowly commoners such as myself fell into the latter category. I felt intimidated by their air of superiority and could sense the pupils' disdain, some of them looking me up and down as if I had no business being there.

Needless to say, I couldn't wait to leave the school and its inhospitable tribe that day. I didn't realise at the time that I was soon going to have to go back there to endure three long years of bullying, humiliation, and abuse from both my peers and members of staff.

The moment my father broke the devastating news, I slipped into a state of high alert which I've rarely left since. I didn't know what was coming towards me; all I knew was that it was so scary I could scarcely breathe, so unavoidable that any feeling of safety I might have had up until then was erased in one fell swoop.

Not that I'd had much of a sense of security before that, having already been uprooted from my birthplace in New Zealand a few years earlier, but what I did have was the freedom to wear what I wanted and to play how and with whom I wanted. That all changed when I was sent to boarding school, an all-girls' establishment with a strict uniform policy. We were to be groomed into a conventional Christian version of God-fearing young ladies with a knowledge of etiquette and manners befitting to our station as the future of the landed gentry.

This was worlds away from the refreshingly rule-free, gender-neutral existence I'd been allowed to lead up until that point. Raised by a liberal Scandinavian mother and an atheist intellectual British father, I'd been largely left to my own devices, used to roaming around outside, semi-feral and often naked!

At the local primary, I'd been allowed to wear my own bright red velour trousers since I refused to attend if forced to wear the regulation grey skirt and tie. At break times, I'd play 'Kiss, Cuddle, or Torture' with the boys round the back of the playground shack. After school, I'd either see how far we could jump down the stairs at home without hurting ourselves or create plays with my best friend to perform to my long-suffering father when he got home from work.

Whilst my parents were largely absent from my daily life, the babysitters charged with my care were kind-hearted people, some with children my age who I could play with and rely on to counteract some of the chaos in my own family life.

Though I can't exactly say I was living my best life at the time, at least some of my basic needs were being met and I felt relatively settled at school and integrated in the local community, despite the emotional neglect I was experiencing at home.

To this day, I still don't know what exactly possessed my parents to send me away from home at the tender age of six. What I do know, however, is that they were going through a sticky separation at the time and couldn't agree on who I'd live with (my dad/my mum/my dad and my aunt), which country I'd live in (Scotland/ England/Spain) or who'd get custody of me (my mum/my dad/both of them). A complicated court case ensued.

With this acrimonious discord as a backdrop, I can see how my father, a former boarding school pupil himself, might logically have come to the conclusion that placing me in the care of a single educational institution would be the 'best option' for me rather than have me batted back and forth between two warring factions whilst they battled out the logistics of my future whereabouts.

As the day of my departure drew nearer, an increasing sense of foreboding and dread engulfed me. Resigned to the inevitable, I instinctively started to withdraw inside myself, desperate to protect something, anything, of what I knew to be me.

The unpredictability of my life before I even went to boarding school had already left me permanently on edge. The prospect of being plunged into yet another unfamiliar environment far away from anyone or anything I knew only served to exacerbate my distress. I had no concept of how I would be expected to behave in this alien system or what the consequences of inadvertently breaching a new code of conduct might be.

I was shaking with fear when we arrived at my new school, months of anxious anticipation finally bubbling up to the surface. My apprehension only heightened when we were greeted with fake smiles by the pastoral staff. Their superficial welcomes were all an act, no doubt put on to pacify the parents. They rapidly changed their tune, however, as soon as my father had driven down the driveway and out of sight.

It didn't help that we'd forgotten to bring Aslan, my cuddly toy lion, who would have been my only tangible reminder of my former life at home. The uniform list was so strict I wasn't allowed to bring any other personal effects which might have provided some meagre comfort or connection with home.

That night, I couldn't sleep. Hardly surprising, given that I'd been allocated one of the worst beds in the youngest girls' dorm, right next to the door. It was left wide open all night, artificial light streaming onto my pillow from the hallway, keeping me awake.

Long after lights-out, I started jumping on my bed in a desperate attempt to tire myself out enough to sleep. It felt freeing! I was re-connecting with the person I knew myself to be.

What happened next, happened so quickly I'm still shocked when I think about it.

Suddenly, the dorm light was switched on and an angry adult stormed in. It turned out to be Matron. Quick as a flash, she'd torn down my pyjama bottoms and started to smack me on my bare bum. She hit me six times and then left as abruptly as she'd entered.

I lay there in stunned silence, my arse smarting with pain, my cheeks smarting with rage and embarrassment.

I felt humiliated and confused. I didn't understand what I'd done wrong or why she'd hit me so hard let alone hit me at all!

I started to sob but also instinctively knew I mustn't make a sound for fear of further recrimination. My six-year old self realised in that moment that it wasn't safe to cry in this hostile environment so instead I gulped down my tears, the first of countless occasions when I would swallow my sorrow, burying my despair deep inside myself to avoid punishment or the mockery of my peers.

I lay there in a state of shock all night, barely daring to breathe. If I allowed myself to breathe, someone might hear it. If I allowed myself to move, someone might hear it. So I lay there stock still all night long, not daring to make a sound, unable to sleep for fear of incurring Matron's wrath again. I felt like a hunted animal, lying frozen in anticipation of the next potential attack.

That was the beginning of my attempt not to exist. I figured that if I didn't draw attention to myself then I wouldn't be hit again. If I could train myself to suppress any form of personal expression then I might have a chance of survival in this perilous place.

Dazed from lack of sleep, I was in for another unwanted wake-up call at breakfast the next morning. As the youngest child in the school, I'd been allocated the most dreaded place in the dining-room: a seat right next to Matron where she could keep a watchful eye on me. Already silenced into submission by her actions from the previous night, I endeavoured to make it through the meal without drawing any negative attention to myself.

Alas, my plan to remain inconspicuous was disastrously thwarted by what I was expected to eat: a bowl of steaming-hot, lumpy porridge. Despite my best efforts to consume what was placed in front of me, I simply couldn't keep it all down. Halfway through eating what was virtually inedible, I started to bring it back up again. Clearly an outward manifestation of inner rebellion, the ever-increasing pile of puke was unequivocal evidence that my body had had enough of this vile substance.

Unfortunately for me, Matron saw things differently. As far as she was concerned, I'd only had enough when my bowl had been scraped clean. I was to stay seated at the dining-room, porridge bowl in front of me, until I'd eaten its entire contents, vomit and all.

Long after the other girls had finished their breakfast and vacated the room, I was still sitting there, struggling to eat not only the remains of the now stone-cold porridge but also my lukewarm sick which kept topping up the bowl and hence exacerbating the situation. I felt like Sisyphus, stuck in a seemingly endless loop of eat, retch, repeat.

I managed it though, after what seemed like an eternity. I ate the bowl clean, puke and porridge lining my belly as I was finally released from my ordeal to arrive at the first lesson of the day and further castigation for lateness.

Within the space of 12 hours, I had begun to harden inside until I had compressed the essence of 'me' into a tiny, tight ball of rage deep within myself.

So angry was I at the violations I'd experienced in those first few hours at boarding school that I vowed to wage a silent war against those charged with my 'care'. Whilst they'd already proven that they had the power to abuse my body, they would not touch my inner core. I wouldn't let them.

I only began to emerge again decades later when it felt safe enough to start coming out of hiding.

Even now, almost 40 years on, I'm still in the process of reintegrating the parts of myself I was forced to hide and have only recently felt safe enough to tell people around me that I'm non-binary.

\#

4.3.8   On rage

... THEY WANT TO TELL PARENTS HOW THEY HAVE SUFFERED, BUT THEY CANNOT, BECAUSE THE PARENTS WOULD FEEL BLAMED. BESIDES, ENGLISH CULTURE, AND THE INNER PARENT, HAVE FORBIDDEN THIS. BUT BLAME, IF NEITHER FEARED NOR INDULGED, IS ONLY A STAGE OF RELEASING RAGE AND ANGER, AND IT DOES NOT LAST. IF SOMEONE CAN ALLOW YOU TO EXPRESS IT AND YOU CAN BE HEARD, IT IS INEVITABLY FOLLOWED BY GRIEF WHICH IS A DEEP HEALER, AFTER WHICH HUMOUR OFTEN FOLLOWS.

RAGE IS HEALTHY FOR A SPECIFIC REASON; IT IS THE NATURAL AND CONGRUENT RESPONSE TO THE BREAKING OF NATURAL LAWS, SUCH AS THE ABANDONING OF A CHILD.

THE MAKING OF THEM, NICK DUFFELL, LONE ARROW PRESS,
3RD ED., P. 279

\#

4.3.9   Jane H

This document is about my earlier days before I went to boarding school.

So many children can remember before they turned five, but that was not the case with me. I think there were a lot of factors involved.

My father was in the British Army and had been posted back to Aldershot in Hampshire from Malaysia. Because my mother had suffered from ill health, with dysentery, my father flew back to the UK with my sister of about nine months and my mother travelled by sea in order to recover. She felt quite off colour and put it down to the fact she was not getting enough nutrition, but found out on arrival in the UK that she was pregnant with me.

I was born in the military hospital – my mother went immediately into a fever and it was three weeks before she came out of it. I was fine, but obviously could not bond straight away with her, and when we came out of hospital, my sister was not happy that I had taken so much of my mother's time from her. My mum would tell me stories of how Sue would give me black looks, and once she found her putting an electric fire into my cot – 'Mummy I was just keeping Janey warm' she said.

When I was eight months old, my father was posted back to Malaysia and we undertook the journey back by ship, settling in Malaysia until just before my fourth birthday. I remember very little about living there, just the odd feeling about playing with dinky toys under the house which was on stilts.

The worst part of leaving Malaysia (told to me by my Mum) was that we had an Amah called Leeja who was like a second mother to us. Our departure from Malaysia to Hong Kong caused an enormous separation rift and Sue and I both felt it.

I did not seem to fret as (again my Mothers' words) I was a happy little thing, full of sunshine, telling all and sundry that we were travelling by train to Hong Kong! Because that was what I believed we would be doing.

We arrived in Hong Kong and again there are no memories until my father left the army and joined the HK Prisons department. I have no memory of the school that we attended with the other army children.

We arrived in Stanley. Memories there are very strong, as we made lots of friends. We lived in a flat in a complex where all the children had ease of contact with one another, and also travelled to the local school, Quarry Bay. We used to travel in the back of a lorry or a Black Maria which was driven by one of the prison personnel and we took turns in being the guard. It was great fun and we had lots of friends, social events, parties, and beach barbecues. My dad was in charge of the Stanley Club entertainment and they would put on the most wonderful Christmas parties, with my Mum dressing up as the rear of the reindeer. It was so funny because we always knew who she was.

One time we were all on the beach playing and swimming when a typhoon warning came in. There was only one car, and about ten of us. So, we piled into, on top of, and on the bonnet of the car in order to get back home before the typhoon hit. We ended up going up the drive of the Commissioner of Prisons and sheepishly returning back down the hill, to go to our flats.

There were fairs and my Mum would make lots of ginger cakes – all of the prison personnel loved her cakes because they were so delicious. She also sewed and made us the most wonderful Christmas presents, dressing up dolls and covering cribs with net, because there was not a lot of money.

Sundays were amazing because we often had American pancakes (hot cakes we called them) which she cooked on an electric frying pan in the dining room, with lashings of butter and golden syrup.

My best friend was Christopher, who I have found out has sadly passed away. We would play for hours around the flats, and I remember his father was a doctor, who had to stitch my mum's finger back on after she almost chopped the whole thing off with a small chopper. The families would all get together and have house parties, and ours were always curry parties – most of the food made by my father, with loads of cold beer around. The inevitable happened and the adults fell asleep and the kids played and got up to mischief.

Diane was my best friend at Quarry Bay, although I do not remember a lot about her. She was Japanese and we swopped sandwiches in the lunch break because we each thought the other's were better. On the odd occasion we were allowed a school dinner, that would be the day when we had fried rice.

My sister and I did spend some time together but as she was two years older than I, although we shared a room, we did not seem to be that close. She was quite a moody child. On one occasion she actually cut my hair – 'Janey let me cut your hair for you' – and I ended up with the world's first mullet at the age of six.

Memories come and go of Stanley, the smells and sounds of the market, the children playing together in the playground and also the beach, the children's beach barbecues, and the odd visit into Hong Kong itself. Life seemed quite idyllic, and my school reports said I was a happy little thing. My Mum also said I was quiet and she nicknamed me Mouse.

Memories of a birthday cake, made by my Mum which was supposed to be purple and turned out blue – royal icing and very complicated, but she really tried to give us as much as she could, despite the circumstances. Fancy dress outfits were made by her for the whole family. She was resilient, hardworking, and still not well from dysentery.

When I was seven we were told that we would be going back to England, and having a lovely holiday in India, so we would miss a whole term of school. India was amazing, although we landed in Delhi and were asked questions by the customs people, because they were very strict at that time.

Once we made it through customs we headed for the most glorious of hotels, with the waiters cutting the top off our eggs with white gloves on. Sue and I were in awe of this. The smells and sounds of Delhi fascinated me. I loved the colours of the women's clothing and the buildings from the colonial era as well as the temples. We respected the customs and took our shoes off before entering the temples, and I learnt from my father to respect all religions as well as cultural differences.

After India we headed for England to visit family. Whether we knew there was change coming, I cannot remember, nor can I remember arriving in the UK. I vaguely remember going to the uniform outfitters in Liverpool. They could not find a uniform small enough for me, because I was to become the youngest boarder in the school, aged eight.

The holiday in India and the memories associated with it are vivid, but of arriving in England, very little remains. I know we visited both our grandmothers, and we prepared ourselves for school. My Dad sewed all our name tapes on our clothing at my Nana's house.

Trunks were prepared, and everything carefully packed, our names stencilled on; then it was all shipped to the Isle of Man, with us following on the boat.

It seemed such a marathon event and there are no memories that are clear after that, except the day that we arrived at the school. We must have been staying at my gran's, because there is a photo of us, and our trunks must have been sent ahead, because on that day in January when we were finally ready, kitted out with everything that was required, we were taken to the school. I do not even remember, after all these preparations and being so busy, whether my parents took the time to tell us what was happening, and that we were now not going to see them for six months. That memory may have been put aside in order for me to start coping. The memories of a child are so selective, as I have discovered, by talking to friends who were at school with me, many years later.

The big day arrived, and it was so peculiar because although my aunt had a car and my parents did not, she did not offer to help. We got the bus out from Douglas, walked from the bus stop to the school gates, and walked down a long driveway with hedges of bamboo on the one side – making a rather eerie sound as we walked down in the dark. My parents were clutching two small mini hamper baskets with our tuck in. Being a lover of cake, I was keen to see what we had been given, and I think that was more on my mind than anything else.

We arrived at the front door of an old Victorian House, with a portico, and my parents took us in and we met the matron and assistant matron. Strangely. I have no memory of my parents looking at our dormitory, but going directly into the common room. Arriving in the common room there was a new girl, Caroline, who had also just started. She had come from Uganda, but her dad had settled on the island after retiring from the Ugandan police force. My father started chatting to him and they got on really well, and Caroline and I hit it off straight away, although she was a year older. We were placed in the same class and we became firm friends for our school days. We made contact later as well, meeting up for lunch or a school lunch with all the people who were not only boarders but also day girls.

Caroline and I played a game, which I brought with me, 101 Dalmatians, with others joining in. My parents left, seeing us settled, and that was the last we saw of them until the following July. After that I only remember the routine of getting settled, and a very unkind matron who punished me for talking after lights out, without much of a warning. She gave me no second chance, just hauled me out and made me stand in the dark for what seemed like forever to a little eight-year-old, but was probably no more than 30 minutes.

My parents had sent me with all the required equipment, including a rubber sheet, as I had started bed wetting and so they wanted the school to be prepared! My bed wetting continued until just before I went to senior school, and was a cause of great shame to me. The matrons and pupils never said anything, but you could sense it when you had to let them know the sheets were wet after a night of deep sleep. I found that I was sleeping so deeply, I dreamt that I had actually got up and been to the toilet. What started this I will never know, but I was so relieved when it was all over.

We settled into school life, changing outdoor for indoor shoes, changing into our non-uniform clothes (civies or mufti as it was known at boarding school) after school, and also school meals, which to be honest were not too bad. We had a routine of getting up in the morning as a group, sharing bathrooms, and walking in a crocodile when we left the school grounds. A lot of heckling came from the pupils in the High School across the road from us, but we 'took it on the chin' and things did not look too bad.

Apart from the bullying from one of the girls in my dormitory, Stella, all was OK; not fantastic, but manageable. I had suffered a lot of torment from my father, who was always criticising me, so I suppose that this was just another version.

Stella seemed to take a dislike to me, and would pull my hair, push me around, and generally make life uncomfortable. She would encourage others to gang up on me, and there was an occasion where she almost swung me around by my pony tail, and tore the ears off my pink rabbit, which was all I had from home. The rabbit did not stay at school after that and was left at my granny's house.

I learnt very quickly to become the happy little girl that nobody saw as a threat, and went into survival skill mode, foraging for flowers in the woods with Caroline, and watching spring with such joy as neither of us had seen it in our hot countries. We explored and lived in our imaginations, and escaped from the things that may have troubled us. The birds that nested in the woods would often lose a young bird from the nest, and we would take it to the stables, feed it, keep it warm, and inevitably kill it, as kids do from lack of knowledge. We would then ceremoniously take these little fledglings that did not make it, creating a burial ground mainly for the ravens as they were in abundance.

My parents phoned to say they were returning to Hong Kong, and suddenly there was a realisation that this was happening and we would not be seeing them until mid-July. I seemed to take everything in my stride at that time and did not show if I was upset. Whether I cried at night or felt sad, I cannot remember. I had become quite resilient so I made the most of the time I had with my friend Caroline, with the knowledge that on my return from our six-week holiday, there would be someone there for me, a trusted friend. I was not a dramatic child, unlike my sister, so can never say when that watershed moment came, but I think it was the phone call my parents made. I do remember being called to the Matron's office, and we spoke to them, with her monitoring, so we could not say anything bad.

The weeks of letter writing were the same, keep your chin up, and let them know how much you are enjoying the school. My sister wrote letters from school, and from Granny's house, but anything negative about our life at boarding school was not allowed and she had to rewrite her letter. When she wrote to my parents asking if we could come home, she discovered my grandmother never sent them, in later years.

Exeat Sunday came and we were picked up by my aunt and taken to Granny's. They were very good with us and spoilt us, but as time wore on you could see it became a chore rather than something they wanted to do.

Easter came, and we were farmed out to my other grandmother in Yorkshire. I hated going there because she disliked me and showed it – many years later she told my mother she had made a huge mistake by branding me as trouble from day one. I think often that I was the quiet one, and my sister the outspoken one, so she got it all wrong.

My aunt as well as my father were both sent to boarding school. My father left and joined the army, and my aunt never married and stayed with my Granny, and continued to live in my Gran's house until she passed away. A month before that she phoned me – having had a fair few drinks – and told me that they never wanted us and that my parents had dumped us on them. You can imagine what a knock it gave me, as my parents were no longer alive and she was all I had left in the way of family of that generation.

Although I made the most of what I had at boarding school, made friends, sat on the fringe of it all, I know that I had that awful feeling that my parents did not want me, and in later years neither did my grandmother and aunt. It is a strange feeling, when you are a sunny upbeat little thing, to suddenly have taken from you the dearest thing to you, and that was my mother.

4.3.10 On homesickness

NEAR THE BEGINNING OF COLIN LUKE'S FILM (*THE MAKING OF THEM*)* ... WE SEE A LITTLE BOY OF EIGHT ON HIS FIRST OR SECOND DAY, FINDING A PLACE IN THE PLAYGROUND WHERE HE CAN BE ALONE AND LET HIS TEARS RUN. THEN WE SEE SOME OTHER BOYS APPROACH HIM, PROBABLY IN THEIR FIRST YEAR RATHER THAN THEIR FIRST TERM. "ARE YOU HOMESICK?" THEY ASK HIM, IN WHAT SEEMS QUITE A TENDER MANNER. "NO", HE IMMEDIATELY RESPONDS. "NO-O", HE SAYS AGAIN, MORE EMPHATIC IN HIS DENIAL. THIS IS THE DELIBERATE BEGINNING OF A MECHANISM THAT WILL SOON BECOME UNCONSCIOUS. HE HAS TRIED TO CONTROL HIS FEELINGS AND HE REFUSES TO IDENTIFY AS ONE WHO IS HOMESICK. HE IS NOW, AS IT WERE, WRITING THE LINE OVER AND OVER AGAIN IN HIS BRAIN: "I AM NOT THE ONE WHO IS HOMESICK/VULNERABLE/NEEDY, ETC". IT REALLY HELPS HIM NOW, BUT HE WILL FIND IT DIFFICULT TO ERASE OVER TIME.

* *THE MAKING OF THEM* (PRODUCED AND DIRECTED BY COLIN LUKE) WAS FIRST SHOWN ON THE BBC'S *40 MINUTES* SLOT IN JANUARY 1994 AND HAD A CONSIDERABLE NATIONAL IMPACT. IT IS STILL GRIPPING VIEWING TODAY AND IS NOW FREELY AVAILABLE ON THE INTERNET. THE FILM IS AVAILABLE ON YOU-TUBE. HTTPS://WWW.YOUTUBE.COM/WATCH?V=2URR77VJU8U

WOUNDED LEADERS, NICK DUFFELL, LONE ARROW PRESS, 2ND ED., P. 80

4.3.11 Jane P

I can't recall if my parents and sister accompanied me to prep school on my first day there in September, when I was eight years ten months old. I *assume* they did, based on a cine-film my father took, which shows me visiting a zoo with my parents and sister, wearing the school uniform. The film must have been taken on the day my parents drove me to the new school and one last treat, before we had to say our good-byes. Dad perhaps wanted to keep a memory of that day to look at later with my mum, back home in Iraq, when they would be missing me, as well as my younger brother, very much. When I look at the film now, I see a happy child, with neatly cut, short blonde hair, in her dark green winter coat, green corduroy beret, and brown lace-up shoes, darting about, eager, curious, and living in the moment, thrilled to be peering at monkeys in a cage, laughing alongside her little sister.

My prep school in Yorkshire was about 3,000 miles away from where my parents lived, in Iraq, the country where I and my siblings were born and that we called home. We lived there because of Dad's work, as an engineer in Iraq for an oil company. But that day in September, a chilly boarding school in Harrogate became my new 'home', if an institution can ever really be a home.

My initial sensations, arriving at the school for the very first time, must have included hearing the crunch of the gravel drive-way as we drove through the wooded dell, and over a stream, followed by the first glimpse of the imposing mock Jacobean façade, with its stone mullioned, leaded box bay windows. The main entrance was to one side; here we would have entered the large, dark entrance hall, in wood panelling, with a wide oak wood balustraded staircase, ascending upstairs to the dorms. Adjoining the entrance hall, at ground level, was the main Hall, again panelled in dark oak, with a large stone fireplace. Looking out from the Hall, through the bay windows at the lawn below, I might have noticed the enticing, leafy evergreen shrubs and thought 'Perfect for hide and seek!', and further beyond the wood and stream. It wouldn't be until later that I would find out that these areas were all Out of Bounds, areas we could only visit when out walking in crocodile, supervised by a teacher or matron.

How different from the *first* eight and a half years of my life in Iraq, when my siblings and I enjoyed such freedom. We played outdoors from dawn to dusk and roamed the gardens and alley-ways of our compound, playing with the other children who lived there. We explored the river banks by the sailing club. We spent all day outdoors in the sun, jumping into blue, sun-lit swimming pools, and only came in for meal times or for a break from the searing heat. My toes wriggled freely in the sandals I wore, to protect me from poisonous insects or reptiles, that might be hiding in the long grass. Lizards, camels, donkeys, goats, packs of pye-dogs were daily sights, and occasionally we spotted or heard more exotic creatures such as parakeets, kingfishers, or mongooses. On Fridays, we savoured delicious curries at the Club, served buffet-style on a long table, with piles of delicious accompaniments, such as nuts and large, juicy dates. Or we went out for the day on the motorboat that Dad, ever the engineer, had built by hand; we would motor slowly down river towards the delta of the Persian Gulf, where the Marsh Arabs lived in arched reed barastis. We watched the fishermen standing tall and still in their boats, made from hollowed-out tree trunks, blackened with tar, as they threw their circular nets out over the water then drew them in. We saw the silver sides of the fish glinting in the sun as they twisted and wriggled within the snare. Every morning we awoke to the sound of the call to prayer coming from the minaret of a nearby mosque, or to turtle doves cooing in our garden. Our lives were happy and carefree and our parents were warm and loving. And they naively believed what other ex-pats told them, that boarding school would be the making of us. Such a privileged education would open doors for us in the future. And the expense of sending us both away to school was tax-deductible too, as there was no English school there in Iraq for children older than eight. Dad's ex-pat salary was generous but this was an added perk.

It was probably in the large, dark entrance hall that the headmistress, Miss K, greeted me. I can't recall the moment when I said good-bye to my parents at the new school, and have since heard that it was believed at the time that parents should quietly slip away, unnoticed, whilst the child was distracted with something, to avoid unnecessary embarrassment or distress. I must, at some point, have realised I was now on my own, surrounded by complete strangers. Did I feel betrayed, having been told beforehand how exciting it would all be, how grown-up I would feel? Was I intimidated, or thrilled? The feeling part of my memory is buried deep, frozen within.

I can remember unpacking my uniform from the trunk in the dorm. There were eight or ten beds in the dorm, lined up in regimental style against two opposite walls, with a little chest of drawers between each. My precious possessions consisted of a few porcelain cats and dogs to put on top of my chest of drawers, together with a single photo of my family, as well as my precious Amanda Jane doll, with her voluminous soft red velvety dress, a zip at the bottom, where I stowed away my pyjamas, before placing her proudly on my pillow. The bed is an old hospital-style, cream, metal, creaky bed with a lumpy mattress, sheets, pillow, a few skimpy blankets and a counterpane on it.

My trunk is open and at the foot of the bed. It is green with wooden hoops around it, and a brass lock and clasps; there is a brown card label, tied with string to the leather handle on the side, written in my mother's clear, round handwriting. On one side the label says **Xxxxxxx Preparatory School, Harrogate, Yorks., England** and on the other, **12 Abdul Latif, Basrah, Iraq**.

'Why are you still wearing your beret?' the girl at the bed next to mine asks, as we unpack our things.

'I like it! Don't you like wearing yours?'

'You don't wear berets indoors! It's just for when you go outdoors, didn't you know that?!'

I had no idea, as no-one wore berets at all in Iraq. I quickly realise there is a lot I don't know about this strange new place and I'll need to be on the alert at all times, if I'm not going to be laughed at, or 'sent to Coventry' or worse.

The school bell rings, summoning us all downstairs to the Main Hall. We are told we must line up in our forms, the smallest at the front and the tallest at the back.

Our form teachers are standing opposite us, along the wall in front of us, with the headmistress, Miss K, in the middle. Miss K stands very erect. She is somewhat over-weight, in twin set and pearls, her white hair scraped back in a bun, her fleshy hands clasped together in front of her, her nails are so short I wonder if she bites them. Her skin has a marble-like pallor, smooth and fleshy, like a raw whole chicken, deathly pale. Her eyes bulge, ice-blue.

Miss K tells us we must stand in silence in our form line for five minutes until the bell rings. There is no question of disobeying her. I am standing in the line for the youngest form, all new girls like me. Suddenly I realise a girl close by is desperate to have a pee. She has crossed her legs tightly and is jiggling around uncomfortably. But we have just been told to stand up straight, in silence, 'without moving a muscle', for five whole minutes. I feel her panic rising, her face white with shock. As new girls, we don't yet know if we are allowed to put our hand up to ask to go to the toilet, during the five-minute line-up in silence. The next thing I know, the inevitable has happened: she has peed onto the dark, parquet floor. In tears – this sort of thing hasn't happened to her in years – she hides her face in her hands. At once, Miss K reproaches her sternly and orders her to stay behind to clear up her disgusting mess, whilst the rest of us file past her, in silence, to the dining room for tea. I glance back as I leave the Hall and catch sight of a matron, with a bucket and cloth, telling the girl to get down on her knees and clean up.

I cannot face eating the flabby white sliced bread and sickly bright red jam after this. It's hard even to talk to other girls nearby. After tea, we are ordered to single-file upstairs, in silence, to our dorm.

We pass the new girl, who has missed her tea, and been told to stand all this time in a dark corridor, her face to the wall. In disgrace, for all to see. The sound of some 80 pairs of shoes scuffing the lino tells her that the whole school is filing past her now, and seeing her for what she is – nothing better than a baby. I'm relieved I'm not her, I don't want to be her. I'm a big girl now, and soon I'll have new friends.

But in my bed a while later, huddled up under the sheet, blanket and counterpane, I must have done all I could to stifle my sobs. The 'me' looking back on this as 'observer' sees it all happen, and knows that it did. Yet I have no real memory of how I felt, I can only imagine that I must have felt afraid and very alone. And learnt from that very first day, that I must not show my feelings of distress, fear, or bewilderment. I must behave as expected, and wear the mask of a busy, chatty boarder, in order to survive.

A term is a long time for a young teenager, but to a child of eight or nine, three and a half months is an *eternity*. Knowing that I would not be seeing my parents and siblings for such a length of time, I must, at some point, have decided to deny and suppress any longing to be with them, as that feeling was too painful. By the time I did return home for the holidays, I had learnt to cut off those feelings and to distance myself from the people I loved most in the world. I see myself flinching slightly when my mother hugs me, and talking to my parents and siblings in a rather detached and superior way. Photos show that I looked different too, when I returned, a little taller and thinner, with straggly, lanky hair, quite unlike the smiling eight-year-old, with the neat, short hair-cut, beneath that green beret, captured on my Dad's cine-film.

And once home, the count-down would begin, as the day when I would be returning to school came closer, with each passing day, a dark shadow that slowly lengthened.

My school reports are among the only things I have left as proof of my time at Xxxxxxx and I find them fascinating. For example, they record that I behaved 'immaturely', and showed 'lapses in behaviour that were sometimes rude and disobedient', comments which occur on my autumn term report, a year after I'd started at school. Thinking about why that might be, I realise I had just enjoyed my first long summer holiday back home with my family and parents, in Iraq. Hardly surprising then, if I acted out my distress, on my return to prep school. I even feel quite proud of that little girl who managed at times to rebel and express her anger.

My parents and sister naturally wanted to hear all about my posh Yorkshire boarding school. In a grown-up voice, I think I would have said something like this: 'Well, it's a good school really ...' and then listed all the various reasons why that was so. I never dreamt of telling them the painful truth as I trusted their decision totally. And I play-acted the game of 'teacher and pupil at prep school' with my younger sister: I would tell her off strictly when she made mistakes at reading or sums, criticise her 'deportment', express my exasperation at her inability to make proper hospital corners with her bed sheets and blanket. Sometimes I even rapped her knuckles with a ruler.

My stammer worsened whilst at boarding school. I also had a mystery illness, which resulted in having to spend three weeks in a room on my own, frightened and alone. I was so ill, I was unable even to stand up without fainting, and have no idea who came in or out of my room at the time, except that a matron or doctor appeared a couple of times a day, to take my temperature and pulse. I don't think the school even told my parents at the time that I was ill. The first my parents probably knew of this was when they read my end-of-term report, which recorded the days of absence, and that my weight had decreased slightly too that term. Looking back on this now, through a post-Saville lens, it seems obvious how vulnerable I was then: anything could have happened to me during those weeks on my own. And my parents, who were paying a huge sum of money for all this, would have been the last to know.

We had a very limited library, consisting mainly of abridged versions of the classics. There were no lively, illustrated children's books, as you might find in a usual children's library. Lessons usually followed this format: we were instructed to read a few pages from a text book in silence, then copy it out into our exercise books *neatly*, then learn off by heart what we had written, so that we could regurgitate it the week after, in a test. Fortunately for me, I had a good memory which helped me secure a ranking in class, that my parents were pleased with. Such unimaginative, regimented teaching made life easy for the teachers, but hardly fostered our creativity or critical-thinking.

There was an obsession with deportment at the school. Whenever we had to line up in our forms or proceed around the school in single file, in silence, we had to do so with a rod-straight back. Pupils were rewarded for good deportment with badges, and the highest award of all, was the 'blue girdle'. We were never allowed to run around, to hop, skip, and jump on the grass like children would naturally do. Our bodies, like our minds, were being schooled from a young age, into prim and self-conscious, future 'young ladies'.

However, I had one outlet for self-expression at school, which was ballet. My ballet teacher, Miss T, seemed to understand the importance that dance held for me. I felt enormous joy when listening to the music, and letting my body express it, through dance, whether it was joy or sadness or longing. I was thrilled when Miss T gave me a starring role in a *pas de deux*. My part was to be 'The Dying Swan'.

I have many other memories of my time at boarding school which I have written about elsewhere – the canteen slop we were forced to eat daily; the school toileting and washing facilities which offered no privacy; the weekly bath in a few inches of warm water; the daily diet of Bible, hymns, and chapel on Sundays at the senior school; the early rises on very cold mornings; the obsession with ranking us all from best to worst in each subject; the requirement to go to bed early every night, long before it was dark in summer, and not to talk at all, after lights out; the weekly letter writing on a Saturday morning, in class – all our letters were read by a teacher before they were sealed up, to ensure we only said positive things; the daily ration of a few sweets from our tuck box, which we lined up to collect each day after lunch; the lack of any toys or board games to play with, except jacks, not even being allowed to throw a ball on the lawn, let alone do cart wheels or handstands; not celebrating anyone's birthday ever – I think I probably forgot it was my birthday, when the date came around – it was a day like any other, certainly no cake or balloons.

When the time came finally for me to leave boarding school for good, after four years, I recall my mother and sister coming to the school to collect me, my mother's warm and radiant smile, happy that we'd all be together again now. My parents had returned to the UK and I and my siblings would now be at day schools near our family home. I think I even felt a little sad to leave – I had become institutionalised. Xxxxxxx Preparatory School had been my home and I had been a part of that strange boarding school 'community' for four years.

My parents really believed that going to boarding school at age eight or nine was a privilege that led to academic success later. My own view is that my secondary education, after the boarding school, as a day-girl at a state grammar school, was what enabled me to then win a place at a top university in the country. In any case, the negative effects of boarding *far* outweighed any positives. The experience of being sent away from a happy family and home at such a tender age affected my mental health and well-being for my entire adult life. My relationships with my closest family members were never the same again. From being a once sunny, joyous, generous-hearted little girl, I developed, at a young age, negative, self-destructive habits of mind and body. My parents little realised, when they sent me away to boarding school, that they were bartering away my future *happiness*, as well their relationship with me, in exchange for so-called 'success'. Surely too high a price to pay?

Like many other survivors of boarding school, I have learnt how to keep it all well hidden beneath a cool, calm, if somewhat reserved exterior. It was not until decades later that I started to realise that I had experienced emotional and physical abuse there as a child. But I would never have dreamt of telling my parents at the time, and kept up the pretence that I was perfectly happy there. At that young age, I simply did not question the wisdom of their decision.

4.3.12   On splitting

SPLITTING ALSO VERY USEFULLY HELPS US TO RECOVER FROM SHOCK AND LOSS. WE CAN DIVERT OURSELVES BY TEMPORARILY SHIFTING OUR ATTENTION, COMMONLY KNOWN AS 'TAKING YOUR MIND OFF THINGS'. BUT PERMANENTLY ORGANIZING ONE'S INNER WORLD LIKE THIS DOES INVOLVE A HUGE LOSS OF EXPERIENCE IN EXCHANGE FOR A SENSE OF BEING IN CONTROL ... CHILDREN WHO BOARD TEND TO CUT OFF FROM FEELINGS RAPIDLY, EFFECTIVELY, AND SOMETIMES PERMANENTLY. THIS IS SPLITTING AND ONCE LEARNED IS VERY HARD TO UNLEARN.

THE MAKING OF THEM, NICK DUFFELL, LONE ARROW PRESS, 3RD ED., P. 76

4.4   Missionary

4.4.1   Linda

On a morning cycle, I was startled by a family of moorhens scurrying across the track just in front of me. The parent birds quickly shepherded half a dozen babies across the cycle path and into the safety of the long grass. As I went past, I heard contented chirruping and saw the family enjoying lush green shoots, the parents keeping an eye out for danger and showing their young what to eat. My mother and father were that kind of parent. They shepherded, protected, and instructed.

\#

Until I was almost seven, I lived on and off in Africa, in the country that is now the Democratic Republic of Congo. My parents were medical missionaries and I am a missionary kid. Back then it was the Belgian Congo and I lived there on and off because my early life was punctuated with civil unrest and evacuations back to my then passport country of Scotland. I was born in Belgium while my father was studying in Antwerp. He had to improve his French to take a course in tropical medicine before he was permitted to work in the Belgian colony. I don't remember Belgium because after Dad passed his exams, we moved to Scotland to say goodbye to my grandparents and extended family. I was five months old when we travelled by train, ferry, ship, and river-barge to a small settlement astride the equator on the banks of the River Congo.

Our house was basic. It had three rooms, a covered-in veranda at either end, and behind it, an outdoor kitchen with a wood stove. There was no modern plumbing, and water had to be collected in buckets, boiled, and then filtered before drinking. We heated water on the wood stove for washing up and for baths, which we children often had in an old tin trough outside the back door. My mother made her own bread, washed our clothes by hand, and cooked for her family. Unlike some other missionary or expatriate families, we did not have servants. My mother liked to be independent, but she did pay for help collecting wood and water and cutting the grass to dissuade the snakes from coming too close to the house.

Stephanie Vandrick, a missionary kid who grew up in India, says that missionary kids often highlight the exotic aspects of their lives overseas when they write about their childhoods. What some might call exotic was my normal in Congo. It was all I knew. I grew up just a few hundred metres from the River Congo, the second-largest river in the world by volume and the second-longest river in Africa. It was a mighty presence, wide and fast-flowing, and bounded on its banks by thick tropical jungle. Palm trees grew along the bank between the river and our house and in our garden, there were fruit trees, pineapples and bright, scented tropical flowers. I occasionally travelled on the river in canoes paddled by expert oarsmen who could manage the dangerously strong currents and shifting sandbars, or, even better, in a large canoe powered by an outboard motor. As a child I loved the feeling of the wind on my face as we skimmed quickly and smoothly along the surface of the water, a far gentler ride than in a vehicle on the rough and deeply rutted unsealed forest roads.

On the river, it was possible to see for some distance in either direction, and to look up at an expansive sky. In the jungle, this was impossible because the trees and vines met above the tracks creating dark, green tunnels and impenetrable walls on either side blocking out the sun and any hint of what lay beyond the narrow strip of road. Driving was also dusty, and in the days before air-conditioning we kept the windows down. We would arrive at our destinations with red dirt sticking to the sweaty patches of our clothing and streaking our faces.

Although I remember travel, it stands out because we did not actually do very much of it. Fuel was expensive. We did not, for the first three years, own a vehicle, and my parents were busy with their day-to-day work. Dad conducted clinics and surgery in the hospital and regularly visited the leprosy hospital across the river and the many spread-out bush dispensaries. When Dad visited all the dispensaries, he was away from home for ten days. Both my parents also taught in the allied health worker training programmes for Congolese students. We stayed in the community most of the time and lived a routine life marked by the daily drum calls from the nearby villages and by the watches the missionaries wore and reset to an agreed time at each Sunday evening prayer meeting.

I played mainly with my siblings. We set up logs between frangipani trees and learned to walk between them, starting out with poles for balance, but eventually running all the way across without support. We played elaborate games that went on for days with my doll and my brother's teddy. We didn't have many toys and there was no television. My parents kept in touch with the outside world by listening to the BBC news on the radio, reading newspapers which arrived several weeks out of date, and through letters exchanged with mission staff and our relatives and friends in Scotland.

Following the civil unrest at the time of independence, my mother, my younger brother and I were flown 'home' to the UK. It didn't feel like home to me. It was an alien other world that was completely different to my normal life in Africa. My brother and I revelled in the attentions of our grandparents, aunts, and uncles and in the television shows for children such as *Sooty and Sweep* and *Bill and Ben*. We loved the unfamiliar sweeties and cakes given to us by our relatives and spent hours watching cars, buses, trams, and trains. We marvelled at the milkman's float pulled by a large Clydesdale horse, and the grocery, fish, and ice cream vans that came right to your door and we climbed hills and walked on moors where we could see for miles in every direction.

We were not keen on the cold and rain, which we were unused to and which kept us cooped up inside. We missed our outdoor play, and the rhythms of our life in one small, familiar place where we didn't have to move house all the time. We didn't have a home in Scotland and so we shuttled about living with our grandparents and in various empty church houses where we used fruit boxes for furniture and wore hand-me-down and borrowed clothes given to us by family and church friends. We also missed our father, who had to stay behind in Africa to work for the mission. It was especially hard for my mother who, as much as she could, shielded us from her worries about Dad's safety and well-being when the news about Congo was frightening, post was unreliable, and she had no other means of contacting him. Overall, I learned to love Scotland and I was sad when we left to return to Congo. It was especially hard to say goodbye to our grandparents. We loved them, and they loved us and we saw them often when we lived nearby. We all missed our extended family connections when we went back to Congo.

\#

Not long after we returned to Africa, my parents began thinking about boarding schools. They, and other missionary families in the region, had been lobbying their various missionary organisations to set up a joint English language school in the area where we lived, but by then most missionary organisations were struggling to find and fund enough staff for the work they already supported. The organisation my parents worked for had a policy that children should be sent to boarding school. For most children from the UK, this meant being left behind with guardians and sent to boarding school in their passport country and, if they were lucky and war and other international incidents did not intervene, one visit to their parents each year. Instead, my parents decided to send me to an American missionary boarding school four days drive away.

I had no idea what my new life would be like. I had never been to any school. My siblings and I spent all our time together, and I shared a bedroom with my two brothers. I was not used to being with people other than my family and a few close friends. We had never had a nanny. Other than when my second brother was born on a furlough in Scotland and my father looked after me, I don't think I had slept a night away from my mother in my life before the day I had to get into a truck with strangers for the long drive to boarding school.

Leaving my family was a dreadful shock, and still, decades later, I cannot recall the moment of parting without a tight feeling in my chest and a lump in my throat. The people who gave me a lift to boarding school did not seem kind to me. One of the boys in the car was particularly cruel, amplifying my fear by sticking a small knife into my leg as we sat together on the back seat of his parents' car for the long, uncomfortable drive. I was terrified, and I wonder now why I didn't say anything. I think I expected the parents of the boy to notice his behaviour and stop him. That's what my mother would have done.

Perhaps I was shocked into a submissive silence, or subconsciously remembered that only a few years earlier, when Dad was in Congo and Mum, my brother and I were in Scotland, there was a real fear that he might be killed in the violence reported in the papers and on the news. The relief of having him come back to us the following year was profound. The world was back in its proper place – for a while. But now, we were split up again, and it was me who had left.

And it was a death of sorts. I was no longer my former childhood self. As the car accelerated off in the dust, and during the long journey, I left my secure childhood self behind. I split in two; my home self and my leaving-home, terrified self. All of me wanted to be back with my family, but the leaving-home me was sitting wedged between two bigger boys, in a car that belonged to another family. I don't even know their names, and nobody in my family can now remember who they were. I probably couldn't remember their names on the journey either. I probably avoided calling them anything. I was probably too frightened to talk at all.

But I can't remember these details. The journey took four long days. We would have stopped for three nights. We must have eaten almost a dozen meals together, but I remember nothing of those things.

I do remember, at some point in the journey, sitting as still and small as I could, keeping my body away from the boy who hurt me. I was on the left-hand side of the car with half-closed, out of focus eyes, willing myself out the window towards the light that occasionally sliced through the canopy of trees. I ached to be in the tops of those trees. I would not be where I was. I would not participate in this moment. I saw myself from somewhere outside of, and above, my body. I remembered this moment in an intense clarity of recognition when I read about another death in Congo in Barbara Kingsolver's novel, *The Poisonwood Bible*. The youngest daughter of the missionary family escaped into the treetops just before her death. I did not know it at the time, but I had just done something similar.

School felt painfully lonely and the ache inside continued. I was teased by some of the other children, regarded as a lesser being because I was not American, had a Scottish accent, and came from a different missionary organisation to the ones their parents belonged to. The other children all seemed to know each other and where they fitted in the patriarchal missionary pecking-order. I did not fully belong in their world. The two girls I shared a room with looked down on me and teased me when I cried that first night and then, shockingly, discovered my wet bed in the morning. I was not a bed-wetter at home, but it added a new layer of anxiety and shame to boarding school. I was frightened to make the long walk to the toilet in the dark by myself, and I struggled, at the age of six, to manage my personal care and to look after possessions such as my toothbrush and toothpaste. I was used to my parents looking after me and helping me with these things.

I felt completely isolated. I was only beginning to read and write and there was no telephone. I wrote letters to my parents from sentences copied from the board at school. I did not know what I was writing and I could not read what my parents wrote to me. I had little conception of time measured in months, and I could not imagine how long it would be until I saw my family again. At the half-term break, I waited all day hoping that they would visit. I did not understand that they could not make an eight-day round trip to spend one day with me.

Meals were a struggle. I was a slow eater and the food was often unfamiliar, different to the predictable range of things my mother cooked at home. We sat at tables of about eight, with a mix of children from five-year-olds to teenagers. Mostly, a staff member supervised at the head of each table; some staff were better at this than others. At several meals food was served on big plates in the middle of the table to be shared out, and because I was so slow, and not used to how things worked, I regularly missed out. At breakfast, some of the big boys stuffed a whole piece of toast in their mouths, while reaching for another piece which they gobbled just as quickly, their hands out-stretched for their third slice before I had taken my first bite. For a while, I did not know how meat disappeared from my plate, or notice the lumps of less desirable vegetables being shuffled over in its place. Some staff seemed unwilling to challenge the boys' behaviour. They were the sons of their bosses or other important leaders in the mission organisation. It was easier, and less confrontational, I suspect, not to notice what was going on.

One of the Congolese cooks did notice. For a while he kept back a few slices of cinnamon toast which he handed out, cold and soggy, to the littlest children at morning break time. I think he got into trouble for this thoughtfulness. One day, some of the bigger boys saw what was happening and ran over demanding food. When the cook refused to give them any, saying that they had already had their share, the boys complained loudly. The next day, when I ran down to the kitchen, the cook shooed me away and shut the door.

Growing, active children do need plenty of food and perhaps the boys were hungry. Perhaps they were exerting their power and taking what they considered to be a privilege of age and status. Not all the staff ignored bad behaviour and many were kind and caring. Likewise, not all the children were bullies. Many looked out for the younger ones and stood up for them when they could. However, children missing their homes and families and coping with the power imbalances inherent in an institutional setting take out their anger and frustration on each other. Even good and attentive staff are not around 24 hours each day to supervise what is going on in the dorms or the playgrounds.

My first semester at boarding school came to an early end because of a civil uprising in Congo. Parents were asked to collect their children two weeks early so that families could be together should an emergency arise. I was beside myself with anticipation waiting for my family, and I remembered that the last time I had anticipated them, they had not come. Despite reassurances from staff, I was afraid that I would be left behind again. It was late in the day by the time they finally arrived at the school and I had left my sentry post by the driveway to sit in a tree in the orchard gazing westward towards home. One of the bigger girls came to find me to say that my family was here. I scrambled out of the tree and scampered across the grass to the road. There they were; my parents, my brothers, and my baby sister, tired and dusty from the long drive but here.

After boarding school

A few days after we returned home, the rebel soldiers arrived in the community and declared themselves an alternative regional government. In an attempt to gain international recognition for their rule, the rebels took almost 2,000 international workers hostage. Many missionaries and expatriates were held either in prison, or under the protection of rebel soldier guards in their homes. My family, along with many others, was held for almost four months. My father continued to work under the supervision of rebel authorities and my mother tried her best to protect my siblings and me from the increasingly erratic and menacing behaviour of the bored and hungry guards. We were rescued in a multinational intervention at the end of November 1964 and returned to Scotland.

Needless to say, the events I have described have had a lasting impact on my life. The civil unrest and the early separation from my father were obvious triggers for anxiety and an overprotectiveness of my own children. However, as time has gone by, I have come to recognise that boarding school has left the bigger scars. During even the most frightening times while my family was held hostage, my parents were there, with me. They provided comfort and helped me to cope with behaviours and events which I could not understand. As the years have gone by, we have also been able to talk about our experiences, our *shared* experiences. At boarding school, I was alone in my grief and fear. No other family members went to boarding school. No one knew what it was really like. I was without the shepherding, protection, and instruction from loving parents that I needed as a six-year-old. I was, as Joy Schaverien explains, fostered with strangers who did not love me.

Bibliography

Kingsolver, B. 1999. *The Poisonwood Bible*. London, UK Faber and Faber Ltd.

Schaverien, Joy. 2011. *Boarding school syndrome: Broken attachments a hidden trauma*. British Journal of Psychotherapy, 27(2), 138–155.

Vandrick, S. 2013. *The Colonial Legacy and Missionary Kid Memoirs*. In G Barkjuizen (ed) *Narrative Research in Applied Linguistics*, Cambridge, UK, Cambridge University Press.

4.4.2 On dissociation

WHEN A CHILD, NEEDING TO SURVIVE LONG PERIODS WITHOUT LOVE, TOUCH OR PARENTAL GUIDANCE, IS ENCOURAGED TO CUT OFF FROM HIS PRIMARY EMOTIONS AND BODILY REALITY AND TAUGHT INSTEAD A FORM OF EMOTIONAL UN-INTELLIGENCE (TO PARAPHRASE DANIEL STERN'S FAMOUS TERM*), HE WILL NEED TO EMPLOY DISSOCIATION EXTENSIVELY. THE RESULTING ADULT CANNOT AVOID BEING IN DEEP PSYCHIC TROUBLE, FOR HE WILL HAVE DEVELOPED A DEFENSIVELY ORGANISED PSYCHE BUILT ON DISOWNING AND PROJECTION. THIS MEANS HIS STANCE IN THE WORLD WILL BE QUITE RIGID AND PRECARIOUS, DESPITE WHAT IT LOOKS LIKE FROM THE OUTSIDE. HE WILL HAVE DIFFICULTIES DISTINGUISHING BETWEEN FRIEND AND FOE AND THEREFORE IN MAINTAINING AUTHENTIC RELATIONSHIPS. REMAINING ... SEVERELY CHALLENGED BY THE DEMANDS OF EMOTIONAL INTIMACY AND PARENTING, HE WILL BE ETERNALLY ON GUARD.

* STERN, D. 1985. THE INTERPERSONAL WORLD OF THE INFANT. NEW YORK, BASIC BOOKS.
WOUNDED LEADERS, NICK DUFFELL, LONE ARROW PRESS, 2ND ED., P. 78

4.4.3 Raewyn

When my oldest daughter turned eight years of age, I looked at her with horror and indignation. Today I look at my seven-year-old grandson and feel rage stirring in my belly. What I see in these two children, who I love dearly, are my sister and me at those ages. My sister, at the age of seven, had been at boarding school for four months. We were left at the same boarding school on the same day. She was only six. I was, and it has taken decades for me to say, 'only', I was only eight. For many years, I thought that 'only eight' was a rather pathetic way to describe my beginnings at boarding because my sister was only, yes, only six. Four- and five-year-old children were left there for a term and, sometimes, for two terms at a time. So, what did I have to complain about? Eight was practically grown up, and that was what I was forced to do, to be grown up, although no one recognised that an eight-year-old child has neither the developmental maturity nor the resources to be truly and fully adult.

I was born in India, within the old city of Delhi. My parents had been born in New Zealand. They came from fairly ordinary working families. My mother's upbringing was poor and my father's was not affluent. Whereas my dad, the oldest of six sons, was born into a conservative fundamentalist Christian family, my mother, the younger of two daughters, was 'converted' to it in her late teens. Both of them were the first in at least three generations to earn a university degree. They became school teachers. They held education in high regard and clearly expected their two daughters to gain an education and to attend university.

My parents became missionaries and they met and married on the mission field. They believed that they were called by God to go to India and convert people to their specific brand of religion. That was, not only because they believed that their religion was right, but also because they thought that those who did not convert to it were damned to hell for all eternity. India, to them, was a country teeming with the potentially damned. In a way, that is how they expressed care if not love itself, for other human beings, although we never talked about love in our family. Love was what God did in a strict authoritarian parental style, ever ready to mete out punishment to erring children. Born into their context, I absorbed their attitudes and values, although I have long reassessed and rejected many of them.

Part of my wider context was, of course, the country of India, its sights, smells, sounds, its food, climate and landscape, its people, religions and cultures, and its languages. Much of that has also sunk into me, absorbed through my skin and senses. Then there were repeated moves of country, homes, and schools. My child-hood was greatly disrupted even before I went to boarding school. I was left without a solid sense of belonging or a consistent way of being, for there was a disconnect between the places and cultures I lived in. I now know that this gives me a name. I am a 'third culture kid' or TCK.

From my beginnings in India, I stood out as different to most of those around me, simply due to the body I inhabit. I do not look Indian, I look European. My parents, particularly my mother, reinforced difference as a state of being. Their religion encouraged a separation between 'Believers' and 'The World'. Being open to and accepting other religious practices was a sin. I was actively discouraged from, and sometimes forbidden to, play with local children. They might in some way corrupt me. Mum's attitude was somewhat tempered by my father's curiosity and his respectful behaviour when visiting temples, mosques, and other places of worship. Other missionaries became extended family to us, although most of them were from different 'home' countries and cultures.

My parents always assumed that our life in India was temporary. New Zealand, a country I barely knew, was 'home'. Temporary became a theme of my life. The Buddhist doctrine of impermanence resonates completely with me. It was the experience of my early life, imprinted on me. In those days it was usual for many missionaries to work in the mission field for a five-year term. They would then return to their home country for about a year's furlough. Travel was usually by ship, as air travel was not very common and was very expensive. Furlough was not an extended holiday for my family. It included much travelling up and down the country, several moves of 'home' and, when older, of schools. My parents were not given a stipend, as some missionaries received from a mission society. They were in India 'on faith', trusting God (and New Zealand donors) for an income. On furlough we visited extended family and my father, principally, spoke at many church meetings reporting on their work in India. These meetings, and regular newsletters, were the main way of raising financial support for our family and his and Mum's work. As a result, they lived with a high degree of uncertainty. We lived frugally and modestly. I learned very early never to ask for material possessions.

As children we were toted around like mission exhibits and expected to be constantly on show and well behaved. In a sense this was nothing new. In India we were also expected to be such brilliant examples of Christian children that our behaviour alone would help convince others that my parents' beliefs were true. Thus, my behaviour, which was ideally submissive and quiet, staying within expectations of me, had the Highest Authority of All endorsing it.

For me, as a child, 'home' was not always home. On each trip 'home' to New Zealand and on our final 'return' when I was 13, neither journey was to a known home nor a return to something familiar and safe. By the time I was 13 I had moved countries five times. Depending on how I count them, we had lived in at least 15 different homes, although there were many temporary places in which we stayed. I also had attended at least nine different schools. My years at boarding school were the most stable geographically, although I never knew from one term to the next which dormitory I would be assigned to or which bed would be 'mine'.

Two years before our second furlough, we all travelled down to the south of India, to the Nilgiri Hills. We visited the school I was later to attend. I remember sitting in the sun on a grassy bank with my sister while my parents walked by the school swimming pool in a dell below us. They were speaking with the head mistress. I was four years old. I imagine that was when they decided to send us there.

The school was primarily for missionaries' children. Racial discrimination was a social norm in those days and, as a result, they excluded Indians. Some Anglo-Indian children were admitted when I was there. The fees were kept very low, except for those who came from non-missionary families. Staff worked for bed and board plus a small allowance. The school was founded in 1899 when some parents left their children with two or three single women in a holiday home that was otherwise empty out of season. The hills were a refuge from the heat and dust of the plains and children, it is said, thrived there in the temperate climate, clean air, and on the fresh fruit and vegetables grown in the hills. Leaving them there, we were told, provided improved health and an education for the children. We knew, also, that the parents were then free to concentrate on their mission.

After our second furlough in New Zealand and having just turned eight years of age, we returned by ship to Bombay, now Mumbai. After the relative quiet and the social restraints of life on board, the port was a sharp contrast. It was full of noise and smells that I had not sensed for the last 12 months. On the dock there were people everywhere, running backwards and forwards with carts, luggage, and other goods. There was much shouting and noise. We disembarked and stayed briefly with other missionaries in the city. Then with all of our heavy trunks and bags we boarded a train to Delhi and finally arrived in Chandigarh, where my parents had rented a house in which their church meeting room was situated.

Once in Chandigarh, unpacking began and no sooner was that completed but packing for boarding school was commenced. My mother entered a marathon of sewing nametapes on to clothes and linen. Big metal trunks were packed, hand luggage was prepared, and bedding rolls put together. Within weeks of landing back in India, we were on the train heading south to boarding school. The litany of losses that a TCK naturally experiences as a result of multiple moves was about to reach a new and devastating crescendo.

So far in my life, moving both between countries and within countries, I had lost many homes, several schools, and multiple friends, along with the familiar sights, sounds, and smells of each place I had lived. Things I valued and was attached to were left behind. In moving countries, the foods I was used to and enjoyed were no longer available. I had lost my sense of place and belonging. I had lost Sooty, the stray black kitten that had adopted us in Christchurch. Immediate contact with my beloved grandparents and cousins had disappeared. And, during our last furlough, I lost my established grasp on the Hindi language, both spoken and written. The last loss I regret even today. Starting at boarding school I then lost my family – my parents and, although we were at the same school, I lost my sister too.

Our journey to school began in our black Standard Vanguard car. My sister and I sat in the spacious back seat, my parents in the front. What did not fit in the boot was loaded on the roof of the car and so we made the long slow drive to Delhi. We passed villages and fields full of sugar cane and flowering mustard, farmers working either in the fields or drawing water from wells using bullocks or camels. There was something meditative in the drive, when we were not squabbling, as we passed other's lives and homes, a cloud of dust following us. Other traffic included busses, horse or camel drawn carts, and trucks which were usually overloaded. Sometimes there were accidents or a truck had tipped over. It was noisy on the road, horns blown with abandon, announcing that the vehicle is there and approaching. In the car, because it was winter, the windows were closed and we were insulated from the world outside. We stopped for a picnic lunch of processed Chesdale cheese that came in tins from New Zealand, pickled beetroot, bread, margarine, vegemite, jam, and banana. There was tea in a thermos and we carried our own pre-boiled drinking water with us.

I remember little, specifically, of the first journey to boarding school but we underwent the pilgrimage there five times and the journey was always basically the same. In Delhi, where the kerbs on the city's roads were painted in black and yellow stripes, we would often spend several days staying with other missionaries. Sometimes we arrived there in time for Republic Day. At least once we enjoyed watching the Republic Day parade down Rajpath from the Presidential Palace. India Gate was lit up in lights and the drama and glory of the occasion gladdened me intensely. I felt an exciting sense of patriotism.

We went by train from Delhi and we travelled third class. First class travel was a luxury. The school insisted on our travelling by first class for our end of year journey 'home' because staff from the school chaperoned the parties that set off in different directions across the subcontinent. They were not expected to rough it. To travel to school, parents bore the responsibility of booking the train journeys, forming groups or 'parties', which some of them chaperoned. They organised large baskets of food and big milk cans full of safe drinking water for the journey.

We travelled with the 'Delhi Party'. Although my parents sometimes chaperoned us, the separations began in our journey. The children in our party attended one of two single sex schools in the Western Ghats, although my school did accept, until the age of ten, the brothers of girls who were boarding. We picked up children who joined our party from various places on the way through central India and part of the east coast of Andhra Pradesh to Madras (now Chennai). Parents would bid farewell to their children at the railway station and hand them over to the care of the chaperones. The children may not have known the chaperones at all. Possibly the parents had never met them either. I recall the atmosphere of sadness and distress that was never fully expressed.

The trains were drawn by steam engines that belched out smoke, soot, and sparks. The soot was everywhere in our carriages. As a child, the uncleanliness did not bother me in the least. Like so many other things, I just accepted it. The rhythmical rocking of the train and its clacking as we moved over the tracks brought a soothing sense that was devoid of human contact. Encased in my own world much of the time, we journeyed in the same direction, staring out of the window as the landscape changed. We passed villages, towns, and temples; buffalos in water holes; farmers out in their fields; women going about their daily tasks; labourers working on or near the railway line; and young boys jumping and playing in rivers. The temperature increased as we moved inexorably southwards and we folded away the warm winter clothes which we wore in the northern winter. Sometimes there would be stops on the way, in the middle of the countryside for no discernible reason. The boys would then jump out and set up a game of cricket or softball. And when the train tooted to signal impending departure the players quickly upped stumps and ran to jump on board again as the train began moving again, slowly chugging and gaining speed. When we stopped at or near stations, our white skins attracted hopeful beggars, including naked or rag-clad children with bellies swollen from malnutrition, but we had no money. On station platforms vendors walked back and forth calling, '*Chai, chai, garam chai*' (tea, tea, hot tea). There was bedlam as people with their luggage struggled to alight as others pushed to enter the carriages.

At Madras we often had a full day's wait for our connection to Mettupalayam where we, again, changed trains to the, now, world heritage train up the Western Ghats to our schools. The wait in Madras was sometimes spent on an outing. One time we visited the compound of a church where we were allowed to submerge our grubby bodies in a water tank and some of us guiltily trespassed in the church itself. Another time we were loaded onto 'tongas' or horse drawn carts and transported to the beach and the vast wonders of the ocean for a few hours. Then it was back to the train station, to the big piles of trunks, water cans, baskets of food, small hand cases and bedding rolls. Chaos ensued as the train was boarded and we spent another night of swaying and clacking along the line to Mettupalayam, at the base of the mountains.

At Mettupalayam our connection was made to the little blue hill train that ascended more than 6,000 feet. As the train climbed up the *ghat* not much faster than walking pace, the air became clearer and cooler, the vegetation greener. Goose bumps appeared on my arms and we reached for warmer clothing. The final part of the trip was to board a bus, the luggage loaded on the roof in piles, for the short ride to the school itself and its moon gate entrance. The whole journey, from my parent's home to school, had covered almost 2,000 miles. It took more than three days.

At school, I was taken to my dormitory. My trunk followed, carried by bearers employed by the school. I was shown my bed in a room that six or eight of us shared. The only windows were several clerestory windows. There was a bathroom attached where we bathed twice a week in a tin tub, but the toilets were some distance away, through other rooms and along a veranda. In front of the converted cottage was a wide expanse of green lawn, a border of bright fragrant flowers and some trees. We overlooked the valley, the slopes of which were full of tea bushes, and we could see the nearby town on the opposite hillside. Our geographical surroundings were beautiful. My mother bid me farewell, saying: 'Here's a present for you, don't cry'. She shoved a wrapped toy into my hands. She disappeared. I was abandoned. I was in the way, in the way of God's work. I was not wanted and had no place in their life. I sat on my bed not knowing what to do. I had been told that I must wait for a specific member of staff. I felt lost and forlorn. Stunned. One of the other girls came over and showed me where I was to put my clothes and linen in a large communal wardrobe. There was a locker beside my bed for my Bible, teddy bear, and doll. A stool had been placed at the end of my bed. At night I had to fold my counterpane, lay it on the stool along with my uniform of blue gingham and matching bloomers. Someone sang: 'She'll be coming round the mountain when she comes ... she'll be wearing red shoes when she comes'. When the teacher turned up to take me to the dining room for supper, she was, indeed, wearing red shoes. She took me by the hand and walked so fast, I feared I might just leave the ground and fly. The dining room was at the other end of the compound and I learned very soon how strict and unbending the school was.

The menu for that first supper consisted of egg. I could not eat eggs without awful nausea. Eggs were served several times a week in various forms. There were watery scrambled eggs with spinach, and 'igloo' that was hard boiled eggs in white sauce. They, and the lemon sago that we called 'frog's eggs', were, to understate it, unappetising. I preferred to go hungry rather than eat the eggs served me. At that first meal I was told that I absolutely must eat the igloo. I sat staring at my plate. A staff member came and sat next to me, reinforcing that I must eat it all. The rest of the children had been dismissed from the tables and I was not allowed to go with them. I sat and sat. It was an impasse. Eventually, I gave in, but not without coming to the arrangement that I eat one mouthful only. Over those years I put a lot into my body that I did not want. I soon discovered that we could ask for a 'small' helping as our food was being served up, so I did not have to force down any more than required of a disliked dish. I was always hungry.

In those first days at boarding school, activity and busyness kept us afloat. Our lives were ruled by the bell. There were two, one at the top of the school and one the other end, at the 'bottom'. They signalled when to rise in the mornings, breakfast, classes, other meals. At night, after dorm prayers and Bible reading, once the lights were turned off and we were in the dark, I was surrounded by the sounds of sobbing. I do not remember crying.

My sister was placed in a dorm at the other end of the school. From that first day at boarding school on, we had little to do with each other. Our family was fractured and we became isolated from each other. In my childish lostness, I had no idea that my sister might be suffering too. I didn't even know that what I experienced was suffering. I ask for her forgiveness for not being a good big sister to her.

We had to write to our parents each week. Our teachers read and censored our letters until we were in the senior school. Complaints or any emotional upset were forbidden content. After all, it was God's will that we be at boarding school and you dare not challenge God. Letters may need to be rewritten. Writing 'home' became a perfunctory task. Little of any import was communicated. I have no idea what my parents thought of our letters, or if they were relieved to hear from us each week. They, in turn, wrote to us each week and the letters arrived regularly. My memory of them was that they supplied a list of 'what we did this week'. Other girls got letters full of endearments and emotional sharing of being missed in their parents' lives, of felt shared loss. One exception was a letter from my parents when I got chicken pox in my first year, at Easter. My Dad sent me a phantasy-full story about chickens, Easter bunnies, eggs, and pox, complete with drawings, full of the warmth I craved. I wish I had kept that letter.

As a school for missionaries' children there was, naturally, a heavy emphasis on fundamental evangelical Christianity. Not only was church attendance compulsory, there was Sunday school, daily dorm prayers, grace at meals, and we were expected to have a daily 'quiet time' in which we read our Bibles and prayed silently. Everyone was required to learn an assigned Bible verse each week. I ran afoul of the system within a week. I simply didn't learn mine and could not quote it back to the matron when told to. My humiliating punishment was to sit outside my dorm on my stool that Saturday afternoon, the Bible on my lap to learn the verse by heart while the other girls played in the orchard and on the lawn. After that I complied each week, spouting forth whole sections of the King James version whether or not I understood what I was saying.

In that first year boarding, the Indo-Pakistan war broke out. We were largely protected from that in the south as the fighting and bombing was in the north, where my parents lived. I was told that if anything happened to my parents, we would be sent back to New Zealand to live with my uncle and his family. Instructions had been given to the school on how they were to proceed. I dreaded that. We were always conscious of the immanence of death and destruction, how unsafe living in India was. I knew a number of children and adults who became seriously ill and some died over my time there.

I adjusted to school. My parents came to the hills for the May holidays and usually for the August holidays. When they did not come in August, we stayed at school. I liked that. We had a relaxed life with friends and outings. At the end of the year, we all returned 'home' for the long Christmas holidays.

The equilibrium that I found was horribly upset when my mother decided to come to the school as dorm matron. She did that twice when the school was short staffed. One time she was matron of my dorm and she remained distant to me during that time. Being a staff member's child made me ripe for bullying. There was no escape from what had become a prison. It is hard to forgive that she put me (and my sister) in harm's way like that. In recent years I was told that some other mothers saw what was happening to me so they refused to help at the school, to save their children the same fate. I am not aware of anyone intervening at the time.

Over the years there, I did receive a good education. The curriculum was from the UK and they offered GCE O level exams. I developed a serious illness. It was picked up by the school nurse and I was finally treated for it in a mission hospital. Once I recovered, I found study was a pleasure and I had the strength and energy to enjoy and do well at sports. I ran in the inter school's athletic competition and played hockey. I loved Latin and Scripture classes, became enamoured of maths. I took piano lessons and sat a Royal Schools of Music theory exam. My terrifying piano teacher said that I was so bad at playing the piano that I was wasting my parents' money taking lessons. She said I should stop lessons. I agreed. What choice did I have? My parents were informed. I received a letter from them telling me off for being ungrateful for the opportunity to learn how to play an instrument. I was devastated at that accusation. My first period arrived in the loneliness of boarding school. I was the first in my class to reach menarche. I did not tell even my parents at the time. It was too private a matter to put in a censored letter, so I dealt with it alone, shamefully and with little information and no support. In spite of the difficulties, school was, paradoxically, a refuge in another way. There I escaped from the sexual abuse perpetrated by a church elder who lived in the same house as my parents over several years.

Now, as an adult, I believe that I was sacrificed to the harsh God of my parents. In ancient times the Canaanites practised child sacrifice. The Bible tells the story of Abraham journeying three days into Moriah to sacrifice his son, Isaac. I believe that God demanded the practice of child sacrifice to cease in the Judeo-Christian religions on the day that his angel intervened and stayed Abraham's hand. The cost was too great and God did not require it. It was a heathen and barbaric practice.

I left the boarding school when we left India. I knew we would not be back. Exciting though our move was, I wanted to stay with my friends and teachers at school. I longed to go back. Those who continued and finished school there have a special bond that I do not have. I wish I could have remained there with them.

Part of me is still there. That part is still standing outside my first dorm, not long after being left there. I look up at the mountain behind the school. On it was a huge rock that looks like an elephant head and trunk. We call it 'Elephant Rock'. I look at that rock, solid and dependable. I realise I'll be at boarding school for at least five years. I feel despair. I know I have to get through it. I turn my attention to doing just that. My grief and sadness move into part of me that is a windowless room. The door slams shut and locks. Those emotions stay there for decades. I am still that little girl standing outside, looking at the Elephant Rock. The despair is with me even until today.

4.4.4   On growing up too fast

… IT IS A REVELATION FOR THE PSYCHOLOGICALLY MINDED OBSERVER TO SEE HOW A YOUNG CHILD CONSTRUCTS A STRATEGIC SURVIVAL PERSONALITY TO BECOME THE APPARENT CHILD-ADULT HE IS EXPECTED TO BE. IN THE RAPIDITY OF THE JUVENILE PROCESS, WE CAN OBSERVE HOW IT INVOLVES BETRAYING THE SELF HE REALLY IS AND SUBSTITUTING A KIND OF PSEUDO-ADULTHOOD. WE CAN IMAGINE HOW HE MAY BE IN DANGER OF NEVER REALLY GROWING UP IN AN ORGANIC WAY.

WOUNDED LEADERS, NICK DUFFELL, LONE ARROW PRESS, 2015, 2ND ED., PP. 103–104

4.5   Military

4.5.1   Nicky R

When I was eight years old my parents shared the exciting news with my brother and I that our dad had been offered the job of Royal Boats Engineer Officer for the Sultan's personal Navy and that we would be moving to live in an extremely hot country called Oman which was somewhere in the Middle East. That really meant nothing to me at the time, but I knew it would be an adventure. I have memories of excitedly explaining to my teacher that I was moving to Oman in Muscat, or Muscat in Oman, I didn't know which but it sounded wonderful … and it really was. In fact, for years after I would tell people that those were the best days of my life; and bar meeting my husband, and having our lovely children, I would still put it up there at the top of the list of my most amazing life experiences.

I enjoyed an idyllic lifestyle, experiencing things that many will never have the chance to experience. One such event was visiting a Bedouin village where certainly the children, and also many of the adults, had never seen white skin before. It was a little scary at times because the children pinched at my skin – I assume that they didn't think it could be real! I remember us being separated, with the men led off to one tent and women and younger children taken to another, where each group were presented with a huge feast of goat and flavoured rice, and we were beckoned to eat first before the villagers joined in.

Other times we would go on banyans – these were picnic trips by speed boat to various coastal shores. One beach in particular could only be accessed by sea at the time. There would always be several families who we would meet at the port where my dad worked, and the adults would load the boat with huge Igloo cool boxes full of food and iced cold drinks to share later. Sometimes my brother and I could convince our parents to let us sit on top of the cabin as we bombed along and waves crashed against the boat and we would hold on to the mast for dear life. Many years later I heard that they had blasted through mountains, built a main road, and stuck a hotel on that beach so I feel immensely grateful to have experienced what I did before the commercialisation.

Whilst living in Oman I attended the Royal Flight School which was situated near to the main airport in Seeb, Muscat. It had been built to accommodate the ex-pat children from the Royal Yacht Squadron, Royal Flight, Royal Guard, and Police Air Wing. I remember it being an early start in the morning, I am almost certain that we left before 7am, and it was a fair way to travel by school bus with no air conditioning. However, the best bit was that we finished school about 1:30pm every day, which left the afternoons free for playing with Omani children or other English friends in our complex, going to the Sultan's Armed Forces Club beach (which was members only and felt very posh), or for going swimming in the Royal Yacht Squadron Club pool.

The club would also put on events for the families at various times of the year, such as a Halloween or Christmas Party, and we would go to our friends' club pool complex where I was lucky enough to get to see UB40 perform. I remember going with my mum to a posh hotel once to meet her friend for coffee and just being in awe as I looked around – coming from a fairly small island I had never seen anything like it in my life. There were marble floors, walls and columns that gleamed with gold and crystal chandeliers everywhere.

I don't ever recall anyone being bullied in Oman and I had some lovely friends. We'd often have sleepovers at each other's houses and twice a year all our parents would be invited to the Sultan's Palace for tea and a formal dinner. I loved these occasions as usually there would be a few kids going to one house so that we could be looked after by one babysitter. I do remember one time telling the servant who was minding us that if he wouldn't let us stay up later then I'd tell my parents on him and he'd get the sack. Generally, we could get away with anything and everything. We did, however, try to make up for being horrid by putting on a show for all the household staff one day which involved my friend Simon's pet mice that we had half trained to do tricks – they seemed to enjoy it.

There were a few occasions which weren't quite so great and one of these happened shortly after first arriving in Oman. I became very unwell and was raced to hospital where I was diagnosed with acute pancreatitis. Oman was still very much a developing country then and the hospital was very basic – not the ideal place to try and recover. I remember being in this huge hall-like room with a few short wall dividers here and there. In that room there were women who were giving birth alongside other sick women and children and I vividly remember the smell which was a mixture of urine, body odour, and curry spices. There was nowhere for parents to stay of course and therefore I would have visitors during the day but be on my own at night, which was pretty scary for a very poorly eight-year-old in a strange country where very few people spoke English. I had been told that I could not go home until I started eating and drinking properly, yet I wasn't used to curried foods for breakfast and couldn't stomach the smell of it let alone eat it. Thankfully, I was visited by the daughter of some commander where my dad worked, and she bought me lemonade and cream crackers. I started eating and drinking and was soon allowed back home again.

Another horrifying incident was when I witnessed my brother falling many feet on to jagged rocks after the ropes that he had tied together in the middle had come apart. I can still picture and hear the blood curdling scream that came out of my body as I watched what I thought was him falling to certain death. By some miracle he had landed on his back and his backpack contained coiled up rope inside – this had literally saved his life and he came away with only cuts and bruises and a fractured arm.

\#

During the Boarding School Survivor (BSS) workshops we were asked to think about our transitional moments. For most this would be the moment when we stopped being our former selves and took on a new persona, one that would enable us to survive – when we stopped being innocent children and instead became the little adults who would be forced to grow up far too soon. At the same time, our inner child would be trapped for years to come and for many, like myself, this was to become the cause of so much misery, mistrust, self-loathing, and self-destruction well into adulthood. It continues to have a presence that at times dominates my thoughts and there are moments when I shed tears for that little, abandoned girl who just needed holding and soothing and to be told that everything would be all right. I appeared to struggle more than most with this idea of an actual transition moment and so my story is not necessarily one of transition, but instead a mix of partial memories which are all that I have to try and build some resemblance of a timeline and attempt to put my few memories into context and order.

I have a memory of a cold, dark evening and pulling into the gated school car park, our parents unloading mine and my brothers' huge trunks, and then dragging them over the bumpy ground alongside scores of other parents and children, all heading the same way towards the long drive that led to the various boarding houses and then them filtering off in different directions. The fact that I started school in September makes me think that I am not remembering the first day but another time, possibly after the Christmas holiday as it would have still been light outside in autumn.

I have another memory of my parents' car pulling in and stopping on the right-hand side of the long driveway by an area of lawn right in front of the Junior School, although I would have thought that this was not the usual practice as there would have been far too many vehicles on what I remember as being a narrow drive. I do, however, clearly recall standing there, crying, and saying that I just wanted to go back home as 'I hated it there', therefore this occasion would most probably have been a return from half term, or again perhaps after a Christmas break.

It frustrates me no end that I remember very few intricate details despite being in that institution just shy of three years. Without looking at a photo I could not have told you what our uniform consisted of, if we wore socks or tights or what colour they were, yet I can still picture my light grey tailor-made suit for Sunday Chapel, perhaps because it was made in my favourite place, Oman. I felt so proud and grown up wearing that suit and I liked that it was different to everyone else.

This seems odd because of the bullying; however, strangely, I do not recall being specifically bullied due to my somewhat bizarre dress sense.

I have a handful of truly clear memories and other fragmented parts. Sadly, what I can recall is the constant mental bullying. I remember well the taunting and belittling and trying to disappear, keeping my gaze to the floor and avoiding eye contact at all costs so as not to be noticed. It took many years to be able to raise my head whilst out walking and I still have difficulty with eye contact to this day. It did not work of course; I was such an easy target as I was so weak, and it really did not take much to break me. I do not believe there was even a single day without one child or another saying something derogatory about myself or my brother, or when I did not feel alone. The continuous feeling of fear and panic, and what I later discovered was severe anxiety, just totally overwhelmed me.

It has been mentioned to me that it is quite likely that I have blocked many of these thoughts in an unconscious attempt to protect myself as it would have been just too hard to deal with the reality. This is more than likely the case; however, I think that it is more than this because from as far back as I can remember I have struggled with my short-term memory. I could remember spellings and times tables for a test the next day but then that would be gone. My exam grades and end of term reports would reflect this, stating 'results do not reflect the effort put in during class' – however, I was never assessed or given any extra help due to my now obvious disadvantage with learning. Rules of sporting games and matches have never stuck and neither have sets of instructions or directions, so I believe that these undiagnosed issues have also exaggerated these memory difficulties.

On that first evening at boarding school, I have a fleeting memory of heading to the refectory for supper, but nothing about eating or drinking when inside. I can then picture being in the dormitory, sat crying on my bed, and a couple of girls trying to comfort me and make me laugh. Then another thought goes to matron hugging me into her huge chest whilst rubbing my back, but I am still unsure that this is the first night. I went to sleep sobbing and did so for weeks, even months on end. There was sympathy to begin with, but I guess it wore thin after a while as I was the only one who continued to cry for home every evening.

During the boarding school survivors' workshops, I was interested to learn that it is unusual for a child to continue to be so outwardly upset because after a brief time survivors usually realise that they just shut down their emotions to survive that transitional moment – but apparently nobody gave me that memo. During the therapy weekend I noted that it was assumed my sensitivity should have put me in a better position to have survived without too much damage as I was able to express my emotions, but sadly that was not the case at all. I was, and still am, overly sensitive and I feel my own and others' pain greatly. What I did learn after a short while was that both the children and the adults would stop listening to my upsets and stop showing that they cared, even if they ultimately did, and therefore, like the rest, I learned to internalise my thoughts and worries as I realised that nobody was coming to save me.

A strong memory that I do recall is of being told off by my mum for writing such upsetting letters home. She had spoken to the Housemaster about it and from then on, all my letters were checked a lot more closely. I do remember thinking at that time that nobody was listening and nobody cared how I was feeling, and this was probably the moment when I really knew that I was stuck there in that hell hole, to be perpetually bullied for years to come.

The bullying was relentless; walking to class, in class, waiting to be picked for team games and never being picked, but instead waiting for the inevitable groans of the team who drew the short straw and ended up with me as their booby prize. I still have that inner voice which screams 'you are useless at sports, you'll make a fool of yourself, everyone is watching you' and even today I try and avoid any competitive games if possible. If I do go out with family or friends to bowling for example then I have to talk to myself to remain calm as the anxiety really affects my performance. I believe that I would have played better at school if I had not felt the shame of not being chosen and the overwhelming feeling of eyes bearing into me, just waiting for me to mess up so that they could continue to taunt me.

Things only got worse when I moved up to the senior school. All my perpetrators were still there as we remained on the same site, just a different house further along the drive. This time though I had the added bonus of not being given a set place at a dinner table, unlike 99% of the other children. The kitchen staff had decided that there would usually be one or two spaces left on tables most evenings as not all of the day pupils would stay to dinner and therefore they did not want to cook extra food when they did not need to. Just my luck that I was to be one of the placeless! Each evening I would find myself searching for a space at a table which I thought may have the fewest bullies on. I remember that feeling of being absolutely petrified and at the same time feeling immense shame – I knew that nobody wanted me to join their table, but if I were lucky, I would get to sit with some older day pupils who would not be nasty to me. This constant fear every evening eventually led me to skipping meals. If there was nothing left in my tuck box then I would make sure to pick up a pack of cream crackers from the local store during one of our increasingly sparse free times.

Before boarding school, I was already an extremely shy child who was incredibly easy to embarrass and upset because I would never answer back or fight back. I was an easy target for those who needed someone to torment to make themselves feel better. I had already suffered some horrible bullying at my first country primary school, long before being sent away to board, and I would seek and prefer the company of adults over children – although I did have one close friend. I really struggled with lack of confidence and never attempted to make conversation with other children, even though I desperately wanted to have friends.

The three years spent in Oman were heaven compared to my first primary and I did make some great friends there. I suppose it was easier because we were all minorities in a foreign land, and we were thrown together in these wonderful complexes with swimming pools and club houses. We did have a lot of fun, although my extreme shyness continued, and I would still prefer the company of adults.

Being sent far away from the place that I called home, my happy place, and suddenly forced to live and attend school with hundreds of strangers was just the worst thing that my parents could have done to me. This of course rings true for any child but especially a quiet and vulnerable child like me and the knock-on effects to my life have been truly devastating. I internalised so much that my own children have only recently heard my story and had no idea what I had been through. My husband also did not know of the main cause which led to me being reliant on antidepressants to stay alive – but how could he have known when even I did not realise the extent of the damage caused by being sent away to boarding school.

4.5.2   On bullying

BULLYING IS EASIER TO TALK ABOUT THAN SEXUAL ABUSE, BUT NOT MUCH. THE TENDENCY IS TO ACKNOWLEDGE THAT THERE WILL ALWAYS BE SOME BULLYING IN SCHOOLS BECAUSE OF THE NATURE OF CHILDHOOD, TO CONDEMN IT, BUT TO SAY THAT IT IS NORMAL. NORMALISATION – MAKING SOMETHING OK BECAUSE IT HAPPENS – IS A FORM OF DISTORTION, AND IS COMMONLY EMPLOYED IN THE MATTER OF BULLYING. AN INDIVIDUAL OR COMMUNITY WHICH CANNOT TOLERATE A THREAT TO ITS SELF-IMAGE WILL TYPICALLY DEPLOY THE MAIN DEFENCE MECHANISMS. THESE ARE; DENIAL, DELETION AND DISTORTION, AND THEY OPERATE IN ALL WALKS OF LIFE TO DEFEND AGAINST CHARGES OF BULLYING AND ABUSE, WHETHER SEXUAL, PHYSICAL OR EMOTIONAL.

\#

... GIRLS ARE RARELY BEATEN OR PHYSICALLY TORMENTED IN THE WAY THAT BOYS HAVE BEEN AT BOARDING SCHOOL, BUT THERE ARE DIFFERENT WAYS OF HURTING PEOPLE. THE GIRLS' WAY IS TO UNDERMINE THE PERSON BY VERBAL ABUSE AND TO WITHDRAW ALL THE QUALITIES OF LIFE THAT MAKE SURVIVAL AS A HUMAN BEING POSSIBLE. AFFECTION, APPROVAL, PHYSICAL CONTACT, THE RIGHT TO PRIVACY AND FREE TIME ARE SOME OF THESE.

\#

PEER GROUP BULLIES HAVE THE PHYSICAL AND NUMERICAL ADVANTAGE, AND THEY ARE ALWAYS AROUND – DAY AND NIGHT.

... PEOPLE WHO HAVE BEEN THE BUTT OF SUCH SCAPEGOATING MAY WELL SPEND A LIFETIME AVOIDING GROUPS, COMMITMENTS AND RELATIONSHIPS.

\#

THE MAKING OF THEM, NICK DUFFELL, LONE ARROW PRESS,
3RD ED., PP. 184–189

4.5.3 *Alyson*

Around the convent was a wall, broken by a gate and the gravel driveway. At the side of the gate was a wooden bench. I remember Daddy hugging me, then he got up and left. I don't know if my mother was there or not; I can't remember her being there. I sat there, not knowing what to do, until an older girl came and showed me where I had to go.

I was eight years old, and just a few weeks before I had been raped by a stranger when I wandered off-camp, and both my sister and I had been repeatedly abused previously by my father's batman [Ed – a sort of military personal assistant and general aide] over the course of around a year; he was a trusted babysitter. We never talked about these events in the family, after the batman had been found out and put in prison. I was sure I had been sent away to school because of the abuse, that it was somehow my fault.

I cried and cried and cried at school. I was so homesick for the life I knew in Germany, and my sister's company, and for home. I even missed my baby brother! I was so upset that I went back to wetting the bed at night; the nuns made me strip it and wash it. I was so ashamed, but there was nothing I could do to stop it. Once or twice, I cried so hard that I was physically sick.

I asked again and again to be taken away, but nothing worked. My father had been firmly told that officers' children went to boarding school; only other-rank's children could stay at day school, laugh and play and be happy. I went home only for the long summer holidays. My parents came over to England for the Christmas holidays, and my grandparents were close enough to take me for Easter and half terms.

My father was posted to Germany almost as soon as I was born, and so all I knew was Army life. Postings were every three years, so people changed around quite a lot; you learned to make friends quickly wherever you were. Some of those friendships have stood the test of time, decades later. I loved both the postings in Germany before I was sent away – I had lots of friends, played with the neighbours' children, did OK at school; I was happy. My sister was only a little more than a year younger than me, and we were close.

When I was ten, Dad was posted to Canada. I had two shillings' pocket money, and I ran away from the convent to the railway station, put my money on the counter, and asked for a ticket to Canada. I was taken back to school, of course. My performance was so poor in lessons that the convent asked for an assessment from an educational psychologist. I found the letter in my Dad's effects, after he died:

... emotional responsiveness was rather flat and withdrawn ... she displays depressed, disinterested and negative attitudes towards her life [at school] as a boarder ... responds to individual attention.

The psychologist recommended that I be sent 'home' to Canada, and not return to school. I went to Canada for one Christmas holiday and back to the UK; then the school asked my parents to take me away. At age ten, I had failed.

Canada was wonderful, though! I could go to a day school, and my English accent made me exotic and interesting – people actually wanted to talk to me and sit next to me at lunch! I had a crush on a boy, and thought he might have one back … I lived there for almost a year, then we were posted back to Germany.

Another convent boarding school. This time I didn't care; I was a rebel, did no work, left school at 16 with no qualifications except in Art. Somewhere along the line they discovered I was severely dyslexic, but no-one ever made any allowance for that; I was always the thick girl, the one who didn't even try.

I look at my eight-year-old granddaughter and wonder, how could anyone do that to a child …

4.5.4   On self-worth

A SURVIVOR'S SELF-IMAGE IS FREQUENTLY EXTREMELY LOW … HER ABILITY TO INITIATE OR MAKE THINGS HAPPEN IN THE WORLD IS OFTEN SEVERELY UNDERMINED … MEMORY OF THE TRAUMA IS OFTEN REJECTED OR REPRESSED, WHILE THE SENSE OF INNER SHAME CAN BE OVERWHELMINGLY PRESENT.

THE MAKING OF THEM, NICK DUFFELL, LONE ARROW PRESS, 3RD ED., P. 223

4.5.5   Joanna

My father was from a prominent Catholic military family, called Godfrey, on his mother's side. The Godfreys moved from Bryn Estyn Estate in North Wales to Bournemouth. In 1938, my father was sent to St Peter's, a Jesuit run boarding school, at age four. At 14 He won a scholarship to Britannia Royal Naval College, Dartmouth. He always wanted to fly and became a highly qualified naval pilot. I blame the Royal Navy for his alcoholism. Rum rations at 14. BRNC operated like a boarding school for officer cadets at that time. "Jews and Catholics fall out". Daddy was fortunate to be allowed onshore on Sundays (i.e. into Dartmouth as the school operated as a ship).

On his father's side military intelligence features for generations.

Daddy had put my older brother John's name down at birth for Sherborne School, and at the time expected the navy to fund our education, the norm for children of the officer class. A man of honour, he was working out how he could still fund the education of his four children, having been pensioned out of the Royal Navy due to a burst peptic ulcer, and so, initially, he took a job with Shell, but very soon thereafter joined QEAF (Qatar Emiri Air Force) – a tax free salary in the Gulf would cover our school fees.

I would say that my grandparents on my mother's side gave me my greatest sense of continuity and they later became my guardians in the UK. I was born on their dairy farm in Woodgreen, Hampshire and prior to that they had farmed the Montagu estate in Beaulieu. They were great friends with the Montagus and shared governesses up at Palace House. A racy set. I often wonder if the idea of Sherborne came from Lord Montagu who sent his children there. My mother and her two brothers had a wet nurse in Beaulieu and a nanny called Nanny Twigg, and after the governesses all the children were shipped off to prep at eight, then the boys to Charterhouse.

I write this to explain that boarding at eight or younger was in the family on both sides, though my grandmother, who was born in India, had a governess, was a debutante, and was never allowed to go to school, used to say how very much she longed to be sent.

Granny was the first person to hold me when I was born, apparently, and I think that I bonded with her instead of with my mother. There were several instances where I turned to my Grandmother for comfort rather than to my mother. I also think my character is very much like my father's. I don't see much of myself in my mother – although I felt tremendous awe and connection when I gave birth. Perhaps characteristics skip a generation.

As a naval pilot my father was posted to various locations along the SW coast and we moved frequently. In Penzance, I remember Larry the fireman and scary farm dogs and my younger brother laughing at him, loving his fire engine. Getting the milk. I remember our last house, Fairview, particularly well, near Fording-bridge in Hampshire. I have some very happy memories of that house – I think from about five to seven years old. I shared a bunk bed with John in a small bedroom at the top of the stairs. We were settled and happy and our life was colourful and full of excitement. My mother is an artist and very creative and great at making things; I remember so much fun she made for us. Birthday parties. Fancy dress costumes. One morning John and I crept in to peek as she'd been up all night making us Mickey and Minnie Mouse costumes. I remember sharing baths with John and making shampoo horns in the mirror, dressing up in bridesmaid and pageboy outfits and thinking we were rather splendid, walking down to the mill past the houses of children we knew.

We loved our primary school in Fordingbridge and we took the bus in from Sandleheath, feeling very grown up. We had a little pocket money to spend and we'd ride whatever bikes we could into Fordingbridge to the very excellent Tuck Shop. I loved going to school with John and all his friends were my friends. I remember the sheer terror of playing kiss chase, hiding in playground loos and the idea boys might trespass, and grumpy dinner ladies dishing out Smash potato with ice cream scoops. I remember a teacher, Miss Kelly, making me go back up to the blackboard again and again because I could not spell 'because'. Publicly shaming me. Before the primary we'd been to a little private nursery in Ringwood called Blynkbonnie and my reports were far kinder. I was seen for me. So, we found some aspects a bit rough, including the bus trip to school, but we belonged in the community and were invited to all the birthday parties around where we lived, and the local children were all invited to ours in turn.

I was a Brownie and John was a Cub. I won my first badge, Hostess, but I apparently didn't really deserve it because I was too shy and my conversation wasn't up to much. I was perhaps too young to be a Brownie at six, but they gave it to me anyway, because I was leaving the Brownies to go to Doha. There was a party in the village hall held by the Brownies and my parents donated a huge raffle prize which my mother won but had to pretend she hadn't. I think that was the last time I remember feeling a sense of stable, not transient, community in my home life. A sense of belonging. Later I would understand that in relocating to Qatar and buying our private education we bought out of community and belonging, which I eventually would try to find again when raising my own children. It has rendered us nomadic as a family. I suppose for the purposes of Empire that would've been a plus. That willingness to relocate at the drop of a hat. Forces and Diplomatic Corps expected it.

It wasn't all that sudden because John went first. A term before me. I remember meeting the revolting Robin Lindsay in his study at Sherborne Prep very clearly. [Ed – Robin Lindsay owned Sherborne Prep School until 1998. He was described as a fixated paedophile by a tribunal that saw him banned from teaching, but died in 2016 before being prosecuted.] I was quite horrified by him and deeply concerned that my brother would be left with a man like THAT! How my parents didn't see through the 'eccentric' confirmed bachelor I've no idea, but I am extremely thankful for one small mercy. He didn't yet take girls. In April 1973, the term I was sent, he only took boys. By 1974, he did take girls so my escape was an extremely narrow one. I remember visiting this school very often as I grew up, for Sports Days, watching vile Lindsay take each of my three brothers from my parents in turn, a reassuring con man grooming my parents out of a small fortune every time. Pitching for children as only a practised paedophile/child catcher can. Roald Dahl describes in *Boy* the 'shark's grin beneath the surface' which is what I caught a flash of.

Later, from Sherborne Girls, I would queue up for my pocket money (50p perhaps) on Saturdays when we were allowed out into town and spend it in Woolworths on my two little brothers. Beano's, Rolo's & Curly Wurly's – I would remember the position of their beds from the start of the year when trunks were taken up and leave the treasure under their pillows whilst they were all out playing sport. I felt so guilty that I could leave via a green back gate that was never locked and my poor brothers could not. I always knew instinctively that something was wrong. Complicit matrons always saw me and said nothing. Perhaps they pitied their charges. My little brothers.

Being a military man, my father was extremely practical and liked the idea of all of us being in one town if he was to be abroad. In fact, our trains didn't exactly coincide but he saw great merit in a prep, boys' and girls' school of single sex all in one town. Stanley Johnson [Ed – Boris Johnson's father] persuaded Ashdown to take his daughter Rachel too. 'All 4 or none at all'. I often wonder what would've happened if my father had insisted upon the same. Would I be campaigning as I am, had I been sent there too? That was how both prep schools went co-educational. One attic room for a girl's dorm and advertising needlework and cookery classes. As if that's all that was necessary to include girls in a boys' prep.

I recently discovered (when I finally found the courage to revisit in June) that my parents had looked quite carefully for a girls' prep for me and it was a choice between Knighton House next to Bryanston School near Blandford; and Hanford. My mother had grown up with horses in the New Forest and had a book written about her family called *5 Proud Riders*, so Knighton House was chosen for me, because children could bring their own horses providing other children could ride them. We had gymkhanas instead of sports days and some memories are of great excitement and anticipation. Granny and Grampa brought a proper picnic and I remember jam jars full of cream and their own delicious strawberries. The manners system at Hanford was possibly what deterred my parents, too – there was a 'pig's table' for when a girl couldn't be trusted to sit decently in company.

What I remember about the process of being sent away is as follows.

My brother was sent first. I remember the sound of my mother's sewing machine sewing on Cash's nametapes, kit lists, uniform buying, trunk packing, and feeling very left out. I think I wanted some of that excitement and attention they were giving John, so busy were they with him – in later years my mother would tell me: 'But you *chose* to go!' I don't see how that can be true – how *could* I know to choose anything at seven?

John was sent to Sherborne Prep and then the house was sold and we spent an amazing holiday in Doha. We had a villa with staff; a household servant, a driver, and a cook. We were members of Shell Lodge where they'd put on movies, we'd have English food like 'mince & mash' and swim endlessly. There was a terrible incident where John nearly drowned because of a mask he'd dived in with which had a ping pong ball in its snorkel as one piece. Suction meant he couldn't remove it and a trainee diver in the pool saved his life. Once, Daddy bought a doorless Mini Moke and straight off a BOAC flight he drove us children at breakneck speed around almost every roundabout in Doha. So fun! We used to ride in the desert at dawn and the English community were excellent at creating weekend fun like camping under the stars at the Inland Sea, Dukhan, or at Umm Said, a sailing club outside Doha. Using trays as toboggans we'd slide straight into the sea down a hot sand dune. Delicious BBQs and makeshift campsites made of sheets tied to broom poles. Sleeping on lilos or rubber dinghies under the stars which seemed so much closer, brighter. Life in the holidays was spent in glorious technicolour, the sounds and smells of the old souq were captured in my mother's brilliant paintings of Qatar. She remarried a British architect when my father died prematurely in 1997. In the end, she left Qatar after 50 years when he also died, in 2019. A woman in Qatar must have a male sponsor.

Expatriate parties and alcohol were never in short supply and the resulting promiscuity meant none of my friends who were all at various boarding schools in UK had parents that managed to stay together.

As I grew older, I found myself in increasingly dangerous and vulnerable situations. Flying out as unaccompanied minors on BOAC with 'Universal Aunts' was safe enough, but then we flew other airlines like Alia via Amman in Jordan to save on costs, which wasn't. I remember deciding very young not to disclose certain information to my parents because I didn't want them to worry. The cost of our education was burden enough. I remember agreeing this with John quite early on and the fact that his complaints about his prep and headmaster fell on deaf ears meant our two younger brothers barely spoke about it. There was no point. It was their inevitable fate, if John, who (good for him!) screamed when he was sent back, and often had to be dragged forcibly out of his seat by a universal aunt, had never been heard.

Whilst still at university I survived a rape attack in Doha, then later during the Gulf War I had to leave my father and fly back to London. Really, I should have been a Sherborne Girls 'success story' as an Exeter graduate in Russian with French. However, in my opinion boarding school set me up to be perfect prey. I would draw a direct comparison between the level of vulnerability I felt abandoned a week after my eighth birthday and my arrival age 25 in London straight off a flight from a war zone with no money, no contacts, and only a suitcase. And my wits.

That was how it happened that I was recruited by UAE Royals top diplomat for their property office in Knightsbridge. I was tricked into a medical check-up including investigation for AIDS and STDs, following a five-month period during which I was raped, and then trafficked to a VIP. I would go as far as to say that my upbringing to be obedient and dutiful, without any protection in the wider world, prepared me to be abused; first in this job and then afterwards (boarding school does not teach you how to set healthy boundaries), so that I needed to frequently change places geographically in order to feel safe. In the end I travelled right around the world alone in 1997 after my father died, and finally found Totnes where I felt safe enough to raise a family. Compartmentalisation is a skill learned early for survival, especially in prep boarding school non-disclosure agreements, death, and legal threats compound this, as if the trauma itself were never bad enough.

A lawyer asked me if I'd ever told my family about this and I needed to make quite sure. I plucked up the courage and asked my mother if I'd ever told her I was raped. 'No'. I was not remotely surprised. She remarried around that time. Clearly, I did not want to spoil her wedding. It was an important day and I did not wish to be blamed for ruining it. Later I asked my mother if she could see how it was that ten years of being raised in girls' boarding schools had led to this happening. She said she could not see any relation between the two.

I was a straight A model student, school prefect, extremely diligent, mainly because it was my academic reports that my father paid attention to. When I was 18, he was *astonished* that girls' A level exams were set to the same standard as boys', and at how well I'd done. I felt that all my childhood effort up to that point had been in vain as he had only then finally understood my achievement. I remember making the choice to be hard-working when I had friends who at 16 were smoking and discovering boys. Through General Studies (woodwork was where I met one of my best friends who was a boy – the school practical joker and good friend of the head boy) I found more freedom and friendship and the Stick (Sherborne School Bar) on Saturday nights, by invitation. Boys always made safer friends, I found. I could trust them not to betray me, generally...

The night of the 'Battle of Brittan' was funny but led to tragedy for another girl. I arrived in the Stick to find boys flying at me like Messerschmitt fighter planes. The popular joker was planning to ask me out. I politely declined. He walked me back to Mulliner, the upper sixth girl's house, and walking back to School House, he bumped into the head girl, declared his undying love for her, walked her back to her house, got drunk, thought better of it, and found his way into her room in the middle of the night. Unfortunately, that was directly above her housemistress' room. He escaped by shinning down a drainpipe and was subsequently gated, but the poor innocent girl was publicly shamed at a whole school assembly and immediately expelled – her early career in tatters. Public shaming was used to great effect as a deterrent in girls' schools as opposed to corporal punishment. I've never felt so powerless, I knew she was innocent and the joker who trespassed entirely at fault, but his family were significant and he baked croissants for the school headmaster in chef's whites on Sunday mornings. So…

My mother flew back to the UK to put John and I in boarding school together in April a week after my eight birthday. I still have all my school reports with the dates on, which are helpful to me for confirmation of these blurred traumatic memories. I had forgotten, until my own daughter was the same age, the depth of the trauma of separation that I had buried. It came back to me 13 years ago in a horrible flashback. I was waving my daughter off for a weekend trip to Dartmoor; she was seven, the same age as me. I began to cry whilst waving and it was literally like the sky fell in. I sat in my car for about 30 minutes sobbing and feeling black although it was a sunny, outwardly happy day. The memory that flooded back was being left in the gloom of the hallway of Knighton House holding Matron's hand whilst my mother walked out of the front door and away into the light carrying my baby brother and holding my younger brother's hand. Flying back to Doha. I'd lost everything familiar in an instant. Matron was a complete stranger. They'd left me!

I think up until that point, the *reality* of abandonment, the excitement had carried me, not my own excitement particularly, but that of others, those buying into this particular cult of private education who would persuade me that I was so privileged and fortunate, that I was one of the lucky ones. Sell it to me. Propaganda. Cult. Sacrifices had been made for me. I was always careful to try not to be obnoxious or carry this conceit which such schools as Sherborne quite deliberately engender; however, the voice I'm left with is hard to disguise.

I remember leaving my primary school and all the questions about where I was going and me trying to explain it. I remember talking to my best friend, the daughter of the town stationer, and how painful it was to lose her as my dear school friend. It was as if by buying an education my parents opted out of community. I didn't belong anywhere and lost all my roots. The most rootless point ever was holding Matron's hand at the time of actual abandonment, and it was a terrible memory to have return. I realise now that just like I shut it out because it was too painful, I did exactly the same thing with anything else that was too much for me, including the terrible crimes committed against me in my 20s. I realise now I was living in survival mode and had to learn to cope alone, and learn for myself whom I could trust. Vulnerability is a key defining attribute in a case of sex trafficking according to ex-Crown Prosecutor Nazir Afzal.

Matron was extremely practical and in truth I really did appreciate that about her; it was comforting in a way. She reminded me of my father in her practicality.

For my father, a prep was preparation for big school via the Common Entrance exam which was preparation in turn for university etc. He was focused on our academic results, always.

Matron used to read to us after baths (three pairs of girls to each of three baths with only about six inches of water). We sat on the wooden floor of her room in our dressing gowns while she read and we could have two biscuits or triangles of brown bread and butter and a drink. I really hated her reading Worzel Gummidge to us because he reminded me of Jimmy Savile.

One of the ways I found out how practical Matron was by making myself vomit on my dormitory floor. She'd come in with Dettol and I'd be put in the san for two days with no food and no visitors. Quite regularly. This was in my first dormitory. There can't have been much in my tummy when I was sick and I must've become very thin. I remember it being like water. But it got Matron's attention. Which must've been what I was after. I remember being unbearably lonely in the school san yet I did this self-harming behaviour repetitively at the very beginning. It returned when I was 17 and lasted until I became pregnant with my first child. An awful, terrible damaging combination of anorexia and bulimia.

I recently returned to my prep school and I asked my mother afterwards (by phone) if they'd ever told her I used to do that. 'No' she replied. And that was the end of it. I think it was a cry for attention and comfort, somehow. Later, Matron would nag me about standing up straight and putting my shoulders back, 'Don't slouch, Joanna. Shoulders back!' Unfortunately for me I was born with a deformity. I had a winged scapula which meant my shoulder was missing a muscle and there was nothing I could do about it. It just stuck out and I slouched.

I remember I was the smallest in the school, tanned from an Easter holiday in Qatar. The prefects made much of me being little and I overheard them once cooing over me when collecting the sweet box for our table's after dinner sweets (two each). I remember deciding that being sickly sweet would serve me well and I wore a mask I call 'Pretty Pleasing Penelope' from that point onwards. It was a painful mask to wear as it was my false self. I must've felt it served me.

One other aspect that served me well was being expatriate, especially as I grew up. In the dorms at night the expatriate children would tell tales of their holiday experiences in different countries which I found fascinating, especially the daughter of a game keeper in Kenya and one whose parents were in Malaysia who told fabulous jungle stories. How much was entirely true I've no idea but it didn't matter as she entertained us so well. (She also read us some racy stories by torchlight.) Importantly the more snobby, titled girls found it much more difficult to pigeonhole us socially when I was sharing about fish souqs, for example, and a crazy fisherwoman throwing dirty water at my mother because she didn't want to be photographed for a painting at dawn.

My very first form teacher was Miss Brown. She said in my first ever lesson; 'Now girls, you must think of me as your new mother because you will see me for two thirds of the year and your mother only for one'. Everything inside me screamed; 'But you're *not* my mother!' And I felt furious but could not express it.

What a terrible thing to say to a child who had the night before been abandoned! I think I was the only new girl that term – I was sent a term early so that John wouldn't be their only child in England and we could travel on BOAC as unaccompanied minors to Doha together.

I was a tremendous tomboy having three brothers and it was the perfect school for a tomboy. Very Blytonesque. We wore red dungarees over our grey skorts and yellow aertex shirts, and mine, which were second hand (so soft not starchy), had more patches than anyone's from climbing the big tree. I think I navigated almost every single branch of that amazing tree, but one Parent's Day tragedy struck and the branch of Spaghetti Junction snapped almost directly beneath me and I watched as it fell to the ground. One of Knighton's best gymnasts broke her arm as a result. An ambulance arrived. That was a trauma unshared. We used to do fantastic gymnastic displays, we had a coach who was involved somehow with the Olympics, and parents would come and give incredibly fascinating talks and slide shows. A Congo explorer parent was always particularly impressive.

When I went back to Knighton, I remembered John and Peggy Booker who were very benevolent and kind, deeply Christian people who had started the school and took me under their wing. I couldn't say I got special treatment but I did feel loved by them which was perhaps rare for a child sent to boarding school with parents thousands of miles away. I was eventually made a committee member (their prefect system) with a little yellow scroll for a badge inscribed 'Committee' and played Mary in the school nativity tableau which was the highest honour (much to the titled girl's disgust, who was certain she would be chosen 'because of who my father is'), and my parents sat in the front row of Durweston church to watch me not move a muscle or sing a note (I wasn't allowed in the school choir because an unkind choir mistress pronounced me tone deaf the first time I ever sang a note for her). It didn't help that Mr. B kept asking me why I wasn't in the choir. 'Tone deaf, Mr. B'.

In fact, when I returned, I stood in the very spot where I'd played Mary in that church and prayed just before I summoned up the courage to ring the doorbell. It was *exactly* the same doorbell and very little had changed from the outside. I'll never forget pressing the doorbell as an adult and being warmly received.

I'd asked my mother, incidentally, if she would return with me because I felt it could be healing for both of us but she refused and said she 'didn't think it would be a good idea'.

My mother hadn't liked me describing drop off as abandonment: 'I never abandoned you, how dare you!'

Well that was how, in truth, it felt to me.

A comment she made about paying school fees and finding she'd been conned by a fixated paedophile was that it was 'a bit rich'.

So you see...

I'm glad I didn't plan it; it was spontaneous returning from Surrey to Devon and I was alone, which was a blessing in the end. The school was empty of children, so memories came flooding back that the building itself held. It was quite extraordinary to be standing there again in the hallway where I'd been left.

Also, on the driveway where I'd said my goodbyes leaving, aged 12. I remembered it so clearly, how close we'd all grown over five years, and yet I never saw any of them ever again.

Some of the good things were the gymkhanas; the awesome cakes on Sunday afternoon that Mrs. P the cook baked for us, especially coffee and walnut and her cherry pastry pies; bonfire nights when we wore jodhpurs and wellies and enjoyed cocoa, jacket potatoes, and sparklers, whilst our guy burned up by the stables; and then amazing fireworks on the lawn of Knighton; gymnastic and dance displays; playing horses in the laurel hedges; climbing Big Ben (the big tree); hopscotch and roller skating down the drive; playing jacks and blowing balloons out of toxic smelling plastic gum; riding out when I was confident, unafraid of my very scary riding teacher Miss Handy (who picked her nose at table); playing mushrooms (a breath holding competition), and swimming in a really dodgy old reservoir; committee trips in a minibus to local beauty spots like Stourhead or local churches on Sundays other than Durweston; being read Thomas Hardy by Mr. B and then being shown Casterbridge (Dorchester) and lots of places mentioned in Hardy country, including graves; watching Top of the Pops; and long walks on Sundays when I learned to love nature.

And yet these are also some of the times when I was very lonely. I wasn't unpopular and I don't think I was unkind to anyone really, at least I hope I wasn't, but my perception might not be accurate. I also loved doing art in the art block which was a room above the stables. It felt like a special place, a sanctuary. The other place I loved was the cellar chapel, sadly now only used for storage. A huge mistake because it felt to me like the heartbeat of that school. Sacred. We used to attend every Sunday evening and always finished with the song 'God be in my head' and the Nunc Dimittis. There was something hugely comforting to a child voluntarily deprived of family in the repetition of divine singing and chanting, candles and holy paintings, icons.

GOD BE IN MY HEAD

God be in my head,
And in my understanding;
God be in mine eyes,
And in my looking;
God be in my mouth,
And in my speaking;
God be in my heart,
And in my thinking;
God be at mine end,
And at my departing
          (Sir Henry
          Walford Davies)

It was a holy way to start the new week.

By contrast we'd have FP (Friday Papers) exams every Friday morning on all we'd learned that week, and I'd usually do well. I was lucky to have received such an education but the personal cost was always too high and I often wonder what my life would've been like had my father never made the monumental decision he did to move countries in order to send us all away. I also sometimes wonder what would've happened had my father accepted a job with Qantas instead of Shell, if we were never involved with Qatar or Sherborne and I'd been raised an Australian.

I must say as far as PREPS go, I got incredibly lucky. The negatives were significant – mental health and self-harming behaviour most of all – and feeling unwelcome and unwanted has never left me.

Making a home and parenting my own children has been hard. Belonging is nothing anyone can buy. I think I found it quite miraculously in Totnes. My children have not been sent away to board at eight and I was very pleased to break that cycle. I try to check in with my children. I cannot bear the idea of them going unheard. They all carry mobile phones which can be great security for a child.

We had no phone calls, just weekly letter writing, on Sunday afternoon after lunch, on our beds. Letters were left unsealed so they could be checked/vetted so I didn't tell any of the things that troubled or upset me; odd situations I was in, for example, exeat weekends with a family who all sat naked in their sauna and expected me to do the same. A school dance at Downside where a Spanish noble had afterwards written asking me to book a hotel for a dirty weekend for him and his friend who had a car – I still have the letter. Phone calls to Qatar were out of the question so the vulnerability was a constant companion, although I tried so bravely never to show I felt it. I've never forgotten my hunger for letters from my parents. My mother's beautiful italic sloping handwriting on a fat white airmail envelope with Sheikh Khalifa's face on the Qatari stamps. They were handed out at breakfast and I'd desperately try to spot an envelope in advance, so hungry was I for love, comfort, news from home. Like a soldier might be. Sometimes my father would write – both their handwriting seemed beautiful to me – and occasionally my brothers. Once John was sent to school, I never recognised him in any of his letters to me. Rugby and cricket scores. Vetted by Skunk, no wonder. I had a few from my little brothers being educated in Doha. I absolutely cherished them, hugely misspelled as they were. It's an odd thing to move from living with your family to writing them letters. So formal. Desperate. Distanced. Later of course I wouldn't recognise either of them as they started prep.

My voice is what I've come away with as the most obvious marker of an upbringing away from my parents. A 'posh girl', as Robert Verkaik might say. It carries with it a superficial confidence which masks that vulnerability and perceived rejection. That abandonment from which one can never recover. Betrayed by one's parents, presented as privilege. Count yourself lucky.

So if the perk *is* to be my education, then I'd better use it for the highest good. And that is why I campaign continuously for legal reform around child protection and mandatory reporting of child sexual abuse. And as a mother, I am still amazed to have three beautiful children I've somehow managed to keep safe yet give them wings.

4.5.6   On disowned feelings

'BUT THE MOST ENDURING EMOTIONAL IGNORANCE LEADS US BACK TO WHERE WE STARTED; IT IS THE ONE MOST EASILY IDENTIFIABLE FROM OUTSIDE THE ISLAND — THE PRACTICE OF SENDING CHILDREN AWAY TO SCHOOL BY THE VERY PEOPLE WHO CAN AFFORD TO KEEP THEM THERE.

ITS CONTINUATION AND NORMALISATION RELIES, AS WE HAVE SEEN, ON TWO MENTAL-EMOTIONAL CONJURING TRICKS: MOTHERS MUST IGNORE THEIR FEELINGS OF MATERNAL ATTACHMENT AND CHILDREN MUST DISSOCIATE FROM THEIR INBUILT INSTINCTS. BUT WE ALSO REALISED THAT DISSOCIATING FROM IDENTITIES LIKE "I AM THE VULNERABLE ONE" IN ORDER TO AVOID THE SECONDARY FEELINGS THAT MIGHT ARISE, CREATES A VERY DANGEROUS SITUATION IN THE PSYCHE. DISOWNED IDENTITIES AND DISOWNED FEELINGS THEN *CONTROL* YOUR LIFE RATHER THAN GUIDE IT, BECAUSE DISSOCIATING DOES NOT MEAN YOU ARE *IN CHARGE* OF YOUR FEELINGS, IT MEANS THESE VERY DISOWNED FEELINGS UNCONSCIOUSLY RUN YOUR LIFE AND DOMINATE YOU, WITHOUT YOUR KNOWING ABOUT IT.

WOUNDED LEADERS, NICK DUFFELL, LONE ARROW PRESS, 2ND ED., P. 265

4.5.7   Jem

My father was an army officer, so moving home was a big part of my life as a child. I was born in the UK, but my family moved back to Germany before I was 18 months old. All my memories of childhood prior to the age of six are of being in Germany. It was largely a happy time. We lived on army camps, but my parents were keen to integrate in Germany society as much as was possible. Before I was born, they had lived off camp and had made lifelong friends with a number of locals, including one couple that we spent a lot of time with. I didn't really ever learn to speak German, but I think I understood it reasonably well; for some time, I went to a German kindergarten and had ballet lessons in German. Eventually I had to go to an English military school which was an hour's coach drive away from home which I hated.

I remember walks in the forest with our dog, playing with my younger brother and other children on the camp and watching my Mum ride horses at the local stables. We used to go to Denmark on holiday and visit the original Lego Land which was hugely exciting. Christmases are prominent in my memory as we got the best of both worlds; presents on Christmas Eve with our German friends and then more presents on Christmas day for our English Christmas. I remember the Christmas decorations being so magical – I am sure that our friends had real candles on their

Christmas tree which seems like a slightly crazy idea now, particularly with children and dogs around! I loved spending time with our German friends; they spoilt us rotten as they didn't have children of their own and so my brother and I benefitted from lots of presents. The smell of Nivea cream is still evocative for me as their house always had a faint smell of it.

We moved back to the UK when I was around six years old and lived in army accommodation in London. This was also quite a happy and largely uneventful time. I went to the local school, as did the other kids on the camp. I remember quite a lot of social events; some which involved the kids and some didn't. My parents used to go to mess nights and sometimes my brother and I would be put into the car in our pyjamas and taken to the mess and left in a room to sleep whilst the partying went on below. I distinctly remember the smell of my mother's evening perfume which reminds me of being wrapped up and put into the car. Similarly, my parents entertained at home a lot and my brother and I used to hang over the bannisters trying to listen in to the adult conversations! There were lots of children to play with and the mess was also a fabulous playground for us as it had extensive grounds.

I recall my parents telling us about our next move, to Hong Kong (which I naively thought was in the UK) but I don't really remember the idea of boarding school being introduced to me and it certainly wasn't discussed with me. There is a long history of boarding in my family, my maternal family were naval and landed gentry, so it was considered the norm. My mother had boarded and had hated it. I later learned that she didn't want my brother or me to board but was overridden by my father. His mother had also been at a very well-known boarding school and I think he felt that it was important for us to board, both on a practical basis due to the constant moving with the Forces, and for social reasons. He hadn't boarded himself.

I went to my first boarding school at the age of eight. I can remember one visit to the school prior to the beginning of term but I have practically no memory of being dropped off for the first time at boarding school. I learned, only a few months ago, that my father wasn't there when I started school. He was in the Falkland Islands and, whilst I remember that he went there, I had forgotten that he didn't drop me off with my mother. I can picture the school, where we would have been dropped off and my first dormitory, but I can't remember the day itself or any of the emotions. Similarly, I can only really remember snapshots of that first term. The girls' floor was at the top of the building (what probably had been servants' quarters) with little dormer windows which looked out to sea. There were attics next to and between the dorms and we discovered that, if you were brave enough, you could crawl between these and scare other children in their dorms, or even make it to the common room if you could get far enough without being caught. The routine was strict and we weren't given much free time. I was horrified at having to go to bed at 6:30 pm, which was far earlier than I had done at home. Each dormitory had a prefect in with the younger children (a practice both the prefects and younger children disliked). There was little sympathy for homesickness, particularly from the prefects. Woe betide you if you were caught talking after lights out; it could result simply in a telling off but often you were sent to stand outside the headmaster's residence door in the dark dining room lit only by the fly zapper which emitted a creepy, blue light into the room. You never knew how long you'd have to stand there and what punishment would be meted out to you; it was not a pleasant experience. The headmaster's wife would prowl the dorm corridors and she was truly terrifying; I remember noticing my heart pounding when she left the room, even if we hadn't been caught talking. We were allowed very few personal possessions, one or two photos and a teddy. I don't recall having any toys and we weren't allowed to receive parcels from home. We wore full school uniform (including uniform underpants) seven days a week until the age of 12 and a half; we did get the 'treat' of a different shirt and tie on a Sunday. Every morning was dormitory inspection and if our room wasn't neat enough or our hospital corners good enough, we lost marks for our house. We did get duvets (which is a step up from sheets and blankets) but they all had the same 'uniform' pattern; there was no opportunity for individuality. The white, metal 'hospital' beds were spectacularly uncomfortable. I remember at the beginning of a new term it would take a good couple of days to get used to being able to find a way to lie on the mattress and avoid the metal springs which had broken and poked up into the bed. Rats or squirrels resided in the attics and roof spaces and I remember lying in bed listening to them scuttling up and down, the sloping ceilings only being inches from my face.

I can't remember exeats, half-term, or Christmas of that first term. This is odd because I have good memories of Christmas before and after that. My family moved to Hong Kong soon after that first Christmas. Once my parents were abroad again, I did spend exeats and half terms with my aunt and uncle, or grandparents, and I have really good memories of those occasions. My aunt and uncle gave us lots of treats and fun. My first flight to Hong Kong is etched into my memory. It was the Easter holidays, I was still eight years old, and the school arranged for a taxi driver to pick me up from school and drive me from the South Coast to a London airport. I was too scared to ask him to stop to let me go to the loo so I have some memory of wetting myself a bit by the time we got the airport (I can't remember how this was cleaned up as I was in school uniform and had no change of clothes). I was handed over to the airline 'aunties' by the taxi driver. I remember getting onto the plane, trying the seatbelt on and then not knowing how to take it off. The flight seemed endless and uncomfortable, but I did get to watch a film which was exciting. I made friends with a girl on the plane who had done it all before and she helped me out. The 'aunties' seemed to have disappeared by the time we finally got to Hong Kong, and I had no clue as to where to go and what to do in the airport. My new friend helped me out as far as she could but she had a Chinese passport and so we had to part ways, and I had to manage the rest on my own. My mother recalled that when I finally found them my eyes were as big as saucers. I had the most immense sense of relief when I was in my mother's arms again. The taxi ride back to my new home is a vivid memory; the heat and humidity, the smells, the sights – and the desperation to get out of my hot, grey, itchy (and probably smelly) winter school uniform. Hong Kong was wonderful;

I just truly loved it there. I am a country girl at heart, but Hong Kong is my exception. I was jealous of my brother as he got to live there all the time. I went back for the three major holidays a year but that wasn't enough; I felt that the rest of my family were having an amazing experience which I wasn't truly a part of. The memories of the days leading up to returning to school, of packing, of going to the airport and of parting are vivid and I can still feel that dread viscerally.

Until relatively recently, I would have said that my time at my prep school (from age of eight to 13) was largely happy, possibly because my public school experience was more overtly unhappy. I had good friends at prep school, and I don't remember being on the receiving end of any bullying. I did well academically and didn't hate lessons. I was pretty hopeless at sport (I once had the dubious honour of winning the 'non-competitors' race at sports day) but I was good at art and music and participated in the school performances. As my own children have reached boarding school age, however, I'm much more aware now of just how abnormal my own childhood was and of the effects of growing up in an institution. I suspect I suppressed the feelings that I had; it was necessary for survival and I guess I quickly realised that hoping for the circumstances to be different was hopeless. I recall only snap shots of my homesickness; primarily the sickening realisation on waking for the first few mornings that you aren't at home as your sleepy brain had first thought. Contact with my parents was limited; we wrote and received weekly letters and were only allowed a phone call from parents on birthdays. I've calculated that I would spend 75% of the year away from my parents. From around the age of 10 or 11, I became convinced that my parents were going to die when I was away from them. Despite all this, I have very little memory of crying. I also realise that I spent a lot of time in a state of fear, which soon became a normal feeling. The dormitory prowling was also a habit of the headmaster and there was behaviour by him, and other teachers, which, at the very least, would be considered inappropriate by today's standards. Baths and showers were open with no privacy and the headmaster would 'check in' on girls' shower times; the matrons were there but were too intimidated to ask him to leave. Corporal punishment was used extensively. Individuality was discouraged. I was told by the matrons that I was very spoiled and opinionated when I first started school. I quickly learned to stay quiet and to blend in. I still fear expressing my opinions.

My parents moved back to the UK whilst I was at prep school, and they moved house within the UK a number of times. I have only sketchy memories of holidays at 'home'; I was quite bored as I didn't have any local friends and we no longer lived on camp. I was increasingly aware of the breakdown of my parents' marriage and was worried about what was happening.

I only spent one year at public school. My parents by this time only lived about 40 minutes' drive from the school. I found this incredibly hard, harder than when they lived abroad, given that the necessity argument seemed to carry less weight. Despite their relative proximity, I still only saw them at exeats and holidays, and I was desperately homesick. I also really missed my friends from prep school; they had become my surrogate family and parting from them felt like grieving.

My mother lent me her watch, its leather strap retained the smell of her perfume and I used to sniff it for comfort. I did experience some bullying at that school; it was not as awful as many accounts I've read, but nonetheless horribly impossible to escape. Perhaps emboldened by age (I was 14 at the time) I pestered to leave and at the very last minute (the trunk was packed) my parents made the decision to send me to the local school.

My memories of boarding and how I felt at the time may be patchy; however, I do know that I'm left with a lingering feeling of 'otherness' and of not belonging anywhere. I'm envious of those that can say where they come from. I cannot connect with many of the social and cultural references of others of my age group as we didn't have radio or popular music at school and TV was so limited. Ironically, given that the justification for sending me to board was stability, I still attended six different schools and lived in many different homes. I enjoyed living abroad, but I didn't belong there, I didn't belong anywhere in the UK, and no-one truly belongs at boarding school.

4.5.8　On insecurity

THE ENDLESSNESS OF TERMS PROVE THAT [SCHOOL] SOCIETY, THE HIERARCHY, THE ORDER IS UNCHANGEABLE ... THE HOLIDAYS, FOR ALL BUT THE MOST UNFORTUNATE, ARE SPENT BACK AT HOME WHERE FRIENDSHIPS MAY HAVE BEEN LOST OR NEVER DEVELOPED. FOR THE CHILD, SHUFFLING BACKWARDS AND FORWARDS IN THE TRANSITORY WORLD OF TERMS AND HOLIDAYS, THE SECURITY OF HOME MAY NEVER BE REGAINED...

THE CHILD'S HOME NOW TURNS INTO AN ALIEN WORLD, BORDERED BY PACKING AND UNPACKING, DAYS SLIPPING AWAY IN THE PREPARATIONS FOR THE ASSAULT OF THE NEXT TERM.

THE MAKING OF THEM, NICK DUFFELL, LONE ARROW PRESS,
3RD ED., P. 34

4.6　Others

4.6.1　Isabel

I chose to go to boarding school, because I was being bullied for numerous reasons at my prep school. Of the schools that my parents had shortlisted and visited, the one I liked the sound of happened to be an all-girls boarding school. So, off I went.

My parents are Catholic and wanted my schooling to reflect their religion. However, this reduced their options quite considerably in the UK, let alone what was available in my local area. They looked around various Catholic schools nearby and further afield, many of which happened to be single sex.

Having, dyspraxia, dyscalculia, and dyslexia – the trifecta of learning disorders (what they were termed when I was growing up) also limited their options. Unfortunately, I was not advised to be entered into the 11+ exams, for fear that I would not pass. This limited my parents' options further still, reducing the pool to schools that would not require an 11+ entrance exam, enabling pupils to start earlier.

The school my parents shortlisted, and that I ended up doing a taster day and night at, was an ex-convent all-girls Catholic boarding school in Dorset. It also catered to local day girls, which did make the social hierarchy a bit more pronounced – widening the chasm between 'us' boarders and 'them' day pupils. Unfortunately, weekly boarding was not offered, which I think would have benefitted me better, allowing me to escape on weekends.

I was eight when I had my taster day at what would become my school and address for nine years. I was having a miserable time at my Church of England co-ed prep school and could not wait to get the hell out of there. At that age, I naturally gravitated to hanging out with girls, and I didn't yet have the maturity or inclination to have male friends – that would come much later.

My rationale for attending an all-girls school, was that I got along with girls better and it would halve the number of kids giving me stick for being bad at school and sports. That and the fact that the school in Dorset had a vending machine and tuck shop. I had an insatiable sweet tooth back then and I hate to admit it now, but that clinched it for me.

My mum likes to remind me that some major decisions I've made in my life have often randomly hinged on appliances. I ended up working for a small wealth management firm in my mid-20s. The impetus for me to start a career change came after the office dishwasher finally packed up.

I was the most junior person in the company at the time and was told by the managing director to 'go out and buy some marigolds' in my lunch. It was the boot in the arse that I needed to Google copywriting night school classes, leading me to quit that job and build a career in content marketing.

I clearly remember when I told the prep-school kids I was ditching them for a school with a vending machine and tuck shop. I made the choice of packing myself off to boarding school at nine, leaving the bullies and my parents behind. There I was, looking forward to a future of limitless Dr Pepper.

Upon arrival, I learned it was going to be much harder than I anticipated. I went from the order of my parents to the relative freedom of my boarding school. This was some adjustment which shook me to my core, although I never would have admitted it to anyone at the time.

It was up to me to ensure that I stuck to the laundry schedule (which weekday would be clothes, bed linen, school uniform, towels, etc.). When I chose to brush my teeth, wash my hair, tidy my room, get my homework done, collect my clothes from the laundry, do my turn-ups (when we would have to put everything on the floor on our beds so the cleaners could hoover the floor).

I had a helicopter parent in my mum, and I was absent minded due to my dyspraxia and general lack of self-awareness, so things did slip out of control. The nits in the junior school were the worst!

I did also feel like an orphan at times. Although I was surrounded by teachers, fellow students, house mistress, and house assistants, there was a general lack of pastoral care. We were very much expected to be fully independent and there was not much truck for those that fell by the wayside. Those in authority were merely there to adhere to school rules and ensure we stuck to the schedule – nothing more.

When I got sick with colds, etc., it was up to me to alert those in charge to get permission to go to the school nurse. To expect that at nine years of age, it is a very Victorian attitude in my opinion. I am still shocked by the general lack of empathy or care that I received back in 1999. I would hope that things have changed since my time.

However, in that environment I quickly learned to become independent. In my first year at boarding school, I had a few nasty cavities and other humiliating moments involving head lice. I learned by age ten, if I did not get my life together, it would slowly fall apart, and my health would suffer. It was very much a culture of being thrown in the deep end.

I was also bad at scheduling my homework and schoolwork. Often missing deadlines, hand ins, I was bad at scheduling in revision time for tests. Although we had scheduled homework sessions after dinner each evening, there was not much focus on ensuring everyone had managed to complete their assignments. We did not have to hand it in to anyone to check it over, which meant that I could get away without doing it for weeks on end.

Another challenge I had was forgetting where the classrooms were and getting lost, as the school, although small, had a rabbit warren layout. I often lost various elements of my PE kit, homework, pencil cases, etc. Added to that, I flunked my end of year exams and very nearly got thrown out.

I found out later that the school took me on as a charity case, because my entrance exam was so poor. As they were a Catholic school, they had this ethos of taking on 'lost causes', where other schools had failed. That made me a shoe in, coupled with the fact my parents did not require me to have any scholarship or financial aid.

After a rough start I turned a corner. Probably a catalyst for this change was when our head of junior school made us watch this ancient video from the 1970s called 'Some of Your Bits Ain't Nice'. Charming, but looking back now, I hope it wasn't specifically chosen because of me but knowing my luck it probably was!

Gradually, my organisational skills, personal hygiene and grades improved. However, my disastrous first year had sealed my fate at the school, for teachers and pupils as a 'special case', which would dog me for the full nine-year stint I did in that place. I was infantilised and treated like a mentally incapacitated person a lot. Occasionally, it would have been deserved but most of the treatment I received was emotionally damaging looking back.

Things that happened to me there wouldn't or I hope shouldn't happen today – since woke and cancel culture have happened. I was also being bullied by the girls in my year. I found out later in my 20s, it was because one girl took it upon herself to blackmail any new girls that joined our year that they would not 'survive' if they had anything to do with me.

Overnight, my year group reached a mafia-level of bitching, with each clique double- and triple-crossing each other. Multiple factions sprung up overnight, only for the queen bees to tire of this and form different factions by the following morning. The best way of describing it was being forced to watch a badly written *Game of Thrones* that dragged on for nine shitty seasons – where Daenerys Targaryen was the good guy.

I found myself cast adrift, not wanting to subscribe to one clique over another. Surprisingly, my emotional intelligence was developing much quicker than my academic intelligence. I could see from the outside how petty and childish it all was and simply got bored of their endless drama. From their point of view, I was mental for not wanting to join in. Although, to their credit, I was often called upon for advice in moments of crisis and on more than one occasion they referred to me as 'wise'.

As a result of being a lone wolf, my mental health declined along with my self-esteem and sanity. At one point I got so depressed I had suicidal thoughts and even chose which roof I would jump off if things got really bad. What stopped me was the thought of ending my story blood spattered in tartan. Our school uniform involved a dodgy brown, green, and white tartan kilt that would make the hardiest of Scots vomit. I also did not want the bastards to win.

I hit rock-bottom at 15. As a result of the extreme loneliness I felt, I started talking to myself. I was 17 around the time that Bloc Party released their song 'Two More Years', which happily coincided with starting my AS levels, when I had just two more years left until I graduated. That song became my anthem and I tried to pull as much of my shredded self-esteem and unhappiness together to avoid the whole experience breaking me. If I could just hang on for two more years, then I would be free.

I could not change schools because I had extra English lessons and extra time already built in for my public exams. My parents were worried what would happen if I also got bullied from boys as a later teenager in a co-ed school. As my grades at GCSE were not bad but equally did not set the world on fire, this would have limited their options again, so it was decided to stick with the prison I knew.

Music became my lifeline during my boarding school years, something I kept into adulthood. Combined with reading, film, and TV, I immersed myself into culture as an escape. The only reason I thought about applying to university was from watching imported high school US film and TV. The plot lines revolved around the main characters applying to 'college', so to me, it became normalised. That was simply what you do as a teenager at the age of 17.

Throughout my nine years there, I knew that the upper sixth girls would leave and that some would even go on to university. However, my school was not particularly academic, and this was not a given. Not many girls left to follow up with higher education.

The teachers certainly did not suggest higher education to me. They still saw me as the charity case that forgot the times for things. My parents were told back in 1999 that I would not even get a GCSE and that A-levels were a pipedream. As I got older, and my GCSE grades were better than what was predicted back then, it was decided to take a risk and let me do A-Levels.

Having a new headmaster and head of sixth form start in the mid 2000s also helped. The headmaster had transferred from a sister school which was very academic and was set to galvanise my old school into joining the 21st century.

Naturally, this involved league tables and scrutinising the number of offered university places. Not having people attend university would be bad for business. Luckily for me, this change coincided with my public exam years, so it was decided by higher powers, that I should sit my A-levels and apply for university via UCAS after all.

However, I did have to push for the right course, as the teachers were stumped as to what subject the charity case would major in. I wanted to do a marketing degree, but my maths grade at GCSE was a D and most ex-polytechnics would only accept a C grade or above.

With a lack of direction or support from the teachers who had given up on me by that stage, I used common sense and cobbled together my A-level subjects into a degree. Somehow this worked and I applied to do History of Art and Theology. I was not going to be a loser defined by the American high school TV and films, as someone not going to university to get a degree and a fair shot at a better life.

I ended up graduating from Oxford Brookes University with a combined honours 2:1 degree in History of Art, Religion, *and* Theology. My little sister was still at the school when I graduated, and she told one of the teachers my final grade. The next thing she heard was a note had been placed on the staffroom notice board: 'Isabel Stanton has graduated university with a 2:1'. It was my mum that told me that story.

At the time, I felt it was a bit patronising (nothing new for my old school) but also like they were taking it as their victory, not mine. I did learn things at that school, but upon being asked, I often refer to the biggest lesson, which was how to pack a suitcase.

After a few missteps and a secretarial course later, I eventually made it to working in digital marketing. Working hard was what got me out of that bad situation I found myself in. I used the negativity and being written off to prove them wrong. Now, I can look back and see how far I have come.

4.6.2   The 'I am not The One' imperative

DISOWNING HAS FURTHER GEARS FOR USE WHEN AN ENVIRONMENT IS SEVERELY HOSTILE, WHEN A PERSON IS BARELY SUPPORTED, OR WHEN THE QUALITIES BEING REPRESSED ARE EVEN MORE TABOO. THE NEXT PROCESS INVOLVES EXPORTING THE DISOWNED PROBLEM OUTSIDE THE PSYCHE. IT IS THEN NO LONGER PART OF *ME* BUT ASSUMED BE PART OF *YOU* ... IN PSYCHOLOGY, THIS FORM OF EXPORTING IS COMMONLY KNOWN AS *PROJECTION*.

PROJECTION ANSWERS THE ENSUING PROBLEM OF DISOWNING SOMETHING, WHICH IS THIS: IF I AM NOT 'THE STUPID CHILD' THEN WHERE *IS* HE AND *WHO* IS HE? ... "I AM NOT THE FOOLISH CHILD" WORKS BRILLIANTLY WELL WHEN A STUPID CHILD IS SHOWN TO HAVE TURNED UP SOMEWHERE ELSE, CLOSE AT HAND – IT'S YOU! ...

> THIS EXPORT/PROJECTION PROCESS TAKES TWO PLAYERS AND REGULARLY TURNS
> UP IN INTIMATE RELATIONSHIP, ESPECIALLY MARRIAGES. IT IS CRUCIAL TO THE
> FOUNDATION OF PUBLIC SCHOOL BULLYING.
>
> *WOUNDED LEADERS*, NICK DUFFELL, LONE ARROW PRESS,
> 2ND ED., P. 82

4.6.3   Olivia

Like the woman at the well I was seeking

"Hi Olivia, it's been a while since we contacted each other. How are you doing? Would you mind following my Instagram account and blog? I am currently documenting my journey of recovering from severe suicidal bipolar depression."

J was a friend from a Cantonese church I attended whilst I was still studying in the UK. One of the reasons we clicked with each other was because we both went to boarding school and loved to vent to each other about how much we hated the experience. Little did I know that she had been so affected by the boarding school experience that it contributed to her mental illness only a few years later.

"The reason why I wanted to reach out to you is I thought you would understand, since we've both gone to a boarding school."

I know I have always hated the boarding school experience but it has never occurred to me that it was so bad that I would end my life. I felt relieved that I hadn't become as fragile as my friend in her pitiful state.

Down the rabbit hole

Not so long after the conversation with J, I coincidentally stumbled across a news article that exposed the psychological damage to children who were sold to orphanages as part of the orphanage voluntourism scheme.

I was shocked that I resonated with a lot of the symptoms mentioned in the article. I was then reminded of a similar red flag that had popped up whilst I was at boarding school. I was reading a kid's version of *Oliver Twist*, and I was struck by the fact I resonated with a scene in the story. It was the famous scene when little Oliver, skinny and famished, went up to ask for seconds after finishing his scanty portion of dinner because he was still hungry, and got shamed and punished for being 'greedy and demanding'.

Despite it being the 21st century, my boarding school was so stingy it only offered cheap processed ready meals to the students. There are times we were looked down upon for taking seconds; there were even times when seconds was not enough for everybody. I still remember the first meal I had at the boarding school; it was a stone hard burger, with a slice of burnt and extremely salty piece of bacon as hard to chew as a piece of leather. Those were the only constituents of the burger. No sauces or vegetables. I took a bite, spit it all back out and started to cry uncontrollably.

Many nights I went to bed feeling hungry and unable to sleep.

So, following this line of thought, I continued my research on the similarities between orphanages and boarding school, and there it was – I found what I was looking for: boarding school syndrome.

The last straw

It's now been four years since I started studying my second bachelor's degree in the Netherlands, and I was spending my summer holiday in Hong Kong as usual and visiting my parents.

I have a distinct hatred for airports and anything to do with planes, so I have always pushed the tasks of booking flights to Hong Kong to my mum. Normally it would be a two-part flight transferring in Dubai or a European country, but this time for some strange reason, she decided to book a flight with transfer at London Heathrow. Most likely it was the cheapest option she could find.

Time flew by; it was September and time to start my new semester again back in the Netherlands.

As soon as I boarded the flight I was surrounded by mostly young Hong Kong kids travelling alone. Obviously not for vacation without their parents. They were still happily chatting with each other and suddenly a calm yet slightly smirky voice spoke in my head, 'they have no idea where they are heading towards'. Then I went back to minding my own business and enjoyed the in-flight entertainments without further interruptions.

The remaining journey was almost OK except the part where I had to run for my life and ruthlessly force my way through the people in front to catch a coach that would take me to Gatwick airport. It was all thanks to my mum (who had also lived in the UK for ten years) who didn't realise the transfer was at a different airport when she made the booking …

After the long travel, I was completely exhausted and glad to be back in my own space and not under the same roof as my parents. As soon as I shut the world behind me, the shock of the dead silence threw me off balance a bit as my ears were already so used to the hustle and bustle in Hong Kong.

A soul wrenching sense of loneliness and sadness rushed in to fill the empty room, resembling the sensation I had the first time I entered my room in boarding school. I don't remember much about what happened afterwards.

A few days later semester started, but something's strange this time. I started to have really bad headaches and couldn't focus on my assignments and I had a strong urge to cry. I hurriedly left the classroom and tears started to come out uncontrollably. I was completely perplexed because I had no reason to feel sad at this point of my life, in fact I was acutely aware that I felt calm as if it wasn't me crying. I am now studying my favourite degree, living in the Netherlands happily with many friends, and an aloof but caring cat. All of these are of my own choice.

After a while the crying stopped and I felt better again, no more headaches and the fogginess in my head disappeared. However, the next day the crying became even more violent, but this time I felt I had split into two persons, the 'real me' standing some distance away, coldly watching a small figure wailing and with her back towards me. I was completely perplexed by this crying child, what could've happened to her for her to wail so hopelessly.

For the next couple of days, I continued to cry on a daily basis; there were times I had to storm out of group meetings because I could sense the tears were ready to puke out from my eyes. There are times I would cry out loud in a busy park, but later on I found a chapel with long opening hours and I decided to go there to do my crying ever since.

I was not able to afford a proper therapist because I was still a student, and I couldn't ask my parents for money either because in the past my parents did not allow me to speak negatively about my boarding school experiences. So, I spoke to a school counsellor and an external one, which helped a bit to understand some stuff but I didn't find the answers I needed.

I continued to cry on an almost daily basis. During the days when I was unable to cry, my temper was super unstable, with extreme highs, getting angry very easily. So, I had to force myself to cry otherwise I would be unable to focus or start lashing out onto people around me.

At this point, I finally had to admit, that boarding school left a wound in me that is far deeper than I had imagined. All of a sudden, a lot of things seem to make sense. It explained the origin of this lingering sense of loneliness that I've always felt, like a deep, deep void. I gaze into a bottomless pit and my entire being becomes immobilised by an invisible force…

Another obsession I had since being a teenager was the search for 'zen' in my mind and environment, by erasing (or numbing) any negative emotions. I would obsessively play games like Tetris, spider solitaire, and Minesweeper. Not because I enjoyed any of these games, but because they are so repetitive that I was able to distance myself from the erosive sense of loneliness.

This is how I had survived. I had to shut down all of my emotions. Until this day I still struggle to have a healthy understanding of why humans need emotions.

One recurring theme in my dreams during my boarding school period was frequently being chased, in life threatening danger, and my responses in my dreams had often been waiting passively for death to swallow me. Although in real life I've never contemplated about committing suicide, possibly I don't feel I'm alive anyways.

I remember a friend recalled that talking to me in our early years of friendship always felt to them like my body was there but my soul was somewhere else.

The boarding school years
Contrary to the aftermath, the boarding school years that had caused the trauma did not live up to the drama I had to go through. It was boring as hell. Or I deliberately made it so.

I was ten when I attended boarding school in the UK. I was already extremely homesick upon arrival, and on top of that I was in a foreign country; I could barely understand the language and, most miserable of all, I was away from my family, my aunt, and my friends.

After the initial greetings I was completely left on my own and completely clue-less. Nobody wanted to talk to me, whether matrons or other students – especially if you are the only foreigner there. Day after day, year after year, you simply just learn to accept that you have been abandoned, you are invisible, your needs, de-sires, happiness, or sadness matter to no one. I had become invisible and I quite enjoyed being away from the spotlight. It's safe, you wouldn't get bullied, but neither would you have any friends.

Whenever I was at boarding school, I felt guilty for allowing myself to be happy or enjoying anything there. I mentally self-sabotaged myself.

Every day was as if it was on auto pilot. Waking up at 7 am for breakfast, school, lunch, then homework, dinner, stay in my room, sleep.

I still remember the day I muttered to myself, only six more years, then I will be out of this place. Then I switched off my emotions and thinking and started my life as one of the living-dead.

In a strange way, this was actually because I held onto a belief that one day I would understand the meaning of this pain.

Only after many years, then I was able to name these feelings – loneliness, empti-ness, meaningless, and even pain. I thought I had numbed myself enough and had lost the ability to be hurt, but it looks like it was only a temporary cure. In reality, the pain wasn't destroyed by my strategy, and I lost the ability to ever feel happy.

Recovery

After wandering in the fog for many years, it was through Christianity that I found solace to my soul. I'm not completely healed yet, but now at least I feel more alive than before. Jesus is the only one who can silence my restless spirit.

Epilogue

Out of curiosity, I wanted to find out how was J doing and wanted to message her via Facebook. The last time we talked she shared with me the good news that her recovery is promising and the doctor has approved her to go back to the UK to continue her studies.

I searched and discovered that she was nowhere to be found on Facebook. Then I thought that people have been quitting Facebook so let's try her Instagram then. Also gone. I started to feel uncomfortable and got creeped out a bit. So, I tried to search for her blog and articles she wrote for an online magazine. Still there, but there were no contact methods. Finally, I sent a WhatsApp to her UK number which we used last time. A chill went down my spine when I saw the message was sent, but was never delivered to the other end.

4.6.4   On repression and splitting

TENDENCIES TOWARDS DISSOCIATION CAN BE SEEN ALONG A SPECTRUM OF DEGREE. PSYCHOANALYSTS AND PSYCHIATRISTS LATER DISTINGUISHED BETWEEN *REPRESSION*, WHERE DISOWNED PARTS OR SELVES WERE MORE CONNECTED ON THE MAP AND SUBJECT TO POSSIBLE INTEGRATION, AND *SPLITTING*, WHERE THE DEGREE

OF DISSOCIATION WAS MORE SEVERE. IN PRACTICE, THE MOST COMMON FORM OF SPLITTING IS CUTTING OFF ONE'S SELF FROM ONE'S FEELINGS ...

SPLITTING VERY USEFULLY HELPS US TO RECOVER FROM SHOCK AND LOSS. WE CAN DIVERT OURSELVES BY TEMPORARILY SHIFTING OUR ATTENTION, COMMONLY KNOWN AS 'TAKING YOUR MIND OFF THINGS'...

CHILDREN WHO BOARD TEND TO CUT OFF FROM FEELINGS RAPIDLY, EFFECTIVELY, AND SOMETIMES PERMANENTLY.

WOUNDED LEADERS, NICK DUFFELL, LONE ARROW PRESS
2ND ED., P. 76

4.6.5 Kate

The little river that ran along the bottom of the garden of my childhood home has become my precious and sacred symbol of pre-boarding-school life. A secluded spot this gentle river, where no adults come to bother me. I am alone here, well, mostly alone, but often a dear little friend who shares my pure pre-boarding-school heart joins me. We wade through the water. It sparkles. We squeal as wellies fill having waded too deep, misjudging the depth of the river. The cold water greets the in-betweens of our small soft-skinned toes. Squeals soon subside as water becomes warm, and later delights us with the sound of squelching on every footstep when, hungry, we finally trudge up the bank towards the house. We go home to sit around the kitchen table, making one another laugh so hard orange squash shoots from our noses, eating oven chips and Bernard Matthews mini chicken kievs, sneaking morsels to our beloved furry siblings, the dogs and cats waiting, sitting atop our feet under the table.

There are other, more distant memories less regularly revisited: swimming with friends pretending to be seals or mermaids until our lips turn blue and we're shivering with cold; more crazed laughing that hurts, my brother's bed transformed into a wrestling ring, us both into Big Daddy – our ultimate hero; flicking the light switch on and off to create the Bedroom Disco, playing cassettes loud and pointing the Anglepoise lamp at each other as if we were under the spotlight on a stage, soon the metal lamp burning our fingertips too hot for us to manipulate it any longer. Dancing, bed jumping, and swimming, these were joyous moments of physical freedom and unboundaried expression.

As a boarding school survivor, these childhood memories feel close. I can stand right now in the very middle of the gentle water of that river; sometimes I still wade unashamedly through it. It was, and has been for decades now, the place to escape to whenever the feelings of loneliness, confusion, or just plain anger surface – not emotions unique to a boarding school child of course, but ones that seemed to surface too frequently for me. This escape, to a scene so alive and present, this life before boarding school, is set in one long and truly endless summer. There are no adults, only the light dancing on the surface of the water, with the midges twirling eternally there too.

Like the boiling hot surface of the Bedroom Disco Anglepoise, in the real world there was pain and perhaps a sense of danger, in the world where the grown-ups were present. It wasn't all squelching wellies, sunshine, and sparkly surfaced rivers. Scared and troubled by the presence of my father, I would hide when he returned home from work, worried about seeing him. In another memory, tonally greyed and less visceral than the river wades, I'm sitting on that rusty swing that sat crookedly on our scorched lawn before being condemned, deemed an acute tetanus risk. My father, returning from a trip away, presented me with a gift. I was reluctant to take it and remember the feeling of being afraid and anxious about what may be hidden inside the box he handed to me; I'm not sure why. Now I wonder whether this was the moment he returned home after being admitted to a secure mental health unit for the first time following the first 'breakdown'. It would be another 25 years before I was told that my father even had a mental health diagnosis, and only then because my own struggles had become so acute, I had to seek help, concerned I may hurt myself. My brother and I always knew something was going on, although we never guessed the 'family secret' we joked about concerned someone quite so close. So, the feeling of being emotionally cut off from, not really part of, the family was present far before being packed off and sent away to boarding school. That decision in itself felt like another emotional barrier put in place by the family, yet another that denied any opportunity for real closeness as well as the ability to place our trust in those closest to us.

Undeniably, the very real presence of middle-class privilege, these adult's judgements and their sense of superiority was also ever-present and had the effect of deepening the divide for me, the obvious pretentions I witnessed being so off-putting. The decision to send their children to very expensive, renowned boarding schools was another result of this preoccupation with social standing, a measure of their success. They had sent my brother to boarding school at seven. It was devastating. He was never the same again; betrayed by his parents, bullied by the older boys, he was disturbed by his experience. Perhaps this was where the deep mistrust of the adults was born, in five-year-old me.

The first time I went to boarding school it struck me as the end of being able to easily hide from these buttoned-up, flawed, overbearing adults. That sense of true childhood freedom, with the ability to escape them, was really gone. I was now always visible, in what felt like a shaming and exposing way, with nothing secret, personal, or sacred any longer. I had always been wary of the grown-ups, and viewed them with mistrust, but we had been left largely to our own devices by our parents. Now, at boarding school, I was shocked that these salaried caretakers searched our rooms, roamed the dormitories under cover of night, gave unsolicited advice, made cruel comments, and even supervised the opening of parcels. The sense of injustice and frustration at all of them – parents, teachers, matron – couldn't be vocalised. We were silent as we had to be; this led to frustration and was internalised, festering to become deep-seated anger. On the very first night in our shared dormitory, we lay in the dark overwhelmingly in states of stunned silence, realising that things would never be the same again. The next morning when we spoke about how we had felt the night before, not one of the five of us would admit to being the one girl audibly sobbing into their pillow. I don't know why; we were all just little children and crying would be the most natural thing in the world. But we didn't even want to admit to one another that we were frightened, and more than that, that we were in fact mourning the death of a huge part of ourselves – a threshold had been crossed. Lost was the squealing, dancing self. We had stepped into only what I can describe as an emotional wasteland. This was us preparing for survival in this new and unfamiliar world.

Even on the long summer holidays, the spectre that was the return to boarding school was present; this ominous shadow, faintly on the horizon at the start of the break, inched closer and loomed larger with every second that passed, the nearer start of term got. Writing this now makes me feel nauseous still. That feeling of dread as you drew closer to the end of the holidays, mentally visualising a calendar and flicking through the days left upon it, willing more pages to appear. I often wonder how this has all affected my perception and attitude to time and time passing, spending so many years in these extreme anxious states of being either at school willing time to pass or at home desperately praying for a miracle and for time to stand still. When I saw that red suitcase reappear and sit open on the spare room bed again, it signalled danger, as it was filled with the freshly washed and pressed (always ill-fitting and uncomfortable) uniform. I can still remember the emptiness sitting in the car on the journey back to school, gazing out the window, tears just running down my face. Weekends at home were dreadful. The thought of going home throughout the week was somewhat fortifying, but no sooner than we were picked up from school to finally head home, did the countdown begin again for the inevitable return, and so the feeling of sickness was there the whole time. Again, this constant state of anxiety had an impact, on my skin which became red and inflamed, and on my nervous system – I was diagnosed with an autoimmune disease in my early 20s.

After starting at boarding school, I can't remember ever wading in the river again. No more waterlogged wellies. I would often run down to the bottom of the garden and watch it flowing by on an exeat or in the holidays. Now more like a passive observer of childhood freedom, not the child that was there carelessly splashing through its deepest waters, cold water seeping between the toes. My childhood life was now so much more limited, palpably stunted, I felt dismembered living under the ominous cloud that was the certainty of returning to school again. And it all felt so relentless and inescapable.

4.6.6   On the cost of surviving

... It was becoming clear to me that in surviving long periods away from loving parents in the hothouse atmosphere of public schools, boarding school survivors had in common that they had needed to adapt themselves by means of a variety of defensive personality manoeuvres that limited their emotional range and the ultimate development of their full

POTENTIAL. IN EXCHANGE FOR THE UNDENIABLE PRIVILEGE OF THE SMALL CLASSES, THE INTENSIVELY COMPETITIVE ATMOSPHERE, THE SOCIAL PERKS OF THE OLD SCHOOL TIE AND THE RIGHT ACCENT, THEY WOULD HAVE HAD TO SACRIFICE SOMETHING OF THEIR *INNER* SELVES. IN THE ABSENCE OF NORMAL PARENTAL SUPPORT THEY MIGHT HAVE BEEN BULLIED OR ABUSED BUT EVEN IF THEY WERE NOT THEY WOULD HAVE HAD TO CONSTRUCT A DEFENSIVE PERSONALITY STRUCTURE TO KEEP THEM SAFE.

#

WOUNDED LEADERS, NICK DUFFELL, LONE ARROW PRESS,
2ND ED., P. 34

4.7   Boarder line

Let you and I dance this way for a while,
along the old Empire line.
Let us walk the tightrope,
arms outstretched,
feet poised in balance.
We can meet, precariously,
    midway.
I see your safety net
lies a little off-centre,
fabricated and
networked

by the stretch
and tension
of lives
in toil and servitude.
Mine embeds itself in words,
nomadic, curious,
and more like a welcome parasite
that might draw
sustenance from
this fragmented brain.
Perhaps words will
purge me
of your pathology,
as they have
of mine.
I am besotted,
like a lover who stalks
alone at night,

obsessed.
Sleepwalking from
one dormitory to
        another.
I am looking
for something
with eyes that
cannot see.
Blind-sided by duplicity.

You beckoned me,
collecting me in
with your 11 plus
and a glutton for high IQ.
You enticed me
into gothic rooms,
lined with virgin paper
and spinsters,
        faking it.
The making of us.
The damned.
The chosen.
We, the children,
we, the elite,
we, the not-so-common wealth.
We reside in your spaces,
gnawing on
dried bones
of ambition.
The rope shudders.
I sense
fear.
Power is not yours
as once it was.
Shame petrifies
the flex
of feeling,
a rigor mortis to
the upper lip,
your long arc,
brittle and unyielding.

Didn't you know
the softness of a pulse

would have been
more than enough?

I shall not forget
that soft night,
curled around unfamiliar
pillows of punishment.
The sanctum
of my own bed,
dissolved
like a refugee in flight;
out of place,
out of time and
split from origin.
In that soft night,
I saw an astral body
hovering over mine
in ghostly shock.
Go in Faith,
you said
to the faceless
ones who,
in devoted strokes
of calligraphy,
wrote in isolation
the tenuous boundary
between belonging and
theft of identity.
An elaborate script
that traces expansion
in inks of entitlement.

Rock. Paper. Scissors.
Cut. Smother. Smash –
the three who are afraid of one another.
        You. Me. Other.

Let you and I dance this way for a while.
Let us twirl in formal pose
across the pitch,
playing dirty.
A quickstep
in perfect time
to the tune of

privilege
there is no medicine like success.
Our hearts and heads,
broken from intimate embrace,
collude with our
divided selves
like a Janus:
open and yet closed.
Beyond your rigid shoulder
I sense magnificent detachment
from a savage past,
a transference
of judgment
to those you deem
still have not.
Let us romanticise
our inhibitions
and corset
the world
in civilisation.

I shall always remember
those hard nights
when, hour by hour,
the throb
of your control
forbade any sense
of being weak,
a sclerosis
upon my faltering heart.

Deborah Warne
5th March 2021

Chapter 5

Insights from the personal testimonies

Gendered experiences of childhood boarding

Linda Devereux

In the two chapters that follow, we offer insights into the long-term effects of childhood boarding which emerge from our personal stories. As the majority of the testimonies in this book are ex-boarders who are also third culture kids (TCKs), and this is an under-researched field of enquiry, that forms a key focus of our analysis and we have devoted the following chapter to this subject.

In this chapter, we discuss how our testimonies build on and extend the work of others. We begin by using Schaverien's ABC-D shorthand for abandonment, bereavement, captivity, and dissociation (Schaverien, 2015; Schaverien, 2021) as a framework to illustrate how these themes emerge in our narratives. Secondly, we explore how our participants describe the long-term effects of their early boarding experiences. In particular, drawing on Duffell and Bassett's work (Duffell, 2014; Duffell and Bassett, 2016), we examine the consequences of boarding school trauma on those who have contributed to our book. Finally, we examine the testimonies for examples of how gender contributes to the particular challenges experienced by those who board.

5.1 Abandoned

Being left alone with strangers, separated from all that is familiar, and without love and access to family support, leaves many who have been sent to boarding school as children struggling with a sense of abandonment that never goes away. As the testimonies in this book so vividly describe, the realisation that they have been sent away by those who love them, by their parents, can feel like an 'abandonment from which one can never recover' (Joanna). It is a betrayal so shocking that is hard to avoid the 'awful feeling' that our parents did not want us (Jane H, Raewyn), or that we were sent away because there was something wrong with us, or because we had done something wrong (Alyson).

Some of us describe the sense of shock we experienced when we were left. Feeling 'lost … forlorn … stunned' (Raewyn), we were also completely alone in our misery with 'no possibility of safety or support anywhere' (Nicky M). Some experienced fear and panic (Nicky R), others felt invisible, lonely, and desperately unhappy (Alyson). Olivia describes being numb and 'on autopilot'.

DOI: 10.4324/9781003533665-5

The measurement of time, as an abstract concept, is hard for young children. The months between holidays at boarding school may be incomprehensible, but many of us remember a realisation that our abandonment was complete and would go on for a long time:

> Day after day, year after year, you simply just learn to accept that you have been abandoned … your needs, desires, happiness or sadness matter to no one.
>
> (Olivia)

> nobody was listening and nobody cared how I was feeling … I knew that I was stuck there in that Hell hole to be perpetually bullied for years to come.
>
> (Nicky R)

The trauma of abandonment can be so severe that some individuals cannot remember it (Duffell & Bassett, 2016; Schaverien, 2021). Amnesia is exemplified through the narratives in this book. For instance, although Linda can recall the pain of the separation from her family – she has a clear visual memory of seeing her family huddled together as she was driven away from them by a stranger – she cannot remember any details of where she slept on the four-day drive to boarding school. Jem cannot remember the day she went to boarding school, or any of the emotions she felt at the time. Jane H cannot remember parting from her parents. She says that this 'memory may have been put aside' as part of a selective process. Nicky M notes that she has only 'half a dozen memories from those seven years … at boarding school' – although there is nothing wrong with her memory of other parts of her life. Nicky R has only 'partial memories', while Morag can't describe being left as 'a memory'. It is more like a feeling or a smell, a sketchy sense of 'atmospheres and light and sounds … the darkness of the long corridors … heavy cloaks'. The words she uses – 'darkness' and 'heavy' – convey poignantly a depth of feeling which many of us still struggle to articulate.

Others among us re-experience the grief of abandonment later in life when something triggers a memory. Perhaps a smell, a sound, or the taste of something will cause an inexplicable sense of unease. Our bodies remember, even when our brains cannot form words to describe the past (Devereux, 2012; Van der Kolk, 2019). Sometimes, when our own children are the age we were when we were sent to boarding school, a new realisation of the depth of our hurt emerges. Joanna describes a flashback to being left at school as a seven-year-old which was triggered when she waved her seven-year-old daughter off for a weekend away.

> I began to cry whilst waving and it was literally like the sky fell in. I sat in my car for about 30 minutes sobbing and feeling black although it was a sunny, outwardly happy day. The memory that flooded back was being left in the gloom … holding Matron's hand whilst my mother walked out of the front door and away into the light carrying my baby brother and holding my younger brother's hand … I'd lost everything familiar in an instant. Matron was a complete stranger. They'd left me!
>
> (Joanna)

5.2 Bereaved

Unsurprisingly, being left alone in an unfamiliar place populated by strangers can cause a great deal of distress for children. Many of us remember an aching sense of grief and loss. Alyson 'cried, and cried and cried'. She cried so hard that she was physically sick. Olivia 'started to cry uncontrollably' when she was served her first inedible meal. She was in a foreign country and the loss of adequate and familiar food brought home the depth of her loss. Raewyn recalls that after the lights were turned off and it was dark, she was 'surrounded by the sounds of sobbing'. Nicky R sobbed herself to sleep for weeks until, eventually, like the other the children in the school, she 'learned to internalise [her] thoughts and worries'. She knew 'nobody was coming' to save her. Jem describes a 'sickening realisation on waking for the first few mornings that you aren't at home as your sleepy brain had first thought'.

Others learned quickly that they must not cry, or must cry silently for their homes, parents, pets, and freedom to avoid upsetting those around them. Nicky M learned to cry silently, completely still in her bunk bed, to avoid triggering the anger of the girl sleeping above her. Children who have experienced the rupture of abandonment themselves may not be able to face being reminded of their own grief and vulnerability by witnessing the suffering of others. In these circumstances, emotional displays are unwelcome reminders of their own helplessness (James, 2023: 6). As Kate explains, 'we didn't even want to admit to one another that we were frightened and ... mourning the death of a huge part of ourselves'. Schaverien argues that this response may be a 'necessary coping strategy' for young children. In order to survive the 'immense losses' they have experienced, they try to 'conceal the pain ... even from themselves' (Schaverien, 2021: 608).

The lack of comfort available to grieving children at boarding school is compounded by denial of their grief and loss by those around them. 'Grief 'is reframed as 'homesickness' and there is 'little sympathy for homesickness' (Jem). As the comments above demonstrate, children can be punished if they do not learn to suppress the expression of their grief. Our testimonies illustrate how both parents and school staff used a number of tactics to avoid witnessing our grief. Several writers describe being given gifts by their parents as a distraction (Raewyn, Jane H). Jane P recalls: 'It was believed ... that parents should quietly slip away, unnoticed, while the child was distracted with something, to avoid unnecessary embarrassment or distress'. This approach on the part of adults means that the children were not only abandoned, but they were denied an opportunity to express their grief and distress and to receive comfort from those they loved.

Morag's narrative illustrates another way in which adult power can manifest itself by privileging the parent's recollections and interpretations of events. Morag's parents like to say that *they* were the ones who were negatively affected by their daughter's behaviour at the moment of separation. At the time, Morag seemed keen to unpack her things and the parents recall that they felt upset by her apparent lack of concern that they were leaving. It is the parents' version of this story that gets told and retold within the family; they are the ones who have the privileged position of determining meaning and evoking sympathy for their position. No doubt they did feel sad about leaving their young daughter in boarding school, but the focus of this story seems to be about them not getting what they needed from a child rather than on an empathetic response to what must have also been a very confusing situation for Morag who recalls that she felt 'bewildered' and 'panicked'. The child was expected to not only cope with being left, but they were also supposed to anticipate and respond to their parents' feelings despite their own bewilderment and panic.

Nicky R recalls that she was 'told off' by her mother 'for writing such upsetting letters home'. Her mother spoke to the headmistress and Nicky's letters were 'checked a lot more closely'. Not only was Nicky's mother unable to acknowledge her young daughter's grief and respond to it with comfort and understanding, she was cross because she was forced to witness it. Nicky's mother required her daughter to protect *her* feelings and she colluded with the headmistress to silence her daughter's distressed pleas for help.

Some of us recall being lied to about what boarding school would be like. Marysa writes that she was 'coerced into excitement' about going to school in the UK by her older brother who had himself been forced to tell her lies by their parents. Examples of these lies and manipulations pepper many of our testimonies.

Isabel's narrative gives another example of the 'family story' that continues to be told about her 'choice' to go to boarding school. She says that she chose to go because she was being bullied at her day school. She explains:

A vending machine and tuck shop … clinched it for me. My mother likes to remind me that some major decisions I've made in my life have … hinged on appliances.

Isabel's tone is self-depreciating. Her testimony illustrates how parents can name and reinforce a particular version of events. It is Isabel's mother who likes to remind her how to frame her move to boarding school. Isabel was eight at the time. Would she have been capable of making a rational choice about where she would, or would not, be bullied? As her testimony illustrates, she was also bullied at boarding school. Was it wise of her parents to let her make such an important decision based on a tuck shop and a vending machine? Would the young Isabel not have needed more input from her parents to evaluate options carefully? Despite this, Isabel has learned to retell the story around this momentous event in her life 'lightly', and perhaps in a way which does not cause unease for her mother. Children learn how and when they must attend to their parents' feelings and emotions. There are many unspoken rules in families around what can be said and how (Devereux, 2010: 132).

Joanna tried to discuss her feelings of grief and abandonment with her mother when she was an adult. She found, even then, that her mother did not like Joanna describing being left at boarding school as 'abandonment'. 'How dare you? You *chose* to go' is her mother's version of events. Even decades later, there is an unwillingness on the part of her mother to recognise that she was the adult in this situation with power over the young Joanna. A number of us were told that we 'wanted' to go to boarding school as if this somehow lays the blame for any subsequent bad experiences with us. Other parents just refuse to engage in conversation about boarding school. For instance, Olivia observes that her parents do not allow her to 'speak negatively' about her boarding school experience. The parents in these situations continue to abdicate responsibility for the consequences of their decisions to send their children away. Moreover, they wish to retain the power to name what happened even when their children become adults. The parents refuse to acknowledge the hurt their decisions have caused in the past, and they continue to reframe their children's experiences in ways that are acceptable to them, but which deny their adult children's grief.

Jessica Stern argues that denial of childhood pain is 'almost irresistibly seductive ... for those who observe the pain' but find it easier to 'ignore or forget' (Stern, 2010: 293). She goes on to argue that these denials are damaging for the child, particularly when they are forced to collude in the denial of their own pain. When bystanders, especially those in positions of power, refute or reframe what they cannot bear to witness, it reinforces the pain of those who have suffered. Survivors, in these circumstances, can no longer trust their own senses. They feel grief for something that was lost, but they are told that these feelings are unacceptable and their loss is unimportant or imagined. Denial, as Zeedyk explains in Chapter 2, helps bystanders feel more comfortable. It does not help those who have experienced suffering.

The term, 'disenfranchised grief' has been used to describe non-death losses which are not acknowledged and/or invalidated (James, 2023: 4). There are lasting consequences for those who experience it. If our parents and the adults around us do not listen to us and do not take our suffering seriously, how can we learn to do so ourselves? Raewyn's testimony illustrates something of this dilemma. She explains:

> It has taken decades for me to say, 'only'. I was only eight ... I was forced to be grown up, though no one recognised that an eight-year-old child has neither the developmental maturity nor the resources to be truly and fully adult.

Because no one else acknowledged how young and vulnerable she was, and because there were others at her boarding school, including her sister, who were younger than she was, Raewyn 'didn't even know that what [she] was experiencing *was* suffering'.

5.3   Captive in an institution

A key issue that emerges from the research into boarding schools is how difficult it is for young children to learn to live away from home in an institution. For almost all, this institutionalisation is outside of their control and against their will. They are held captive.

Boarding schools are money-making entities. In order to maximise their profits and reputations they may conceal their institutional characteristics behind an impressive facade. They often look imposing and cater to an 'enduring English fantasy' of the 'country house and grounds' (Beard, 2021: 22). Many are set in rural, parkland settings like the homes of the landed gentry. Yet, as several of our narratives illustrate, although our schools may have seemed grand and spacious, its pupils were often confined to a 'small plot' (Morag). Even where the grounds were expansive, the use of the space could be tightly controlled. Jane P recalls beautiful grounds – perfect for hide and seek – at her school, but these areas were 'Out of Bounds'. They could only be visited when 'walking in crocodile, supervised by a teacher or matron'.

Rules and regulations govern every aspect of life in an institution. These rules are 'strict and unbending' and the lives of the captives are 'ruled by the bell' (Raewyn). The bell signals when to wake, eat, go to class, go to church, prayers, and when to sleep. These routines are strictly adhered to and pupils are not given much free time (Jem). The rules are enforced by a hierarchical system of control and punishment. Many of us recall the fear, shame, and humiliation which was used to control our bodies and our behaviours. For several of us, this punishment happened very soon after we arrived at school. Kat recalls the first night in boarding school:

> I couldn't sleep. Hardly surprising, given that I'd been allocated one of the worst beds … right next to the door. It was left wide open all night, artificial light streaming onto my pillow from the hallway, keeping me awake. Long after lights-out, I started jumping on my bed in a desperate attempt to tire myself out enough to sleep … Suddenly, the dorm light was switched on and an angry adult stormed in. It turned out to be Matron. Quick as a flash, she'd torn down my pyjama bottoms and started to smack me on my bare bum. She hit me six times and then left as abruptly as she'd entered. I lay there in stunned silence … I felt humiliated and confused … I started to sob but also instinctively knew I mustn't make a sound for fear of further recrimination. My six-year-old self realised in that moment that it wasn't safe to cry in this hostile environment.

The very next morning, 'silenced into submission', Kat had to sit next to the same Matron at breakfast and eat lumpy porridge. Unable to keep it down, Kat vomited into the bowl of porridge. Matron made Kat stay seated in the dining-room until the entire contents of the bowl were eaten, vomit and all.

Jane P remembers the effects of the rules and humiliation on one small girl on their first afternoon in boarding school. The group of new arrivals was made to stand in silence in the hall. The new girl did not know that if she raised her hand, she could ask to go to the toilet. She would have been unaware of the strange new rules in a strange new place. She wet her pants. This would have been humiliating enough, but the small girl was berated, forced to clean up her 'disgusting' mess, and miss tea. She then had to stand facing the wall as all the other girls filed past. She was, Jane P says, 'a disgrace for all to see'.

These acts of adult cruelty imposed on frightened new arrivals were deliberately timed strategies to break the children's spirits. It is easier to control large groups of children if they are passive, silent, and submissive, and if they 'fit in' to the system in place at the school as quickly as possible. Both the examples illustrate how *public* the punishments were. Matron put the lights in the dormitory on before she beat Kat. Even though she was ostensibly punishing the child for not being asleep, she put the lights on, no doubt waking other children, so that they could witness the punishment. Similarly, in Jane P's account, the child was made to stand outside the dining room so that all the other students could witness her humiliation as they filed past.

Our stories offer multiple examples of an oppressive, hierarchical system that relies on a 'poisonous pedagogy' aimed at 'breaking the child's will' in order to create an obedient and respectful subject of adult discipline (Miller, 2001). Boarding schools, like other institutions, rely on creating individuals who will conform to the norms (James, 2023). This approach to discipline relies on staff who will impose a 'command and control' approach (Cross, 2023).

Salaried caretakers searched our rooms, roamed the dormitories under cover of night, gave unsolicited advice, made cruel comments and … the sense of injustice and frustration … couldn't be vocalised. We were silent, as we had to be.

(Kate)

Every aspect of life was controlled. There was no privacy. Some of us used open toilets and showers. Baths, often cold and unpleasant, were supervised and water was restricted. We had no control over who supervised us or when. Jem recalls that in the open showers at her school, the 'headmaster would "check in" on girls' shower times' and, although 'the matrons were there', they were 'too intimidated to ask him to leave'. Phone calls were restricted and often monitored so that nothing bad could be said (Jane H), and letters were censored (Linda, Raewyn, Jane P). If any child 'was to write about how they really felt, that child would be forced to re-write their letter' (Marysa).

Meals were strictly organised and subject to strange rules which varied between schools. Kat was not the only one forced to eat all the food that was served. Raewyn was also told she 'absolutely must' eat all the food on her plate. She recalls putting a lot into her body that she did not want, but after she discovered small helpings could be asked for, Raewyn was 'always hungry'. Many of us found the meals unpalatable and the process of eating stressful and unpleasant. Nicky R, struggling with relentless bullying from her peers, was not given a permanent place at a dinner table and so every evening, she would have to search for a space at a table with the 'fewest bullies on it'.

The captivity was also frequently reenforced by parents who refused to listen to children's pleas to remove them from boarding school. Jane H recalls that her sister tried to circumvent the censoring of letters by writing to her parents from her granny's house. Her grandmother never posted those letters.

Nicky M remembers that she was told by the headmistress that her father had given permission for her to be beaten. Nicky could not believe that her father would sanction physical punishment, but the proof – a letter from her father – was conveyed to her in a public setting to maximise her humiliation. It was read out in front of a group of girls. As Deborah explains, many of us recall being 'blind-sided by duplicity'. Those we thought we could trust, those who were supposed to love us and protect us, had abandoned us to our fate, captive in an institution.

As a result of these experiences, many of us lived with anxiety and fear (Linda, Nicky M, Morag, Kat, Olivia, Kate, Nicky R). Life in boarding school did not feel safe. Staff could be 'truly terrifying' (Jem), and control was not only enforced by staff. Prefects were frequently given the power to punish younger children. Those being punished never knew how long they would have to wait, or what punishment would be given. Many of us, like Kat, were physically abused. This abuse could come from staff, prefects, and/or our peers. We were 'hauled out of bed and made to stand in the dark' (Jane H). We were often so terrified that we noticed our hearts pounding even on the occasions when 'we hadn't been caught' (Jem).

Another negative consequence of being held captive is that unhappy children can take out their frustrations on those who are younger or more vulnerable. A number of us were physically hurt by other children. Linda had a knife pressed against her body, Jane H was swung around by her pony tail. Nicky M was grabbed by the arms and legs and dragged towards a cold bath. She managed to wriggle free, but was caught again and again and more girls joined in the 'fun'. Others had personal possessions damaged. Morag had hers thrown out of the window by a group of girls while a bully tore the ears off Jane H's toy rabbit. As Schaverien points out, even the most devoted staff cannot protect large groups of children for 24 hours a day (Schaverien, 2015: 186).

For others, boarding school was a site of constant emotional neglect and abuse. Our needs for comfort were ignored by staff and many of us were relentlessly teased and/or belittled (Nicky R, Linda, Jane P), excluded (Nicky M, Isabel), or othered (Kat) by our peers. These experiences contributed to us feeling unwelcome and unwanted (Joanna), or invisible (Olivia). When one lives in an institution the opportunities for bullying are constant. Nicky M remembers 'no interaction with a child' apart from being bullied. Olivia recalls that nobody wanted to talk to her 'whether matrons or other students'. Being 'invisible' meant that she did not get bullied, but it also meant that Olivia did not have any friends.

Sometimes, girls encouraged others to target a particular person. Isabel recalls that one of the girls in her year told new girls that they 'would not survive if they had anything to do with' her. Jane H recalls that a bully encouraged others to gang up on her too. Children in day school can also be bullied. However, the difference at boarding school is that there is no escape. We did not have access to our parents and families for comfort in the evenings, or weekends to feel safe at home. In boarding school, attacks are relentless and can happen at any time of the day or night.

Nicky R does not recall a single day where some child did not say something derogatory to her.

> Walking to class, waiting to be picked for team games and never being picked ... waiting for the inevitable groans of the team that drew me ... I knew nobody wanted me ... I was an easy target for those who wanted someone to torment to make themselves feel better.
>
> (Nicky R)

The effects of the constant fear and grief manifested themselves in different ways for each of us. Jane P's stammer intensified. Some of us lost control of bodily functions which we had managed at home (Nicky M). Several of us were so afraid to go to the toilet in the night that we wet the bed (Linda, Jane H). Many of us were unable, at a young age, to manage our personal care and we recall teeth cavities, head lice, soiled underclothes, or struggling to manage timetables and our personal possessions (Isabel).

The uniforms required at boarding schools are a physical and embodied symbol of the homogenising force of the institution. We had no rights to dress as individuals. The itchy, uncomfortable, restrictive, formal and, often, masculine uniforms of many boarding schools impose a loss of bodily freedom. The tight and uncomfortable clothing meant we lost our ability to climb and cartwheel and play. Perhaps most significantly, the mini adult clothes of many boarding schools – suits, ties, blazers, hats, and hard leather shoes – also indicated the loss of our rights to be children. To survive as a captive in an institution, each child has to 'fit in' and look and act like everyone else. As Deborah notes, such is the 'tenuous boundary between belonging and theft of identity'.

Life in an institution is often inhumane. Several of us describe our experiences using non-human metaphors, symbols, or other figurative language. Nicky M recalls a moment when something 'shifted' and she 'stopped being part of the herd'. Over the remainder of the term she became 'like a ghost' living apart from the other girls. Similarly, Olivia describes boarding as 'life as one of the living dead'. Morag says that she was 'like a little cornered animal ... fighting for [her] place in the pack'. Marysa describes being 'trapped', Isabel became a 'lone wolf', and Kat remembers feeling like a 'hunted animal lying frozen in anticipation of the next potential attack'. It is telling that these words – such strong, emotive words – represent us as animals, or dead, rather than as small, living, human children.

5.4   Consequences – dissociation, strategic survival strategies, and mental health problems

Our testimonies illustrate many serious and long-term consequences of our experiences at boarding school. A number of us have clear memories of a moment, or an event which shocked us or frightened us so much that it caused some kind of irreversible shift in how we felt about ourselves and the world. Schaverien, Duffell, and others who have worked therapeutically with boarding school survivors explain that these experiences may be expressions of dissociation. For instance, Morag has noted that when she had to fight a group of bullies to defend herself and her possessions, she felt changed by the experience. It damaged her. Her need to fight so hard for self-preservation created both fear and sadness. She felt she 'had to grow up fast', 'shut down' part of her personality, and 'grow a different bit'. She was developing what Duffell may describe as a strategic survival personality (Duffell, 2000: 10). These strategies, which contribute to survival at boarding school may be destructive in adult relationships. For instance, Morag has noticed that she will 'leave behind people and relationships at the first hint of harm'.

Kat describes the effects of the shocking punishments on the first day at boarding school:

> That was the beginning of my attempt not to exist. I figured that if I didn't draw attention to myself then I wouldn't be hit again. If I could train myself to suppress any form of personal expression then I might have a chance of surviving in this perilous place ... within the space of twelve hours, I had begun to harden inside until I had compressed the essence of 'me' into a tight ball of rage deep within.

Safety, for many boarders, can involve cutting off from their childish spontaneity, their vulnerability, and their previous sense of self (Duffell & Bassett, 2016: 96).

Others recall learning to be mentally somewhere else because it was safer (Nicky M, Linda). Jane H lived in her imagination to escape from the things that troubled her at boarding school. She learned not to be 'dramatic' and to sit 'on the fringe' of her life in boarding school. Olivia recalls that at school, her 'body was there, but [her] soul was somewhere else'. She has since discovered that this strategy has had negative consequences. Her pain was not destroyed by ignoring it, and Olivia now finds that through learning to suppress her feelings so effectively, she has also 'lost the ability to ever feel happy'. In order to survive at the time, many of us cut off from our emotional reality (Schaverien, 2021: 611). As a consequence, there are examples of confusing shifts and out of body experiences in our testimonies, as there are in the narratives of other people who write about trauma (Pederson, 2014: 340).

The experience of boarding school can also feel more like a gradual day-to-day wearing down of our previous selves. A series of 'slow-moving, but highly repetitive non-dramatic bad experiences' (Duffell & Bassett, 2016: 109) can create a cumulative trauma. Jane P explains that she learned to 'behave as expected and wear the mask of a busy, chatty boarder in order to survive'. To do this, Jane had to 'suppress any longing' and distance herself from the people she loved most it the world. As a consequence, Jane's relationships with her closest family members were 'never the same again'. Kate recalls spending years in 'extreme, anxious states ... either at school willing time to pass, or at home desperately praying for a miracle and for time to stand still'. The constant state of anxiety at boarding school has contributed to inflammation of Kate's skin and she has been diagnosed with an autoimmune disease.

5.5   Mental health challenges – at school and in adult life

Unsurprisingly, experiences such as those described in this chapter can have lasting mental health consequences. For instance, Jane P says boarding school:

> affected my mental health and wellbeing for my entire adult life. I developed negative, self-destructive habits of mind and body … I have learned to keep it all hidden … the feeling part of my brain is buried deep, frozen within.

Joanna describes self-harming and an 'awful, terrible damaging combination of anorexia and bulimia'; the sense of feeling unwelcome and unwanted has never left her.

Others among us have lost people who were close to us to suicide. Olivia's friend took her own life after being diagnosed with depression as a result of her experiences at boarding school. Morag's brother also took his own life and she wonders 'what happened to him at boarding school'. Some among us have been so distressed ourselves that we have contemplated suicide. Kate developed an acute mental illness and she had to seek help because of concern that she might hurt herself. Nicky R describes taking antidepressants to 'stay alive'. Isabel says that her mental health declined along with her 'self-esteem and sanity'. At one point she was so depressed that she had suicidal thoughts and even chose which roof she would jump off; she hit rock bottom at 15.

These responses are, unfortunately, not isolated incidents and many of the books about boarding include references to the serious mental health consequences of early boarding (see, for example, Ostini et al., 2020: 84, 230). In addition, as those who have worked therapeutically with adult ex-boarders note, challenging and changing behaviours learned so comprehensively so young is not easy (Duffell & Bassett, 2016; James, 2023).

5.6   Boarding schools and gender

In a podcast interview with Piers Cross, Sara Warmer and Karen MacMillan suggest that boarding school is 'at the extreme end of women's experience of the world' (Cross, 2022). By this they suggest that in boarding school girls are constrained by patriarchal organisational structures and practices which mean that their lives are controlled in very rigid ways and through narrowly defined binary gender roles. However, these same constraints are at work outside of boarding school as well. Many women and girls are controlled within their families (Lee et al., 2023), perhaps more heavily so than their brothers, and, additionally, women's lives are profoundly affected by the structures and practices of the wider sociocultural context in which they live. Much of the research and popular publishing about boarding school has been written by and about men. In a recent literature review, James argues that there is a 'disproportionate emphasis on boys' boarding experiences (James, 2023). As a result, the understanding of women's experiences of boarding school is still developing and requires ongoing research (Schaverien, 2019). There is much we do not know about how gender intersects with the experiences of boarding. As all but one of the contributors to this book identify as women our testimonies, essays, and analysis may offer insights into this under-researched field of enquiry.

A key theme to emerge from each of our narratives is the extent to which almost every aspect of our lives was controlled at boarding school. For some, boarding school was an extension of our experiences at home, as Warmer and Macmillan suggest. There was a great deal of pressure on girl children in some of our families to be docile, pretty, and nice. For instance, Jane H mentions multiple times in her narrative that she was 'a happy little thing' despite suffering from 'torment' from her father, who 'was always criticising' her. She maintains that despite the loss of her Amah, which she describes as an 'enormous separation rift', she 'did not fret' and was 'full of sunshine'. These descriptions suggest that 'being happy' and downplaying upsets was normalised in her early life. Jane notes that she was so quiet that her mother nicknamed her Mouse. Jane's mother's role at home was sewing, baking 'delicious ginger cakes' and making 'wonderful Christmas presents. . . despite the circumstances'. The examples imply that there were gendered expectations of women in her home of origin which favoured quiet, uncomplaining female domesticity in spite of challenges. Jane H's behaviour at boarding school reflects these familial expectations. She learned to take bullying 'on the chin', keep her chin up and make the most of what she had. As part of her 'survival mode', she learned very quickly to become the happy little girl that nobody saw as a threat.

Jem's testimony offers another example of how patriarchal structures impact on girls' lives. Jem's mother did not want her to board, but was overridden by her father who felt it was 'important' to board, 'both on a practical basis due to the constant moving with the Forces and for social reasons'. Father was the decision-maker, and the necessities of his work were an important factor in decisions affecting the family. Jem found that boarding school enforced a requirement for her to be submissive and reserved. She recalls: 'I was told I was very spoiled and opinionated when I first started school. I quickly learned to stay quiet and to blend in'. Joanna remembers that her upbringing was to be 'obedient and dutiful', a role she perfected at boarding school where she discovered being sickly sweet 'served her well'. Joanna was aware that, for her, this was 'a mask', one which she called 'Pretty Pleasing Penelope'.

Jane P remembers that, in addition to promoting quiet behaviour, there was a strong focus on personal presentation at the school she attended. Deportment, silence and a 'rod-straight back' were rewarded. These rewards came in the form of deportment badges and something called the 'blue girdle'. It is not clear in Jane's narrative exactly what the latter was, perhaps the name of another badge of honour, rather than an actual girdle. The name itself is certainly symbolic of bodily constraint, as illustrated by her recollections of unacceptable school behaviour.

> We were never allowed to run around, to hop, skip and jump on the grass … our bodies, like our minds, were being schooled from a young age, into prim and self-conscious future "young ladies".
>
> (Jane P)

Kat recalls being groomed into a 'conventional, Christian version of God-fearing young ladies with a knowledge of etiquette and manners befitting to our station as the future of the landed gentry'.

Marysa remembers that when she tried to spend time with her brother at the co-educational school she attended, she was 'admonished by a very strict teacher' who told her that 'little girls do not play with little boys'. When Marysa asked what little girls did do, she was told that 'they sit on benches'. These examples from our narratives illustrate how our behaviour was curtailed at boarding school through narrow gendered expectations. Many of us lost our freedom to play and be the lively active children we were before we were sent away.

As discussed earlier, the uniforms required at boarding school constrained freedom of movement and included items such as berets which restricted head movement (Nicky M) and double knickers. These 'matching bloomers' (Raewyn), or 'uniform underpants' (Jem) were worn seven days a week on top of the girls' own underpants. As others who have studied girls' experiences of boarding school have noted, this obsession with modesty and constant monitoring could make girls feel like 'heads on legs' (Cross, 2022). There was no discussion about changes in our bodies or our developing sexuality. Rather, these events seemed to produce a terror of girls becoming too close. This contributed to a sense of shame around normal bodily functions. Girls often found out 'the facts of life' from their peers, or they coped alone. Raewyn's testimony illustrates this. Her first period arrived in the 'loneliness of boarding school'. She was the first in her class to menstruate and so she did not have others to confide in. Raewyn did not tell her parents. She recalls that it was 'too private' to put in a censored letter; so she dealt with it alone, 'shamefully, and with little information and no support'.

Girls at boarding school learn neither to be needy nor greedy. Olivia recalls being 'looked down on for taking seconds' of bad food. As others who have written about the boarding experiences of girls have noted, food can be a fraught issue. In one study of 17 adult women who had attended boarding school, 13 reported that they 'struggled with disordered eating behaviours' (Priestner et al., 2023: 70). Messages about weight, body, and shape 'seemed to be compounded' for these girls by being in the competitive environment of boarding school (Priestner et al., 2023: 73). Several of our testimonies refer to disordered eating, and as the contributors to our book have also noted, girls can feel that they are constantly on show and being judged by staff and their peers. Kate describes feeling that she was 'always visible in what felt like a shaming and exposing way'.

My experience of the dining hall in a co-educational boarding school illustrates another aspect of gendered behaviour at play. It took me some time to realise that the bigger boys at my table not only ate more than their share of food provided for everyone, they also stole the most desirable pieces of food from my plate. Adults, who were supposed to be supervising meals, did not intervene. They either did not notice, or were choosing not to notice. Perhaps they felt the boys needed more food than a small girl? Perhaps dealing with the boys, and their parents, was difficult. Some of the most confident boys with the most 'entitled' behaviour were the sons of the leaders in the missionary organisation which ran the school. As an adult, I wonder whether some female staff were reluctant to challenge the behaviour of these boys because they did not wish to appear ineffectual, or initiate a confrontation with their supervisors. There are several layers of gendered behaviour in this example. As a young girl, I was being trained to sacrifice my needs to those of the boys. The female modelling I observed was of 'not noticing' and 'not making a fuss' when boys behaved badly. Like me, the female staff were perhaps treated as less important than males in the patriarchal missionary organisation. Women and girls were taught overtly and covertly that their needs were less important than those of men and boys.

Joanna's testimony offers another example of the double standards for boys and girls at boarding school. She recalls that when a young man climbed into the bedroom of the head girl in the middle of the night, the girl was 'publicly shamed at a whole school assembly and immediately expelled' while, in contrast, the trespasser, who was 'entirely at fault', was gated. Joanna notes that the young man's family was 'significant' and that the trespasser 'baked croissants for the school headmaster in chef's whites on Sunday mornings'. We learn from an early age that there are different and rigidly controlled gendered expectations at school, as in life.

Warner and Macmillan (Cross, 2022) note that not all girl's boarding schools had an academic focus. Some gave mixed messages about what the girls were being prepared for – work or marriage. These mixed messages come across in our testimonies too. Jane P recalls that there was not a strong focus on academics at her school. The library was limited to abridged classics and included nothing lively to stimulate the interest of the girls. Marysa recalls that she lost her voice, her confidence and her 'ability to focus … on the educational aspect' of her life at boarding school, despite this being the reason she was sent there. Joanna recalls that there was a lack of recognition of girls' academic capacity and that all that was needed for a former boy's only prep school to become co-educational, was 'One attic room for a girls' dorm and advertising needlework and cookery classes'. This lack of interest in girls' academic achievement was mirrored by her father. He was '*astonished* that girls' A level exams were set to the same standard as boys' and he was 'amazed' by Joanna's own academic achievements.

This gendered and narrowly focused education could mean that girls left school feeling vulnerable and without the life skills they needed to manage in a patriarchal world. Joanna, in particular, stresses that she felt boarding school set her up to be 'perfect prey'. She was groomed to be an upper class wife, but struggled to cope working in the international world of men where she was tricked into an unsafe position and 'trafficked to a VIP from the UAE'. Joanna argues that her upbringing did not prepare her for the world. She did not know how to set healthy boundaries or where to access safe and appropriate support.

Our narratives highlight many negative consequences of growing up in boarding schools. Abandoned, bereaved, held in captivity, and subjected to the demands of an institution while our grief and distress was denied by those around us, many of us struggled to cope. In hierarchical, patriarchal institutions some of us were not able to develop the academic or social skills we needed to flourish beyond school. In order to survive the emotional and physical losses we faced, we learned to hide our fears, feelings and emotions; some of us did so through dissociation. We have each, in our own ways, developed strategic survival strategies which helped us to endure being sent to boarding school. Some of these strategies have not served us well, neither at the time, nor in our adult lives. Each of our stories bears witness to the long-term effects of sending young children to boarding school.

Bibliography

Beard, R. 2021. *Sad Little Men. Private Schools and the Ruin of England*. London, Penguin Random House.

Cross, P. 2022. *An Evolving Man*. Podcast series. https://www.piers-cross.com/an-evolvingman. *The Female Experience of Boarding School*. Interview with Karen Macmillan and Sara Warmer.

Cross, P. 2023. *An Evolving Man* Podcast Series. https://www.youtube.com/watch?v=4cSthMeTEjQ Interview with Person Irresponsible. Podcast

Devereux, L. 2010. *From Congo: Newspaper photographs, public images and personal memories*. Visual Studies, 25, 124–134.

Devereux, L. 2012. *Stuck Between Earth and Heaven: Memories Missionaries and Making Meaning from an African Childhood in a Post-colonial World*. Axon.

Devereux, L. 2015. *Narrating a Congo Missionary Childhood (1958–1964): Memory and Meaning Examined through a Creative Non-Fiction Text and Exegesis*. Doctor of Philosophy, Australian National University.

Duffell, N. 2000. *The Making of Them*. London, Lone Arrow Press.

Duffell, N. 2014. *Wounded Leaders. British Elitism and the Entitlement Illusion – A Psycho-history*. UK, Loan Arrow Press.

Duffell, N. & Bassett, T. 2016. *Trauma, Abandonment and Privilege: A Guide to Therapeutic Work with Boarding School Survivors*. Abington, UK, Routledge.

James, G. 2023. *The psychological impact of sending children away to boarding schools in Britain: Is there cause for concern?* British Journal of Psychotherapy, 39, 592–610.

Lee, J., Wardman-Browne, J., Hopkins, E., Mcpherson, S. & Cavenagh, P. 2023. *It's not all down to boarding. Early family and peer relationships among boarders*. In: Cavenagh, P., Mcpherson, S. & Ogden, J. (eds.) *The Psychological Impact of Boarding School. The Trunk in the Hall*. UK: Taylor and Francis Group.

Miller, A. 2001. *The Truth Will Set You Free: Overcoming Emotional Blindness and Finding Your True Adult Self*. USA, Basic Books.

Ostini, J., Dainton, B., Chenoweth, J., Smith, J. & Watkins, B. 2020. *Sent. Reflections on Missions, Boarding School and Childhood*. Brisbane, Queensland, John Chenoweth.

Pechtel, P., Lyons-Ruth, K., Anderson, C. & Teicher, M. 2014. *Sensitive periods of amygdala development: The role of maltreatment in preadolescence*. Neuroimage, 15, 236–244.

Pederson, J. 2014. *Speak, trauma: Towards a revised understanding of literary trauma theory*. Narrative, 22, 333–353.

Priestner, A., Ogden, J., Cavenagh, P. & McPherson, S. 2023. *The impact of boarding school on adult eating behaviour*. In: Cavenagh, P., Mcpherson, S. & Ogden, J. (eds.) *The Psychological Impact of Boarding School. The Trunk in the Hall*. UK: Taylor and Francis Group.

Schaverien, J. 2015. *Boarding School Syndrome. The Psychological Trauma of the 'Privileged' Child*. Hove, UK, Routledge.

Schaverien, J. 2019. *Foreword*. In: Simpson, N. (ed.) *Finding Our Way Home. Women's Accounts of Being Sent to Boarding School*. Abingdon, UK, Routledge.

Schaverien, J. 2021. *Revisiting boarding school syndrome: The anatomy of psychological traumas and sexual abuse*. British Journal of Psychotherapy, 37.

Stern, J. 2010. *Denial: A Memoir of Terror*, US Harper Collins.

van Der Kolk, B., Ford, J.D. & Spinazzola, J. 2019. *Comorbidity of developmental trauma disorder (DTD) and post-traumatic stress disorder: Findings from the DTD field trial*. European Journal of Psychotraumatology, 10(1), 1562841.

Wharton, N. & Marcano-Olivier, M. 2023. *An exploration of ex-boarding school adults' attachment styles and substance use behaviours*. Attachment & Human Development, DOI: 10.1080/14616734.2023.2228761

Chapter 6

Insights from personal testimonies

Third culture kids and boarding school

Linda Devereux

As the majority of those who have contributed their testimonies to this book met through a therapeutic setting, a boarding school survivors' workshop, it did not surprise us that they found boarding school challenging. What did surprise us was that out of 16 contributors, 12 are third culture kids (TCKs), that is, they spent a significant part of their growing up years living in a country that is not their passport country because of their parents work (Pollock & Van Reken, 2009: 8). Another contributor is a cross-cultural kid (CCK) (Van Reken, 2011: 33). She was sent from her passport country to boarding school in the UK with the assumption that she would return home when she had completed her education. That means that all but three of our participants experienced transcultural childhoods and were sent to boarding school in different countries or geographical regions to where their parents lived. Most were sent 'home' to school in England.

As we discussed in the introduction to this book, when we began the review of the literature about boarding school, we realised that TCKs are strongly represented in texts that emerge from therapeutic settings (Laughton et al., 2021; Ostini et al., 2020; Schaverien, 2015; Simpson, 2019). The high number of TCKs suggests that something about the combination of having a transcultural childhood and being sent to boarding school in a different country may be driving individuals to seek therapeutic help in adulthood. In this chapter, we examine the themes that emerge from the personal narratives in this book – our testimonies – which shed light on this conundrum. In particular, we highlight the cascade of losses and the multiple adverse childhood experiences (ACEs) and other trauma that many TCKs experience even before boarding school. We argue that these early challenges put pressure on entire families. The frequent moves demanded by many employer organisations mean that parents may not have the resources or support systems to be emotionally available to their children. These early challenges also mean that TCKs themselves may arrive at boarding school feeling different to their peers and vulnerable in an unfamiliar setting and country (Ernvik, 2019: 109). Being different at boarding school may set a child up for bullying and

DOI: 10.4324/9781003533665-6

exclusion in an institutionalised environment where students must fit in to have the best chance of survival.

6.1 Multiple losses and unacknowledged grief of TCKs

Many TCKs experience a high degree of mobility in their early lives (Crossman et al., 2022; Crossman & Wells, 2022; Musil, 2011; Pollock & Van Reken, 2009). As Pollock and Van Reken point out, however much a move has been anticipated and thought of as a good thing, it can be difficult for families. A move to a new place inevitably involves some degree of loss. Families lose homes, friends, pets, and possessions; sometimes, they lose everything (Ernvik, 2019: 195). They may miss activities that they have enjoyed and places they love and these losses may be compounded for children who lose all that has become known and familiar during their formative early childhood years. Additionally, expatriate communities are filled with people who come and go, contributing to many more goodbyes.

Where there is a loss, there is also grief (Pollock & Van Reken, 2009: 74). However, these losses and the resulting grief can easily fall into the category of disenfranchised grief discussed in the previous chapter. These non-death losses may be invisible to others and they can be dismissed and invalidated (Ernvik, 2019: 195) in similar ways to the loss and grief associated with being sent to boarding school. Those who live expatriate lives may be judged as 'privileged' in the same way that children sent to prestigious boarding schools may be seen to be privileged. Indeed, the children themselves may feel privileged when they compare their lives to the lives of children in their adopted countries (Den Hollander, 2019: 10; Devereux, 2012: 272). The stereotype of a glamorous and financially lucrative life lived overseas may obscure and invalidate the loss and grief associated with it, particularly for children.

In their large survey of TCKs Crossman and Wells found that almost all TCKs moved homes multiple times; the average TCK in their sample moved house every two years (Crossman & Wells, 2022: 28). However, those who moved most experienced significantly higher ACE scores than those who moved less. Nearly a third of TCKs who moved more than ten times had an ACE score of four or more. putting them at higher risk of a range of negative mental and physical health outcomes (Crossman & Wells, 2022: 40). Those in their survey who attended boarding school had the highest mobility of all. This suggests that many TCKs who are sent to boarding school have already experienced more grief and loss than most 'monocultural individuals do in a lifetime' (Gardner, 2014: 122).

There are many examples in our testimonies that illustrate these issues – high mobility and consequent loss and grief. Nicky M moved countless times and attended nine different schools by the age of 11. The moves were always on her father, or his company's, timetable and Nicky's needs were not taken into consideration. This meant that she frequently arrived at a new school after the start of term when everyone else had already made friends. This made it more difficult for Nicky to develop peer relationships.

Raewyn's experience illustrates the transient early life typical of many TCKs:

I was left without a sense of belonging or a consistent way of being ... there was a disconnect between the places and cultures I lived in ... temporary became a theme of my life ... impermanence ... by the time I was 13, I had moved countries five times ... lived in at least 15 different homes ... many temporary places ... [and attended] nine different schools.

(Raewyn)

Morag also recalls impermanence because her family moved frequently. She lived in nine different homes in seven different countries by the age of 10. Homes were frequently dismantled at short notice. On one occasion, the Christmas decorations were taken down and packed up three weeks before Christmas because the company demanded a move. Morag's family was then homeless. They lived in a hotel, in a different country, for five months.

The challenges of moving are compounded when the TCK must adjust to a new country and a new culture when they are sent to boarding school in their passport country without their parents and siblings (Walters & Auton-Cuff, 2009: 763). Marysa recalls that she had no chance to say goodbye to her overseas home because her parents split up and moved countries while she was in boarding school. She particularly missed her 'father's cook' and his family because she had grown up eating in his kitchen along with his family. She says, 'we couldn't go back to our beloved Nigeria, which had been our home, or to our Nigerian family, who had nurtured us and cared for us as though we belonged to them'. Marysa not only lost her home when she was sent to boarding school, she was denied the opportunity to say farewell to a country and people who meant a great deal to her. Additionally, she had to deal with these multiple sources of grief and loss while separated from everyone she loved, on her own, and adjusting to life in boarding school in an unfamiliar country.

Moving home can be difficult for any child, but it is even harder when the child is not part of the move and when they can never go back to the place that was their previous home. Jem also experienced the sadness of having her parents move from Germany – which had been her home – to Hong Kong, while she was in boarding school. Jem felt she was not 'truly part of' her parents' Hong Kong home where they lived with her little brother. That huge transition had taken place without her and the family was now split. She had lost the last familiar home where she had lived with her complete family and she had no established place in their new lives in a different land. Jem did not know and understand her parents' new life in another new country, and they did not know and understand her life in boarding school. Events such as these make it difficult for families to have shared experiences and this reduces their capacity to have shared memories of family life.

Jem recalls that she attended 'six different schools and lived in many different homes'. She spent her exeats and half terms with her aunt and uncle, or grandparents –

two additional unfamiliar locations. She only spent the long holidays with her family. Jem says that as a result of this mobile childhood,

> I am left with a lingering feeling of 'otherness' and of not belonging anywhere. I'm envious of those that can say where they come from. I cannot connect with many of the social and cultural references of others of my age group.

Those who have studied TCKs suggest that feeling 'other' is not uncommon. (Pollock & Van Reken, 2009: 103). Many TCKs struggle to 'fit it' with a peer group when they are sent to boarding school in their passport country because, like Jem, they have not grown up with the same shared cultural knowledge that their peers take for granted.

Morag makes another important point about change and loss. She says that even boarding school, sometimes justified as a choice offering constancy to a TCK from a mobile family, is not a 'stable place' devoid of disruptions. Her life in boarding school involved constant change and the need to adapt to 'another boarding house, another chapter, another dorm, another home, different rules'. Children in boarding school have no control over which dorm they will be placed in. During the term they may be moved about on the whim of staff, or as a punishment (Jack, 2020). They may end up in a dorm with different groups of children for each year throughout their schooling and are continually subject to the 'friendship lottery' (Cavenagh & McPherson, 2023: 160), which we discuss in more detail below.

6.2 Loss of place and belonging

Another loss which is often invisible to others is the loss of a childhood place or 'homeland'. The loss of a childhood host country can by keenly felt by TCKs. This sense of loss is illustrated through our narratives in a number of ways. We comment on it directly, but our testimonies are also peppered with detailed descriptions of the places where we grew up and the things we did there with friends and family. The language we use illustrates the visceral, sensory memories of children who feel 'place' through bodily senses as they learn about their world (Bartos, 2013; Grimshaw & Mates, 2022).

There are two aspects to this understanding of a sense of place: people, and the physical environment (Grimshaw & Mates, 2022). The people part relates to social interactions with family and friends and the memories of special activities and traditions unique to a particular area. The physical environment includes memories of the natural landscape, scenery, climate, geographical features and wildlife (Grimshaw & Mates, 2022). The sense of place developed in childhood influences later adult understandings, and 'familiar places from childhood may act as reference points and memories to which adults may return' (Grimshaw & Mates, 2022, drawing on the work of Schofield and Szymanski). This makes sense as humans draw on what they know to make sense of new experiences and environments. For the rest of our lives, we may compare new places and experiences to those from our earliest years (Devereux, 2015: 13). This tendency can contribute to challenges for TCKs if they draw on experiences from their adopted country which may not serve them well in trying to make sense of their passport country.

The child sent to boarding school in the unfamiliar environment of their passport country loses both aspects of place; the people and relationships, and the physical environment. The melancholy characteristic of this type of loss has been likened to the sense portrayed in the Welsh word, *hiraeth*. This word, without a direct English translation, describes a type of homesickness that goes beyond just missing a person or a place. It includes a sense of grief for a past that has been lost and which can never be recreated. Hiraeth creates a 'pull on the heart' and contains an element of grief for a 'unique blend of place, time and people' (Crossley-Baxter, 2021). It is accompanied by a deep longing for home, but, for TCKs sent to boarding school, home has moved on in their absence (Foster, 2019: 132).

There is a similar sense in the Portuguese word, *saudade*. Saudade is described as 'a vague and constant desire for something that does not and probably cannot exist'(Gardner, 2014: 116, drawing on Bell). Like Hiraeth, it is a hard concept to translate or explain to those who have not experienced it. Gardner argues that saudade captures the sense of loss unique to TCKs. Because we are neither of one world, nor the other we may always feel 'displaced'. As TCKs:

> ... our earliest memories are shaped by sights, sounds and smells that we now experience only in brief travels or through movies and television. All of those physical elements that shaped our early forays into this world are of another world.
>
> (Gardner, 2014: 117)

Our testimonies refer to both the people aspects of place and the physical environments we experienced. For example, Nicky M combines both when she recalls the 'warm bark' of African trees and camping in the bush with her father 'listening to elephant tummy rumbles' with 'stars so bright they cast a shadow'. These descriptions draw on the senses – sounds, sights, and bodily sensations of place – but they also relate to a happy memory of time spent doing something special with a loved parent. Joanna describes a similarly special memory of play with family and friends with 'tray toboggans' that slid 'straight into the sea down a hot sand dune'. She recalls that 'stars seemed so much brighter' in her childhood home and 'life in the holidays was spent in glorious technicolour'.

Jane P also draws on memories of people and sensory memories of the physical environment in which she grew up.

> My siblings and I enjoyed such freedom, We played outdoors from dawn to dusk and roamed the gardens and alleyways of our compound playing with other children ... we explored the riverbanks by the sailing club ... all day outdoors in the sun, jumping into blue, sun-lit swimming pools ... toes wriggled freely in

sandals ... lizards, camels, donkeys, goats, packs of pye-dogs ... Occasionally, we spotted ... parakeets, kingfishers or mongooses ... silver sides of fish glinting in the sun ... the sound of the call to prayer [and] ... turtle doves cooing in our garden ... [We] savoured delicious curries ... nuts and large juicy dates.

Jane's evocative description, and her choice of words, demonstrates her love for the people in her memories of place and a deep awareness and appreciation of the flora, fauna, and climate of her childhood home.

Raewyn sums up the loss many of us feel when these places are wrenched away from us.

India – its sights, smells, sounds ... food, climate and landscape. Its people, religions and cultures, and its languages ... has sunk into me, absorbed through my skin and senses ... In moving countries, the foods I was used to and enjoyed were no longer available [and] I had lost my sense of place and belonging ... sugar cane and flowering mustard ... cloud of dust ... part of me is still there ... my grief and sadness move into part of me that is a windowless room.

India was the place where she felt that she belonged. It was 'home'. Raewyn's testimony describes a concept of home which is 'rooted in a complex web of sensory stimulations ... that connect children with their bodies, place and others' (Bartos, 2013: 94). It also vividly captures the sense of loss, the 'windowless room', which now holds her grief for her childhood place.

Many of the descriptions of the UK in our testimonies symbolically mirror our strong sense of grief for these places that were previously home. The new is not contrasted favourably with what we have lost. For instance, Morag compares 'cold, dark, wet Scotland' with the 'light and turquoise sea' of her adopted country. Nicky R contrasts 'cold and dark' with the warmth of overseas, while Marysa juxtaposes 'bright, yet thundery rainy-season skies ... dramatic downpours' with 'utterly grey, depressing sky and endless rain ... unrelenting damp', causing her to feel 'chilled to the bone' in the UK. Olivia, describes the '*dead* silence' (our emphasis) of the UK compared with the lively 'hustle and bustle' of Hong Kong. A deep, emotional state is captured in the words we choose to describe the physical environment of boarding school in the UK. It is 'cold', 'dark', 'depressing', 'endless', 'unrelenting', 'chilling', and 'dead'.

TCKs are sent to board in an unknown land with unknown people who do not share their understanding or experience of the world. They become what Van Reken has called 'hidden immigrants' (Van Reken, 2011: 38). They may look the same as many of their boarding school peers, but they think differently because their experiences of the world, their sense of place, and their self-concept and identity are different. Furthermore, as these characteristics are hidden, staff and other students do not understand the grief and culture shock that the TCK is experiencing (Ernvik, 2019: 195). The child may find that there is no interest in their stories of home and that they are despised for their 'idiosyncrasies' (Den Hollander, 2019), or judged as deficient because they do not share the language (Olivia) or accent (Marysa) and/or the cultural capital of their peers (Tanu, 2015: 22). TCKs may learn that at boarding school it is safer to remain silent about childhood homes. Instead, we keep them alive in other ways. Caroline Giddens expresses a desire to remember which many of us share: 'I try and capture every detail of home, so that I can take it with me in my memory; how a flower looks, how a breeze feels, how the kitchen smells, how my bed feels' (Giddens, 2019: 25). The yearning to keep our childhood places 'close' is evident in our stories.

6.3 Travel

A number of TCKs have traumatic memories of travel between home and boarding school (Linda, Raewyn, Olivia, Jem, Joanna). Some parents chose the cheapest options for travel and these were not always comfortable (Raewyn), easy (Olivia), or safe for unaccompanied minors (Joanna). Often, to make things easier for our parents to continue working, or because they could not take leave, we were sent off with strangers (Linda, Raewyn, Joanna, Jem). Some trips took days (Linda), and involved complex transfers (Raewyn). They were often frightening for young TCKs.

Jem remembers her first flight to Hong Kong – an unfamiliar place to which her parents had moved while she was away at school. She was sent to the airport from school in a taxi. Feeling too frightened to ask the driver to stop for her to go to the toilet Jem wet herself by the time they arrived at the airport. She can't remember how this mess was cleaned up as she was in school uniform with no change of clothes. Jem was then handed over to 'airline aunties'. On the plane, Jem tried on the seatbelt and then did not know how to take it off again. The flight to Hong Kong was 'endless and uncomfortable' and when she reached her destination the aunties had disappeared and she had no idea where to go and what to do in the airport. Jem says that she met up with her family with 'eyes as big as saucers' feeling an 'immense sense of relief' when she was in her mother's arms again. This harrowing trip was long and stressful and it was too much for such a young child to deal with alone without adequate support from a parent or trusted caregiver.

The narratives illustrate that some of us remember these trips to and from home in great detail, while others have very few memories of the travel. Each of these reactions – amnesia (Schaverien, 2015: 115) and the recall of excessive detail (Pederson, 2014: 339) – can be a response to trauma.

6.4 Multiple sources of trauma for TCKs and their families

In their survey of just over 1,900 adult TCKs Crossman et al. were surprised to find that many of their respondents experienced emotional and physical neglect as children. This was despite the fact that ACE measures of household disfunction – other than household adult mental illness – were 'generally low' (Crossman et al., 2023: 4). This suggests that expatriate parents were providing 'good homes' but not 'meeting their children's emotional needs effectively' (Crossman et al., 2023: 4). The relationship between these factors makes sense. Living overseas can place unique and often unseen pressures on families (Crossman et al., 2022; Crossman & Wells, 2022; Crossman et al., 2023; Devereux, 2015; Devereux, 2017; Ernvik, 2019). The geographical, cultural, and political environments in which some expatriate families live and work can expose them to poverty, crime, disease, violence, and political instability (Carr & Schaefer, 2010; Devereux, 2015; Devereux, 2017; Schaefer et al., 2007). There are also challenges that come from a lack of infrastructure in some countries such as poorly maintained roads or inadequate medical services. Such conditions can make encounters with trauma more frequent for many expatriate families and can lead to stress responses 'akin to [those] of combat veterans' (Rosik & Kilbourne-Young, 1999: 165).

In addition, although strong family structures can act as a buffer when challenges occur, when a trauma is experienced by a number of different family members, relationships can suffer because everyone is suffering. Some families can pull together, while others are torn apart (Robinson et al., 2008). Several of us experienced the separation or divorce of our parents. Often, this coincided with being sent away to boarding school. Jem and Kat were in boarding school when their parents' marriages broke down. Marysa was also in boarding school when she was called to the headmaster's office to be told her parents had split up and that she would, therefore, not go back to the overseas country that had been her home. In addition, she was made to sit an IQ test just after being given the news about her parents. The school did not take into account her distress, and Marysa's teachers concluded that she was 'not smart enough'. Joanna's parents also separated and she suggests that the expatriate lifestyle may have contributed to their relationship difficulties. She felt that the number of parties and the regular alcohol consumption added to challenges to relationships. She notes that none of her friends from this time had parents who had managed to stay together.

A number of the contributors to this book experienced other traumatic events in childhood. Some were exposed to war, either directly (Linda, Raewyn, Morag) or because a parent was in the military (Jem). Raewyn was at boarding school while her parents were working in the north of India where the Indo-Pakistan war was taking place. She recalls that she was 'always conscious' of the immanence of death and destruction and how unsafe living in India was. Jem's father was serving in the Falklands when she was sent to boarding school. She remembers that she became convinced that her parents were going to die while she was away from them and she spent a great deal of time in a 'state of fear'. Fear became her 'normal' feeling. Children, especially children alone, can become very fearful for the safety of those that they love when they are aware of the dangers faced in overseas countries.

Some of us experienced serious health issues in countries with limited health care (Raewyn, Nicky R). Nicky R recalls being left as an eight year old in one big ward with adults and sick children and maternity patients all in together. She could not speak the language and was left there alone at nights. Jane H's mother was seriously ill with a tropical disease and was so unwell that she could not look after baby Jane for her first three weeks, affecting the mother/infant bonding. Several of us also witnessed serious accidents (Raewyn), or other traumatic incidents (Nicky R, Linda). Each of the events described above and in our testimonies contributed to stress for us and our families. The frequent moves we experienced also impacted our capacity to form stable peer relationships.

6.5 Peer relationships

A growing body of research suggests that the importance of childhood friendships may have been underestimated in the past. Children who build and maintain strong peer relationships benefit from them in a number of ways (Neilsen-Hewett et al., 2017; Wren, 2020). For instance, there is a strong link between peer relationships, well-being, and resilience. Strong and stable friendships are protective for children in times of stress and adversity (Perry & Szalavitz, 2006: 230; Wren, 2020: 71, 74). The benefits from having supportive peers throughout childhood are also long lasting and can lower the rate of adult depression by almost a fifth (Crossman et al., 2023: 23). Conversely, children who are lonely, those who do not have access to effective peer relationships, may experience difficulty building and maintaining relationships in adulthood (Rosik & Kilbourne-Young, 1999). They also have increased risks of ill-health (Crossman et al., 2023: 24).

Access to peers who share their mother tongue is important to children and, unsurprisingly, access to these friendships can be difficult for some TCKs (Crossman et al., 2023). Crossman et al. asked just over 1,900 adult TCKs about their access to peer relationships growing up (Crossman et al., 2023). Of the TCKs they surveyed, 11% had only siblings for friendship and an additional 10% had no access to an appropriate peer group. A fifth of the TCKs in Crossman's study were, therefore, at risk of childhood loneliness. One in three of these TCKs at risk of childhood loneliness had 'a high risk ACE of four or more' (Crossman et al., 2023: 25). In contrast, the TCKs who reported having peers growing up had lower ACE scores, despite all the other ACE risk factors for TCKs.

Our narratives illustrate a range of experiences with peer friendships before boarding school. Some of us had only siblings to play with for much of the time, had rarely been separated from our families, and did not attend school before boarding school (Linda). Some were 'actively discouraged' or even 'forbidden' from playing with local children (Raewyn). Others remember with joy the sense of living in a compound (Nicky R, Jane P, Jane H, Morag) or camp community (Jem, Alyson), with access to 'ready-made friends' with similar life experiences (Nicky R). Jem and Alyson both remember having lots of friends on the Army camps where they lived, while Nicky R recalls that she went to school with other children from the compound where they bonded through all being 'minorities in a foreign land'. Alyson explains that all she knew was Army life where postings were every three years and the people around her changed frequently. She 'learned to make friends quickly' wherever she was. In these settings, everybody around us understood the lifestyle of expatriates, and some of us had little experience interacting with people from outside our compound confines or TCK communities.

However, as discussed above, one of the most striking features of compound life is impermanence. The compound/Army camp community around us changed often and most of us also moved frequently due to the demands of our parents' employer organisations. This means that children who grow up in highly mobile families which are part of highly mobile communities become used to 'moving on' with friendships (Musil, 2011). Where everything is temporary, we may have more experience making *new* friends than working on maintaining relationships. It may even feel risky to invest emotionally in friendships that will inevitably lead to grief when they are lost. Some of us, like other TCKs, did not have long-term, stable peer friendships. We may not have had opportunities to develop the skills necessary to resolve conflicts, work at difficult relationships with peers, or fit into complex and varied group dynamics. Children who grow up in highly mobile families, and those who rely heavily on their parents and siblings for company, may not develop the skills necessary to survive peer relationships in the competitive, pressure cooker environment of boarding school. As the previous chapter makes clear, many of us were bullied, excluded, or ignored at boarding school. It is an area that warrants further research.

Those who have studied peer relationships at boarding school have concluded that friendships in such a hierarchical environment without enough adult support and intervention can be problematic. For example, in a series of interviews with 16 self-selected adult ex-boarders, Lee et al. examined participants relationships with peers (Lee et al., 2023). These ex-boarders reported that their relationships with other children at boarding school were characterised by 'impermanence' (Lee et al., 2023: 62). The children did not know which dorm they would end up in when they went back to school after holidays and this made establishing friendships 'dangerous'. Rather than establishing close trusting friendships, the interviewees describe being forced to 'ingratiate themselves' with a group of peers more as a 'matter of survival' (Lee et al., 2023: 63). A number reported developing a sense of 'emotional hypervigilance' with their peers. They were unable to escape the bullying at boarding school because they lived with those they found intimidating (Lee et al., 2023: 63). Others, described themselves as 'loners' and 'this isolation, combined with the absence of adult support, left them vulnerable to bullying, further deepening a distrust of relationships' (Lee et al., 2023: 64). Significantly, these relationships with peers were not in addition to positive relationships with adults, but *instead* of adult relationships. Relationships with peers were 'formed out of lack' (Lee et al., 2023: 66). The authors conclude that at boarding school children must learn to 'assimilate' rapidly or risk being bullied and isolated (Lee et al., 2023: 62).

Cavenagh et al., describe boarding school friendships as a 'lottery' where 'jungle hierarchies' operate. Those who 'loved boarding school tended to be alpha males, the "silverback gorillas" of the tribe' (Cavenagh & McPherson, 2023: 161). The less dominant individuals had to remain hypervigilant and they learn, 'as a matter of survival, to fit in with group norms' (Cavenagh & McPherson, 2023: 161). Reading this reminded us of the section in the previous chapter where we highlighted the use of non-human language in the narratives of our contributors to describe their response to bullying at boarding school. Not many are afforded the status of 'silverback' in a tribe, and this leaves many more children vulnerable to bullying and harm. Having to be constantly hypervigilant is not a condition conducive to healthy and happy childhood development (Duffell & Bassett, 2016: 46; Schaverien, 2015: 81) and unhappy children may find it hard to form supportive and nurturing friendships (Foster, 2019: 128).

James reviewed the existing literature on the psychological impact of sending children to boarding school using child development and peer victimisation theory (James, 2023). Boarding schools, he maintains, do not have the resources to provide enough attachment figures to children who are separated from their parents. Instead, damaged children must adapt to being part of a group and to the norms of the particular school. Safety comes from aligning with the dominant culture. Children who do not, or who cannot, 'fit in' are targeted, directly through physical and verbal aggression, and indirectly through social exclusion. Each of these outcomes leads to lasting mental health impacts for the individuals involved (James, 2023: 8).

The previous chapter outlines the range of bullying behaviours those of us who shared our testimonies for this book experienced. Many of us were isolated and/ or excluded, or bullied on a daily basis, throughout our years at boarding school. Some us may have been traumatised and dissociated. Many of us describe a sense of feeling like outsiders at boarding school. We may have arrived feeling 'different' because we had previously lived in countries where we 'stood out as different' (Raewyn) to most of those around us due to the bodies we inhabit (Ernvik, 2019: 109). Being different, as the paragraphs above illustrate, does not offer a good match for boarding school. As a result of bullying, isolation, and being made to feel invisible, it is inevitable that some of us added additional ACEs at boarding school to those we arrived with as TCKs.

Perhaps TCKs are more damaged than some other groups by boarding school because they arrive as outsiders, and perhaps this is why they are overrepresented in books about boarding school which emerge from therapeutic settings. We cannot demonstrate a cause and effect relationship and there may be other reasons why adult TCKs who attended boarding school seek therapeutic help. For instance, if TCKs feel like outsiders and are positioned as outsiders by their boarding school peers and staff, they may not identify with the school 'brand' in the same way as others who are from families who have attended boarding school for many generations. This does not mean that those children from traditional boarding school families are not damaged by the experience. However, it may mean that the latter group feel less able to 'speak out'. They are more constrained, perhaps, by the social standing of their families and the multi-generational investment in elite boarding schools.

Donna Musil encountered a range of responses to a film she made exposing the challenges in the lives of military TCKs. Some individuals felt understood and validated, perhaps for the first time. Others saw Musil as a dangerous whistle-blower; they felt very threatened by the content of her film. Musil suggests that some of those who felt most threatened were so invested in the institution – in this case the military – that they could not separate themselves from it. Criticism of the military felt like criticism of who they were and everything they believed in (Musil, 2011: 468). Where individuals or groups feel 'ownership' of something – a school and its reputation, perhaps – where their self-image is closely tied to a living connection with that institution and all that it represents for them, much is at stake. They may have a very strong emotional investment in a particular version of the truth and how it is told (Hirsch, 2008: 110). It is possible that a similar dynamic is at work in some who have been to boarding school. It does not feel safe to criticise the institution and its old boys nor to be reminded that personal privilege may have come at the expense of others.

Perhaps one advantage of *not* fitting in is that it feels more possible to critique the experience. From our 'outsider' position, it may be possible to speak our own truths and seek help and support from others to recover from the trauma of being sent to boarding school as young children.

6.6 Conclusion

This book, and the narratives and analysis presented in it, contribute to a growing body of knowledge about the long-term effects of sending young children to boarding school. Our sample size is small; there are 16 of us. However, our testimonies provide rich data which builds on and extends the work of others. Our testimonies also extend the knowledge of the under-researched experiences of women and TCKs who attend boarding school.

In the previous chapter, we offered examples of how adults – parents and school staff – use purposeful strategies to deny children's suffering so that adults do not have to witness it. In addition, our testimonies give examples of the 'poisonous pedagogies' aimed at breaking a child's will, which are regularly employed in boarding schools. The examples we shared took place in the *boarding houses* of schools – the places where children might expect to feel 'at home' and safe.

The consequences of the experiences we have shared are amply illustrated in our narratives. At school, many of us lived with fear on a daily basis. Others were bullied, excluded, and/or othered. These experiences, lived day after day, year after year, led to serious mental and physical health issues. Several of our contributors self-harmed in various ways and others have experienced suicidal thoughts.

We have also been able to illustrate how boarding schools impose gendered expectations and behaviours on young children. Girls are expected to be neither needy nor greedy at boarding school. They must learn to control their bodies and desires and to be submissive, silent, and reserved 'young ladies'. Subjected to strict binary gender divisions where there are different rules, expectations and punishments to boys, girls are taught overtly and covertly that their needs are less important than those of boys and men. We do not know enough about the long-term impact of boarding school on women or non-binary children. There is a need for more research on these issues.

There are other areas of research which can also prove beneficial to understanding the particular challenges of particular groups of boarding school students. As Susan Zeedyk's chapter illustrates, the growing body of research on ACEs has much to offer an understanding of childhood trauma. Children's brains develop rapidly, and it is becoming clear that trauma and stress may have longer-lasting effects on the under-developed brains of children than they do on adults. Similarly, there is a growing body of knowledge on how stress at different ages can affect children's developing brains in different ways. For instance, the work of Pechtel et al. illustrates that stress-dependent disruptions in neural development may peak at the age of 11, an age when many girls are sent to boarding school in the UK. Moreover, a large review study of trauma illustrates that repeated stressors, such as those inflicted by day-to-day bullying at boarding school, are particularly harmful to children because they occur over multiple developmental periods and thus increase the likelihood of long-term negative outcomes (D'Andrea, 2011). These areas remain underexplored in our understanding of the long-term effects of sending young children to boarding schools.

In this chapter, we have teased out some of the particular challenges for TCKs who are sent to boarding school. There are differences in the experiences of our three groups of TCKs – mercantile, missionary, and military – and more research is needed to understand the particular nuances of each experience. In addition, there are other types of TCKs such as the children of overseas aid workers and diplomats who are not represented here. Crossman et al., even in their large study of TCKs, found that some groups are underrepresented. Almost half of their survey respondents were the children of missionaries and this meant that some of their data for other groups relied on information from small numbers of participants. More research – both large survey research and qualitative studies such as ours – is needed to further understand the challenges facing particular groups.

What we can say with confidence, based on the literature we have drawn on throughout this book and on the rich data provided by our contributors, is that there are some unique difficulties for TCKs who are sent to boarding school. Many TCKs have already experienced significant challenges in their early lives. Some have high risk ACE scores, and others have experienced other trauma such as exposure to war and civil unrest. These traumas were, for most of us, exacerbated by our experiences at boarding school. We each experienced multiple losses and goodbyes in our early lives. As children who relied heavily on family through many earlier moves, surviving boarding school alone was a deep wound. This wound was intensified in the institutional setting of boarding school.

Our analysis also illustrates the deep and often overlooked relationships between TCKs and the sense of place they develop as children in their adopted homelands. Place, as our testimonies illustrate, is absorbed in a sensory way by young children.

Our stories refer to the sights, sounds, smells, tastes, and tactile experiences of the places where we grew up. Place is also shown to refer to both relational aspects of the past – the people who were part of it and the special things we did with them – and the geographical features of landscape, weather, flora, and fauna. Our narratives illustrate that a combination of these elements contribute to a sense of 'home' and identity which is lost when we are sent to boarding school in a different country to our parents. Most of us were sent to the UK from overseas and the loss of our previous lives, communities, and homelands was an immense rupture.

Children who are bullied and excluded at boarding school are likely to increase their ACE load. The fitting in required for success at boarding school, as our testimonies suggest, is particularly hard for TCKs and CCKs. These children *already* feel different; this is a well-documented TCK trait. In addition, we may stand out as different to our peers because, as immigrants – some visible, some hidden – we do not share the cultural capital of our monocultural peers. We do not understand the nuanced social norms required to 'fit in'. Moreover, some of us have additional class disadvantages. Our boarding school education may have been paid for through our parents' employment. We may not come from the British upper class. Some of us are the first in our family to attend boarding school. These differences set us up as outsiders ripe for bullying and exclusion in the competitive environment of boarding school.

Those of us who are TCKs knew we did not 'belong' in our adopted homelands. We loved them, but we were not fully 'of' them. However, many of us feel that we do not truly belong in our passport countries either. Most of us who boarded in the UK felt like we had been sent to an unfamiliar and distant planet. It was worlds away from 'home'.

We have given the last words to Jem. Those of us who have contributed to this book would agree with her.

I enjoyed living abroad, but I didn't belong there. I didn't belong anywhere in the UK, and no-one truly belongs at boarding school.

Bibliography

Bartos, A. E. 2013. *Children sensing place*. Emotion Space and Society, 9, 89–98.

Carr, K. & Schaefer, F. 2010. *Trauma and traumatic stress in cross-cultural missions: How to promote resilience*. Evangelical Missions Quarterly, 278–285.

Cavenagh, P. & Mcpherson, S. 2023. *British boarding schools on trial. Making the case for 'Boarding Family Syndrome'*. In: Cavenagh, P., Mcpherson, S. & Ogdon, J. (eds.) *The Psychological Impact of Boarding School. The Trunk in the Hall*. Abingdon, UK, Routledge.

Crossley-Baxter, L. 2021. *A blend of homesickness, nostalgia and longing, "hiraeth" is a pull on the heart that conveys a distinct feeling of missing something irretrievably lost* [Online]. UK: BBC. [Accessed 11/3/24 2024].

Crossman, T., Smith, E. V. & Wells, L. 2022. *TCKs at Risk. Risk Factors for Globally Mobile Families*. Georgia, USA, TCK Training.

Crossman, T. & Wells, L. 2022. *Caution and Hope. The Prevalence of Adverse Childhood Experiences in Globally Mobile Third Culture Kids*. Georgia, USA, TCK Training.

Crossman, T., Wells, L., Vahey Smith, E. & McCall, L. 2023. *Sources of Trauma in International Childhoods: Providing Individualised Support to Increase Positive Outcomes for Higher Risk Families.* Georgia, USA, TCK Training.

D'Andrea, W., Sharma, R., Zelechoski, A. & Spinazzola, J. 2011. *Physical health problems after single trauma exposure: When stress takes root in the body.* Journal of the American Psychiatric Nurses Association, 17(6), 378–392.

Den Hollander, F. 2019. *Skinny dipping in the Rhine.* In: Simpson, N. (ed.). *Finding Our Way Home: Women's Accounts of Being Sent to Boarding School.* Abingdon, UK, Routledge.

Devereux, L. 2012. *Stuck Between Earth and Heaven: Memories Missionaries and Making Meaning from an African Childhood in a Post-colonial World.* Axon.

Devereux, L. 2015. *Narrating a Congo Missionary Childhood (1958–1964): Memory and Meaning Examined through a Creative Non-Fiction Text and Exegesis.* Doctor of Philosophy, Australian National University.

Devereux, L. 2017. *Overseas missionaries and their families: Can the homecomings for those affected by trauma be reimagined?* In: Jackson, D., Cornshaw, D. & Dewerse, R. (eds.) *Reimagining Home: Understanding, Reconciling and engaging with God's Stories Together.* Macquarie Park, NSW, Morling Press.

Duffell, N. & Bassett, T. 2016. *Trauma, Abandonment and Privilege: A Guide to Therapeutic Work with Boarding School Survivors.* Abingdon, UK, Routledge.

Ernvik, U. 2019. *Third Culture Kids. A Gift to Care For.* Mariestad Sweden, Familjegadje.

Foster, P. 2019. *Afterword. A psychotherapist's reflections.* In: Simpson, N. (ed.) *Finding Our Way Home. Women's Accounts of Being Sent to Boarding School.* Abington, UK, Routledge.

Gardner, M. R. 2014. *Between Worlds: Essays on Culture and Belonging.* USA, Doorlight Publications.

Giddens, C. 2019. *Being sent, then and now.* In: Simpson, N. (ed.) *Finding Our Way Home. Women's Accounts of Being Sent to Boarding School.* Abingdon, UK, Routledge.

Grimshaw, L. & Mates, L. 2022. *'It's part of our community, where we live': Urban heritage and children's sense of place.* Urban Studies, 59, 1334–1352.

Hirsch, M. 2008. *The generation of post memory.* Poetics Today, 29, 103–128.

Jack, C. 2020. *Recovering Boarding School Trauma Narratives: Christopher Robin Milne as a Psychological Companion on the Journey to Healing.* Abingdon, UK, Routledge.

James, G. 2023. *The psychological impact of sending children away to boarding schools in Britain: Is there cause for concern?* British Journal of Psychotherapy, 39, 592–610.

Laughton, M., Paech-Ujejski, A., & Patterson, A. (ed.). 2021. *Men's Accounts of Boarding School: Sent Away.* Abingdon, UK, Routledge.

Lee, J., Wardman-Browne, J., Hopkins, E., Mcpherson, S. & Cavenagh, P. 2023. *It's not all down to boarding. Early family and peer relationships among boarders.* In: Cavenagh, P., Mcpherson, S. & Ogden, J. (eds.) *The Psychological Impact of Boarding School. The Trunk in the Hall.* UK, Taylor and Francis Group.

Musil, D. 2011. *On making BRATS.* In: Bell-Villada, G., Sichel, N., Eidse, F., Schellenberg, C. & Orr, E. (eds.) *Writing Out of Limbo. International Childhoods, Global Nomads and Third Culture Kids.* Newcastle upon Tyne, Cambridge Scholars Publishing.

Neilsen-Hewett, C., Bussey, K. & Fitzpatrick, S. 2017. *Relationships with peers.* In: Grace, R., Hodge, K. & Mcmahon, C. (eds.) *Children, Families and Communities.* Oxford, UK, Oxford University Press.

Ostini, J., Dainton, B., Chenoweth, J., Smith, J. & Watkins, B. 2020. *Sent. Reflections on Missions, Boarding School and Childhood.* Brisbane, Queensland, John Chenoweth.

Pechtel, P., Lyons-Ruth, K., Anderson, C. & Teicher, M. 2014. *Sensitive periods of amygdala development: The role of maltreatment in preadolescence.* Neuroimage, 15, 236–244.

Pederson, J. 2014. *Speak, trauma: Towards a revised understanding of literary trauma theory.* Narrative, 22, 333 –353.

Perry, B. & Szalavitz, M. 2006. *The Boy Who Was Raised as a Dog and Other Stories From a Child Psychiatrist's Notebook*. New York, Basic Books.

Pollock, D. & Van Reken, R. 2009. *Third Culture Kids: Growing up Among Worlds*. Boston, Nicholas Brealey Publishing.

Robinson, E., Rodgers, B. & Butterworth, P. 2008. *Family Relationships and Mental Illness: Impacts and Service Responses*. AFRC.

Rosik, C. & Kilbourne-Young, K. 1999. *Dissociative disorders in adult missionary kids: Report on five cases*. Journal of Psychology and Theology, 27, 163–170.

Schaefer, F., Blazer, D., Carr, K., Connor, K., Burchett, B., Schaefer, C. & Davidson, J. 2007. *Traumatic events and posttraumatic stress in cross-cultural mission assignments*. Journal of Traumatic Stress, 20, 529–539.

Schaverien, J. 2015. *Boarding School Syndrome. The Psychological Trauma of the 'Privileged' Child*, Hove, UK, Routledge.

Simpson, N. 2019. *Introduction*. In: Simpson, N. (ed.) *Finding Our Way Home. Women's Accounts of Being Sent to Boarding School*. Abingdon, UK, Routledge.

Tanu, D. 2015. *Towards an interdisciplinary analysis of the diversity of 'Third Culture Kids'*. In: Benjamin, S. & Dervin, F. (eds.) *Migration, Diversity and Education. Beyond Third Culture Kids*. Bassingstoke, UK, Palgrave Macmillan.

Van Reken, R. 2011. *Cross Cultural Kids: the new prototype*. In: Bell-Villada, G., Sichel, N., Eidse, F., Schellenberg, C. & Orr, E. (eds.) *Writing Out of Limbo. International Childhoods, Global Nomads and Third Culture Kids*. Newcastle upon Tyne, Cambridge Scholars Publications.

Walters, K. & Auton-Cuff, F. 2009. *A story to tell: The identity development of women growing up as third culture kids*. Mental Health, Religion and Culture, 12, 755–772.

Wren, A. 2020. *The importance of positive peer relationships for child well-being and resilience*. In: Williams-Brown, Z. & Mander, S. (eds.) *Childhood Well-being and Resilience: Influences on Educational Outcomes* (1st ed.). Abingdon, UK, Routledge.

Chapter 7

Coming home (a therapist's view)

Roe Woodroffe

When a child is born, she is wild by definition, a part of nature, her senses untrammelled, her behaviours free. As time goes on, society forces her further and further from those nourishing roots. Often, her life's work is to reclaim that wild child's immanence, her connection with soul.

If a child is sent away to boarding school, her roots have been ripped too soon from that early nourishing soil. She is separated from her instinctual animal self. She is unable to grow roots deep within to take sustenance from herself, her companions, or from nature; she is unable to experience her life fully and richly. The gift of loving relationship will likely remain tantalisingly out of reach.

Joan Armatrading and Pam Nestor's song 'Dry Land' resonates deeply with the longing to return to the prematurely undernourished and abandoned shores of our being, our dry land. The song – as I hear it – is an internal back and forth dialogue between self and soul; the wild child is the essential intermediary who can guide and aid in healing the split between self and soul, and so enable our coming home.

Marion Woodman – a Jungian analyst who lived from 1928 to 2018 – wrote:

> Soul to me means "embodied essence" when we experience ourselves and others in our full humanity – part animal, part divine. Healing comes through embodiment of the soul. The soul in matter is what I think the feminine side of God is all about .... The feminine soul is what grounds us; it loves and accepts us in our totality.
>
> (Woodman 1993)

My experience of psychotherapy began in 1981 as a client. I trained and began working as a psychosynthesis counsellor in 1986 and then as an integrative psychosynthesis psychotherapist between 1991 to the end of 2021. My clientele were mainly women and men in the mid-30s to 70s range, including a number of ex-boarders.

I gather much has changed for pupils who have entered the boarding school system, certainly since the millennium. The demography of pupils too has changed. Many more parents from the middle East, from China, and the far East choose to

DOI: 10.4324/9781003533665-7

send their children here in the UK to be educated at boarding schools. The other big change has been in what is now considered permissible language. I'm delighted that the assumption of the hetero-sexual norm, the male-female gender stereotype, has expanded beyond restrictive and false, patriarchal definitions. I believe language is a vitally important factor in how we come to view others, ourselves, our culture, and those of others. It does not mean, however, that I am always going to say or write without causing offence. I'd like to apologise in advance if I do offend, or cause hurt. Also, I want to make it clear that I think everyone is a victim of patriarchy. I also think that men have rather less impetus to challenge the status quo.

I have little doubt that some people go through the boarding experience over a number of years unscathed, although indelibly changed. What makes the experience positive overall I understand as being largely thanks to two major elements: nurture, a sufficiently good-enough parenting of a child in its early years, aiding the formation of what John Bowlby named secure attachment patterns (essentially the ability to form healthy relationships throughout life). And nature: I suspect some of us are born with a robustness of spirit that eases the passage through life. Maybe that is their very good fortune, and I suggest, also their misfortune; for I think pain offers us opportunity to live consciously in its alchemical fire.

> The unexamined life is not worth living.
> (Socrates)

> Sometimes I feel like a motherless child, a long way from home.
> (1870s Civil Rights Movement. 1st citation
> 1880s in Old Plantation Hymns)

> It takes a village to raise a child.
> (a proverb purported to be of African origin)

The preparation for boarding school may last weeks or months but the journey itself, no matter where in the world it is begun, will probably take no more than a few days. The boarding school experience, once embarked upon, like the tanker at sea, will take a long time to turn around, to set out on its return journey home. That journey may take a lifetime.

The younger a child embarking on the life-altering boarding school experience, the greater the impact it will prove to have. Whilst our brains are more adaptable when young it is then that we are most in need of our caregivers' loving support and guidance. We are learning life lessons in our homes that, if our caregiving is sufficiently good, will lay the vital foundations for our entire lives. And home is, well … home.

There are children whose home environment is so appalling that boarding school may be considered preferable, although try suggesting that to the child who is being told that life with restricted or severely restricted access to their primary caregivers will be their new normal. It is these care-givers they know. That much seems certain and certainty gives security, however negative that security may seem to be, or actually is.

The fault lines in attachment patterns established in the family of origin are accentuated by the boarding school experience. What then is that young person's experience of their mother figure and relationship to her? Likewise to their father figure?

There has been much written about the boys' or male experience of boarding. I shall focus on the girls' or female experience but hope to make it clear that I believe and work with the different genders from the same perspective, namely holding central that of our inner masculine and inner feminine, those energies Jung termed the *animus* and *anima*. He thought their inter-relationship, the 'inner marriage' of these energies, was not solely the aim of analytic work but of vital import to our individual and collective relationships across the world, including with that of the natural world.

Most of the world's societies function on a patriarchal model. The self-aggrandising distortion of masculine power, with its concomitant subjugation of the feminine in all her forms, has led us to the near extinction of almost all life as we know it. We are quite simply dangerously out of balance. The desire to control, and the arrogance with which the patriarchy continues to exert its powerful position in the world, has cut us off from that which is most important for all species; the well-being of the planet on which all our lives depend. It has split us off from Mother Earth.

What has this to do with boarding schools and in particular girls educated in this system? In England, during the middle ages, monasteries were the principal seats of education, but their focus – being as it was on producing religious leaders – ensured they were less than efficient at the more worldly, scholarly pursuits. The founder of Eton had a vision of supplying universities with 'scholars from a great grammar school' who in time would take up positions of leadership within business and the military. In British Empire days, boarding schools thrived educating the sons of officers and administrators of the Empire, the focus of their education being diplomacy for the upper classes, and a life in the military for the rest. Girls' boarding schools began in the late 18th century. Their function was to provide young ladies to make suitable wives and mothers to serve the patriarchy; now their task appears to emulate a distortion of the masculine!

A boarding school education was believed to be character-building, and some of the methods used to build that character had the hallmarks of its earlier monastic roots; a strict, often puritanical daily structure, virtual imprisonment, lack of almost all creature comforts, and often less than adequate lighting, and bad food. The character was also believed to benefit from discipline, too often verging on the sadistic, perpetuating a Darwinian 'survival of the fittest' mentality into which bullying fitted all too neatly.

This system served the colonial system well, bringing with it all manner of wonderful discoveries, territorial and culinary. It brought riches and territorial gains, power over other lands and those who lived in them. And so it earned respect and *kudos*, attracting to it many who wanted a piece of such apparent elitism, even if only by proxy. And into this machine in the 20th century were fed the children of the wealthy and the not so wealthy; seduced by the bedtime stories of boarding school high jinks and japes read to them by parental figures who themselves became seduced by lifestyles and the often attractive financial appeal of working in the far east, India, Africa, the Caribbean – just as those in more recent years who live in these places have been seduced by the *kudos* of having their children educated here in the so-called 'public' school boarding system. As commercial airlines proliferated and flights became increasingly plentiful, affordable, and comfortable, boarding schools once again moved with the times, opening their doors a little wider to embrace a broader 'elite'.

As will by now be clear, the boarding school system provided ideal training camps for young men to learn to serve the patriarchal system, socially, politically, and economically. The methods employed by these schools aimed to hone and propagate the cultural stereotypical ideas of masculine characteristics and qualities of their time, namely, mental rigour, physical toughness, resilience and strength, competitiveness, leadership, and self-sufficiency, as well as the ability to suppress and hide feelings that might indicate vulnerability, or be construed as feminine.

And here we have it … denigration of a characteristic deemed unmasculine in a patriarchal system.

And here, our child. She is 5, or 7, or 11 and she has been told some months previously that she is to go to boarding school and that she'll have a wonderful time. Chances are she'll have enjoyed the idea of boarding; she may even have enjoyed the process of being involved in the fitting, buying, and packing of the largest amount of new clothes she's ever had at any time. Words like *Panama* (hat) and *Tussor* (gloves), concepts like *knicker-linings*, will have snuck into her vocabulary and her mind. The smell of the shop and the clothes (be they new, or not quite) will have crept up her nose and may remain lodged there, in her body memory, always.

The physical preparation for the advent of the day that will inevitably change her life is complete. How much emotional and psychological time and support has she been afforded her by those she loves and trusts the most? Has anyone sat quietly, taken time to ask her how she is feeling, really feeling, including any worries, doubts, fears she may have? Has anyone heard attempts she has made to express what she's experiencing? Maybe not.

She sits in the back seat of the car which slowly crunches its way down the long, gravel drive. Ahead is the huge building she's been told will be a home for her. It looks nothing like her home, or anyone's home she knows. Her tummy has very big butterflies diving around at speed and she suddenly feels like crying. The two people she loves best in all the world are beside her as they stand on the drive, now filling with cars spilling out adults, suitcases, trunks, numerous big girls, and a few her own size. She wants to rush back into the car, go home, but her shoulders are held firmly in large hands. She feels their warmth through her crackly new uniform dress and a tear falls from her eye. She wipes it away and hears: 'be brave my little soldier'. Her mother's head is turned away. It is time to part. 'You know we love you' .... 'we're doing this for your own good' .... 'It'll make a young lady out of you'. Laughter. 'It's character building'. Kisses. Hugs. And then they're gone. Nothing now makes sense.

She is bereft. She feels many things she can only name and describe later, sometimes much later, in her life. That night she lies in her narrow bed, curled in the foetal position, and tries to muffle her crying, while all the others in the dormitory seem to be sleeping soundly.

This child and thousands like her are left in an alien environment carrying a profound grief which, as far as they know, they have to bear alone. They have lost all they had grown to trust and rely on. They've been dis-located, uprooted from their 'home land', be that near or far. Their family structure has been ruptured and will never be recaptured in its original form. The sacred realm of childhood innocence has been pierced by acts of abandonment and betrayal – no matter how well-intentioned the parents – its breached walls leave nebulous ghostly shadows of incomprehensible, suppressed memories, free to maraud untethered in the psyche.

I would suggest that whilst suddenly finding yourself abandoned and at sea is not likely to be a happy place in which to wake up, there are many children who arrive at boarding school who appear to slide into the relentless daily routine with a barely discernible ripple. They may have come from another country, another culture, with a different mother tongue, religious, or spiritual difference; and yet they seem to enjoy, even to thrive on the structured timetable, and to relish the near constant human proximity. Whether these youngsters continue to say, and to believe, their school days were indeed the best of their lives, to my knowledge there's been no survey to supply an answer. What seems clear from my work with former pupils is that if, later in life, there is an event which in some way mirrors the major issues inherent in the boarding school uprooting (I'm thinking in particular of loss, or a betrayal) their suffering, both in intensity and duration, are markedly exacerbated. Invariably in the therapy work we'll sooner or later find ourselves back at the school gates, where five or more years of their essential growth towards maturity took place.

The child, the children who keep their fellow dormitory companions awake with their crying, often night after night and especially after a visit from parents or parental figures, are those whose uprooting from their home land and family of origin are, in all probability, those whose grief is embodied in their own origins. I'm intimating here bonding patterns, laid down in infancy (perhaps even starting in utero) continuing during the early months and years and generally known as (Bowlby's) attachment theory.

In our culture the primary care-giver is still usually the mother, or mother figure. It is they who hopefully will learn to respond sufficiently quickly and consistently to the baby's needs which principally, initially, are the physiological needs. But if these needs are consistently met the baby has already learnt something about trust and safety. Being held close to the care-giver's body, the child uses her senses, a number of which are already well developed; although her internal thermostat is not yet up to scratch she'll respond to warmth, and to chill. Her sight is not yet fully mature but she'll gaze at her mother's face and come to recognise it, as she will her voice. Using touch she explores skin and cloth and in so doing comes to know a little about her own face, hands, the other being/s, and her home. If the care received at this stage is erratic or neglectful the child learns mistrust. People cannot be relied upon. The world is not a safe place. I am not held.

Observations indicate that sometime in the second half of their first year a child will display a preference for, and strong attachment to, one particular person, often that principal care-giver, the mother or mother figure. When separated the youngster will show distress, and exhibit signs of separation anxiety. What these observations fail to take into account is the state of the mother, who may herself be suffering an anxiety state; possibly even separation anxiety. She may be cut off from her work environment, social networks, mental stimuli, and emotional support. Not everyone has an available partner, 'suitable' parents, siblings, or extended family members able to help out, or indeed the money to pay for child care. Too many women, for a variety of reasons, know they can't cope. Many suffer postnatal depression, and attempt to cover it up out of shame; for the pressure to feel unequivocally delighted with your new born is strong. Then there is the woman whose own mothering has been insufficient. She may find herself alone with a new born whose desperate cries for feeding and nurturing echo her own inner child's desperate unmet needs for the same. The infant's cries underscore her feelings of inadequacy and helplessness.

Now let's imagine that little person, the baby and young child of insufficient mothering, who finds herself at boarding school. She has already learned she cannot trust her care-giver to meet her needs, viscerally knowing abandonment and betrayal. Experience has taught her the world is unsafe. And now she is to be subjected to a second serving of the trauma.

The wild, instinctual child experiences herself through her body, her senses. If we live in a city we'll turn our own little patch of homeland into whatever our imagination can create. If we have access to, or live in, a rural environment we might climb and make tree houses, hold warm eggs from the blackbird's nest, shit in the woods, play doctors and nurses, pick blackberries from the hedgerows, jump and splash through muddy puddles, roll in virgin snow, swim in the rivers, and run barefoot on hot sand. From the sheer physical exuberance and voracious curiosity of childhood innocence we follow the demands that we, from an early age, 'taste' everything. We bite into life.

True that this wild, natural child needs to hone her instinctual self, learn how to temper her instinctual behaviour when in the home, the homes of others, and to be able to respond appropriately, kindly to the people she meets. If she is fortunate she will have learnt much from the natural world, by being in and with mother nature. The girl child's connection runs deep. Here is her rootedness. She needs too to learn about the strange world of adults, and what it means to be female in a world where males are king. She does not need to learn how to distance – or worse, abandon – her wild child in the pursuit of seeking patriarchal approbation.

The patriarchy thinks otherwise. Understandably, It means to hold onto its power and privileges. It is fearful of woman's power; of her innate connection with Mother Earth, her healing mysteries, her ability to cure, to kill, and her 'miraculous' ability to bring forth life into the world from her own body. 'He' is also very threatened by the sexual allure of the woman.

The body, the female sexual body, is that which causes her and Adam to be unceremoniously ejected from the Garden of Eden. She carries the blame and the shame in old testament biblical proportions. As our bodies change through puberty from child to woman we are destined to carry the vestiges of both the shame and the blame.

If our girl child was at a boarding school up until relatively recently her uniform would have had a fair bit to say about what was what in the world. Around her neck would be a tie. A skirt or dress all year round was the only option (and not to be worn any shorter than two inches/five centimetres from the floor when kneeling). She would be expected to wear two pairs of pants, a white inner pair and over these, a pair matching the school uniform colour. Both pairs, high-waisted.

The return to her unsmirched identity as a female being entails casting off the layers in which the patriarchal system will have clothed her. First, she will need to recognise this is indeed what has occurred; she will have more or less lost sight of her wild child, and so failed to realise she has emerged a fully-fledged daughter of the patriarchy. Ask her what she understands by the term the 'deep feminine' and she may have no concept of its meaning. Only very recently has the word soul (linked to the feminine) entered common parlance, previously almost exclusively associated with the church and the writings of romantic poets. But in Celtic myth, as in Pagan culture, the soul connection has held on to her place, and her dignity.

In the Garden of Eden the role of the serpent is often overlooked. Interesting, as whilst snakes represent many things in world mythologies, they're most commonly connected with the life, death, life cycles of the natural world!

Eve, we're told, accepts the apple and bites into it. In so doing, she awakens from her unconscious state of innocence, seemingly accepting the call to enter into her own central role in the natural world's life, death, life cycle. Temptress? Certainly initiator. She falls into matter (Mother Earth), and here we are, with Eve, carrying the blame for tempting poor Adam out of his state of bliss, and with the shame forever associated with the female body. The couple have lost their innocence in the fall but gained knowledge of many things, including awareness of themselves as sexual beings. It seems that inherent in the myth of the fall is the mental mechanism of splitting. In Judeo-Christianity the use of all manner of things are held as opposites: innocence/knowledge, either/or, virgin/whore, black/white, body/mind, good/bad, innocent/guilty. This simplification has obviously been easier, especially for those holding power. However, it has proved more terrifyingly damaging than the alternative: the more complex, more nuanced, but closer to reality, use of paradox.

Inevitably by the age of 11, 12, or sometimes earlier the girl boarder will compare her own body with those she sees around her. She'll notice among her contemporaries that what were once more or less androgynous bodies are now developing a new more curvaceous shape, a figure. Some girls have considerably more hair on their legs, and their pubic area. It probably won't escape her still acute sense of smell that some girls' games shirts have a stronger body odour than others. And if she feels that her body in some way differs from others, she may quite suddenly wish for privacy. That could prove nigh impossible in the boarding school setting.

She is aware of girls emerging from the matrons' sitting room holding packets of sanitary products. And now in the dormitory there is talk of periods. Some use the word, the 'curse'. Most talk about having or not having 'started'. It is often spoken about in hushed tones, as if there's something shameful about the monthly bleed. To have the topic talked about at all is for some a relief, a wonder, a cause of excitement even. She may have learnt the very little she knows about periods from older sisters or friends at home. One such explanation of periods was: 'You'll start bleeding when you're about eleven, and stop when you're around fifty'.

Surging hormones are no respecter of girls parted from their social set and the different genders of home. The topic of boys arrives; who has done what with whom, the question, 'how far did you go' often asked, and the answer quite probably lied about almost as often! This is a new source of competitiveness. Along with it comes clothes and make-up talk, nail care, experimentation with hair-styles and 'smellies'. Then there's the desire for physical contact, so someone tells a romantic or a sexy story while others climb into one another's beds. Adolescence has made that need acceptable, or maybe just too strong to deny.

It is not purely sexual stirrings making themselves heard. The soul is hungry for expression. The romantic dormitory story-telling, the sensual exquisitivity of skin against skin, gives her a voice; romantic yearning fuels the imagination, often finding a safe enough harbour when the heart's desire is another pupil.

The school hopefully will provide sufficient soul food as an integral part of the communal building spaces, as well as in the curriculum itself: art, craft, literature, poetry, wood-working, gardening, outdoor activities, nature walks. There may be prints of well-known paintings on the walls. The library may cover a wealth of subjects that can satiate the soul's desires as well as the mind's quest for knowledge. No doubt there'll be ceremonies, rituals, music lessons, plays, choral singing, contemplative space/s.

However, this separation from home for most of the school year is neither a natural nor a healthy way to spend down-time in teenage years. Relationships with a different gender are overheated by sudden release from the confines of the stable, to the apparently limitless meadow. Boys are an alien species (having a brother may be of some use)! Finding you are a stranger amongst those who would otherwise be your peer group is difficult at the best of times, but extra tricky when self and body confidence may be at all-time low.

Marion Woodman again:

My soul is the bridge between spirit and body and as such is, is a unifier of opposites. Without soul at center, I would either transcend into spirit or become mired in matter.

(Woodman & Mellick, 2001)

Imagination is that which tethers the personality of the wild child to her soul, growing away from childhood, increasingly conforming to our society and its cultural norms, the soul connection becomes considerably looser, in some people appearing to be lost altogether.

Key to soul work is the remembering of and reconnecting to that wild child. She retains the knowledge of who we most quintessentially are. because she has learned more or less what is expected of her in her everyday life, she can perform her various allotted tasks and has probably found a way of complying, adequately at least. But the fact she has accomplished this, and it has taught her the rudiments of positioning herself at the helm of her adapted personality, doesn't mean she's not considerably more engaged when using her imagination; daydreaming, utilising her 'what if' curiosity. She likes, needs, to create, to play, to stretch, and exercise her body, particularly outside, in the natural world. She enjoys exploring, using her senses to touch, sniff, just as she did as a baby and small child.

* * *

I am sitting in the room in which I work, about to begin an introductory session in what I regard as soul work, but which my client thinks of as integrative psychosynthesis or, more likely, just therapy. Frances (51) cuts an imposing figure, immaculately dressed in tailored jacket and skirt suit with knee length boots. She's tall, slender, with, I note, an unnaturally upright posture.

We greet one another then I enquire what brings her here today. She replies that she has no problem speaking on behalf of those who find it difficult, or impossible, to speak up for their own needs. But when it comes to herself she sometimes finds she opens her mouth and no sound emerges. This is particularly obvious at present in her relationship with her friend and co-CEO in the charitable organisation they set up to support the education of girls and women in the Democratic Republic of the Congo.

Frances's father had died the previous year. She describes him as the backbone of the family and says that with his death she felt she had lost both parents; when in fact, although elderly, her mother was alive and in reasonably good health. As she talks it becomes clear to me that she has taken on a fatherly role, not just shouldering the responsibility for the well-being of her mother, but also for her alcoholic daughter whose father, Francis's former husband, suffers a serious disability. Frances care-takes her daughter's young twins whenever she's needed. They often stay overnight with her and her partner, a man 25 years her senior.

I'm curious about Frances' relationship with her mother, and whilst she says she feels they had, and continue to have, a good relationship, she is eager to tell me more about her relationship with her father. She says he was the only person in her life who ever made her feel special. With warmth in her voice and a distinct mistiness in her eyes she recalls how the two of them liked to sit together, she on his lap, embraced in his arms.

Now already with the aid of several clues, and most importantly Frances's own metaphorical description of her father's position in the family as 'backbone', a working hypothesis is starting to emerge.

I ask if she recognises this inability to find her voice at any other time in her life and she tells me she does. She went to boarding school aged seven, as did her other siblings, and it was here she came across a matron who appeared to have not an ounce of human kindness. Not only did this woman have a loud, commanding presence and accompanying voice, she also knew how to belittle, humiliate, and shame her young charges. This in Frances's case produced bed wetting at night and sometimes during the day. When this occurred she was required to hang the knickers over the iron bed-head for others in the dorm to see, and for her to sleep beneath.

As she recalls this her voice falters and becomes quiet, not much louder than a whisper. Not wishing to interrupt I lean forward to hear. My body has given me another clue: initially my task now is to listen, hard.

As our session is coming to an end I ask her how she got through. Was there anybody she could talk to?

'Pip, my stuffed rabbit' she said. 'She was as scared as I was. We comforted one another'.

... Another clue, possibly the origins of her care-taking others as – in part – a comfort to herself.

I asked if she still had 'Pip' and if so would she bring her to the next session. Frances looked askance at me, said she'd have a search. That she was in a box somewhere and added that Pip was looking rather sad these days, she'd lost much of her stuffing.

... Like Frances must feel, I thought.

After she left I sat contemplating Frances's experience; questioning why I had not asked many of the questions I usually do in an initial session; for example did she grieve her father's death? How much room was there in the family for expressing vulnerability? What feelings were acceptable, welcomed? What role did she think she played for her family of origin ... and now in her present family? I noted that these questions left me enervated which corroborated my instinct that essentially just to listen was the right course of action. Plenty of time for questions. Frances said she wanted to begin the six initial sessions I offered as soon as possible.

I jotted down a few notes to give me some kind of a map as to the likely territory we'd be travelling through.

Father's daughter: *animus* rules. Any place for *anima*, imagination, play, creativity? Possibly with her grandchildren?

Father died recently. F's life and her role appears to be paying homage to the feminine (carer) in herself. But is this over-ruled by the masculine/animus by her role as CEO in the organisation?

When Father died, F felt her mother had also died. I read this as he provided 'motherly' warmth. I surmise F's modelled herself on him, the caring, loving, protective masculine ... Thank goodness she's had this.

Boarding school. Young to be physically leaving Mother's realm. What feelings has she towards (each) parent about this?

Age:

Midlife. Is the life she's living still responding to her needs? Is it the life she still desires?

51, menopausal: the autumn of fecundity. What does that mean to/for her. What is her relationship with her inner feminine/woman?

51, entering the second part of life, the return journey. Leaving the realm of Sun/ascent. Now entering the realm of the waning moon (moon = feminine), the return to Mother Earth ....

Her chosen work: as good father/mother to those children whose voices may never otherwise be heard? And, F is working in education! < possibly an attempt to redeem inner child from an educational set-up in which she had no voice.

Is her daughter acting out the vulnerability she could never allow herself? All around her seem rather helpless – or are they? .... In time query: does role of care-taker-in-charge give sense of self-worth plus protection from her own vulnerability?

Frances returned a week later for her first session.

She sat looking expectant, waiting for me to begin, as many people will when starting therapy. Usually I'll sit waiting for them to speak. Often they might start by letting me know in one way or another how uncomfortable they found the silence. An opportunity for me to explore what hopes and expectations they may have about the work. Also their feelings towards me as some kind of authority figure who has not taken the initiative, as this may relate to unresolved issues with other 'authority' figures in their lives. It also flags up what feelings are likely to get projected onto me.

With Frances I felt pleased she had not stepped straight into handling what she may or may not have experienced as an uncomfortable silence, so I took advantage; asking if anything in particular had stayed with her since we last met. She said she'd been surprised at how emotional she'd been speaking of her boarding experience. Surprised too that I'd suggested she bring Pip to therapy! It had apparently taken a considerable hunt to retrieve the rabbit from her 'burrow', a shoebox which looked in rather better condition than the threadbare, one eyed, limp soft toy that emerged from the towelling cot blanket. Frances placed Pip on her knee, a protective hand preventing the toy from flopping forwards!

I deliberately chose the words Frances herself had used when describing the rabbit in our initial meeting: 'Pip has lost a lot of her stuffing. And she's looking rather sad'.

Now Frances too looked sad.

"I wonder why she's looking so sad."

"No-one's taken care of her in a long time'."

Francis's voice was cracking, informing me that she was identifying with her rabbit's state and in so doing opening up a potential therapeutic pathway. But was there yet sufficient trust in me? A risk worth taking.

"I'd like to hear Pip's story. Do you think she'd be willing to tell us?"

"From when. What point?'"

"Is it OK to let Pip decide where to begin?'"

An affirmative nod. And after a short time, Frances began telling me her story. (It soon became clear she was a natural story-teller. I imagined her grandchildren must love hearing her tales.) ....

When I was a kit, I lived in a burrow deep in the Marram grass on a sandy beach, in far-away Africa. I had many brothers and sisters, and there wasn't enough grass to feed us all as we grew. One by one we left the burrow. When it was my turn, I hopped for a long time until I came to some houses. Right in front of me, smack-bang up against a house was a garden full of things that smelt amazing. I was just pulling a juicy carrot from the earth when a huge human hand pulled me from the earth! I squealed as loud as I could, and then I heard a little girl squeal too. That little girl was Frances and I was allowed to live with her in her huge burrow, as long as I promised to learn how to behave like a tame rabbit. That was difficult because Frances behaved much like a wild rabbit, except she climbed trees and loved swimming in the sea. She liked to shout as loud as the waves. She took me on all her adventures, and I'd sit beside her ayah watching as Frances splashed in the water and danced on the sand, my little rabbit heart bursting with happiness.

Then one day Frances, her Mummy, and her Daddy packed up their beautiful burrow. Frances didn't let anyone pack me up! She held me tight all the way to the far away country called England. She held me especially tight all the time we were in the tummy of a huge, noisy bird that flew over clouds. She was scared. I was scared but we had one another so it was ok. But soon it wasn't at all ok. ...

Frances had clearly enjoyed telling the story thus far. Her face had softened and her shoulders and back looked more relaxed. I'd learnt much about her in the tale I'd just heard: her early bond with and love of nature; how she had relished her freedom; enjoyed her body, and her senses. Most importantly her imagination was in good health. Unlike in Pip's story, Frances thus far had remained untamed and had given me the ideal opportunity to introduce and name the wild child in the context of the soul's journey.

Leaving space for her queries I probably briefly outlined the tenets from which I work, namely: all of us born into and raised in a patriarchal system are implicitly and explicitly taught what is expected of us. This tutoring entails distancing, or even splitting, from our wild, or natural, inner child, inevitably resulting in distortions of the 'true' feminine and 'true' masculine, in both female and male genders. And how, with particular care and attention paid to relocating and reconnecting to that wild child, we can find our way 'home' to those natural roots of ours.

Possibly at this juncture – although far more likely, further into the therapy – I'll introduce a model, a way of thinking about not only soul therapy, but a way of looking at life's journey. I'll sketch a little sailing boat with a figure at the helm. The figure represents the personality. Above the boat's bow I'll sketch a star; it depicts that of the soul. I'll draw zig-zag lines in the 'sea' to represent the tacking her personality will do as her life journey continues. Many times her personality will want to venture in a direction that appears to be way off course. And at times her soul will try to alert her, in the form of symptoms that may affect her body, mind, feelings, or spirit. Eventually her personality will listen, sometimes too late.

In my work with Frances I follow up on the theme of the imagination, exploring with her the part it plays in her life. She tells her grandchildren stories, she plays with them – often outside, often on the beach where she lives now. I ask whether she has other playful relationships. And I ask about favourite films and stories from her childhood. It is fascinating to me how often a favourite child's story in a book or film has remained strong in their mind because, although usually not recognised as such, it is their very own metaphorical story....

Like this, another type of rabbit story ....

A baby rabbit whose apparently useless wings twitched and stuck into the bodies of her brothers and sisters every night as they all crowded together in the one bed, big enough for them all, had it not been for those pesky and totally non-rabbit physical characteristics. Her siblings got crosser and crosser as her wings grew and they got less and less sleep. Their mother became more and more exasperated as those wings became impossible to accommodate in any clothing ever made for an ordinary rabbit. And this poor little creature became increasingly more miserable, until one day she packed her spotted handkerchief, hoisted it onto a stick across her shoulder, and went off to seek her fortune. Eventually after days of seeking, not finding her fortune and by now exhausted, she fell asleep on a doorstep belonging to a kind-hearted stranger, who not merely sheltered her new arrival but admired her wings; each morning fussing over them just as the little rabbit's mother had fussed over all her babies' fur coats before sending them off to school each morning.

Often the 'journey' begins with a sense of not 'fitting' in the family and it's this sense of not belonging that initiates the call to journey. ('The Ugly Duckling' is an archetypal tale of journeying.) In any woman's story, particularly if she is a 'motherless' child, she will do well to find herself on the doorstep of a woman (sometimes a female therapist) who will come to recognise and appreciate the true nature of this traveller. If this unique essence is given house room to merely be, time will probably do the rest, eventually fostering the shift in the individual's growth from surviving to thriving mode. The sense of not belonging in the family of origin is likely, as stated earlier, to be reiterated in the boarding school experience where less than helpful attachment patterns are prone to arise, triggering behaviour almost bound to further alienate the child from her new 'family'.

In the story of the winged-rabbit, given encouragement, warmth, and space, she learns to fly. Then although she gathers sufficient confidence to fly almost anywhere, and although she has built up thousands of rabbit air miles, she now comes home to the roots she has fostered deep within her self.

I always feel optimistic when a client tells me the central character in their favourite story is a young animal with wings. In my experience it speaks of the person's desire to move beyond whatever it is that is limiting them, and often indicates a commitment to reach for the skies of their potential. An animal as the central character suggests that the person's instinctual animal self, although untethered, continues to live on in their psyches, even if only in their memory.

Working with people's dreams is, as Freud put it, 'the royal road to the unconscious'. If someone recalls their dreams – and I encourage people to write down remembered dreams, or snippets of dreams, when waking from them – it's of great use to the therapist, giving, as it will, a view of the psyche's landscape. Surprising how often a person embarking on the therapeutic journey, when it's suggested by the therapist that they are likely to have an important 'therapy' dream, will indeed have their psyche oblige, returning to their next session with a dream that lays out a map of the therapy journey to be travelled! (Always wise to remember the map is not the territory.) As the client begins to learn the language of their 'dream-maker' it is useful to them too, as dream images are often powerful gifts which may be brought to consciousness and worked with in the therapy. Sometimes a particular image may reappear several times over the client's work, gradually, or sometimes radically, altering as the work progresses.

Occasionally a client is dubious or blatantly disdainful about the value of dreams, including their own. I tell how once Jung was seeing a client who continued to feed the analyst his dreams for many years until one day he decided to let Jung know dream analysis was a waste of time saying he'd been telling Jung any old story and Jung had fallen for his ruse every time. Jung is purported to have responded: 'And who do you think was making up these stories?'

I understand Jung as saying that images and stories, whether told in a waking or unconscious/semi-conscious state, were gifts from the person's imagination and therefore of great value to the therapeutic journey. And so learning to make good use of that gift is another great tool for contacting the client's own story. From time to time I have asked a person to write their own story in the style of a fairy tale. This will often link to archetypal myths and stories, the themes of which are collective repositories of universal human wisdom.

The imagination is the bridge between the concrete and the abstract mind: between our present reality and what we might be, or maybe have been, offering another perspective; another way of experiencing our reality.

In consultation, Frances and I decide to continue our work together on an open-ended basis.

Pip, it transpired, had played her part in the sessions and by session 12 we were able to move on – to confront her nemesis, the matron who had so shamed and frightened her that she had stolen Frances's voice.

The Gestalt 'chair method' as it's often called is a way of using the imagination to explore internal issues and gather another perspective. In the case of an inner argument this can lead to the opening up a new or third position, or as in Frances's case would offer an opportunity to say what she never could to Miss Pring. The method usually involves the client moving back and forth between her own chair and that of her protagonist's, thus to a greater or lesser degree identifying with the other. And a third chair is made available for the client's sage or disidentified position to comment on what she's noticed and learnt from the interaction.

I chose a more containing version of the 'Gestalt chair' method to work with Frances on this issue, she being the victim of childhood bullying and humiliation, behaviour compounded in its severity by the fact of the matron's position of authority and role of pastoral care. Integral to the containment, it was essential that Frances's inner child's voice was listened out for. And if she did appear, that she should be not merely heard but her feelings responded to. That may well have been the sole focus for that session; for Frances needed to be sufficiently in touch with her own adult inner authority to be in the best position to overcome her fears and speak out. Ideally, that voice of inner authority comes from the authentic feminine and authentic masculine, heart and head speaking as one.

By the end of our work together, a period of about two years, Frances had regained her voice, and had chosen a very different life for herself, one that involved considerably more self-care, less of carrying others. Hard to know who was more delighted, her or me!

There are numerous ways to make use of imagination in soul therapy work. A major component being 'child's play'! Children are usually daydreaming experts and are, overall our best teachers when it comes to using this amazing gift in all its forms. It is often in moments when we're not aware we're thinking anything at all that inspiration drops in; could be the result of an apple falling on your head, a solution to a problem, an entirely new perspective on an issue.

A few ideas. Using the imagination in the therapy room (and outside it).

- Creative pursuits, for example, drawing. painting, especially with bold colours, and with broad brushes, fingers or, indeed whatever might be fun to experiment with.
- Collage making: photos, paintings, pictures, writings, or sketches of anything that touches your soul.

- Clay modelling. Ticks all the boxes for me. There's the earthy smell, the feel and sound of the wet clay in the hands, and the joy of creating something straight from mother earth.
- Gardening. Most of the benefits of playing with clay but with the added potential to give all senses an outing.
- Singing – off-piste! Making up dances to soothe, to enliven, to let the body move how she wishes.
- Swimming, Preferably the wild sort!
- Sand play. A sand box with plenty of figures and animals.
- Free, or stream of consciousness, writing/journalling.
- Recording dreams. Dream on (e.g. dialoguing with a dream figure, free associating with a dream image, or draw, paint it).
- Walking, sitting in nature. Letting the mind move, or be still, just as she pleases.
- Cooking using fingers to mix and tongue to taste. Make up new recipes, or variations to those tried and tested.
- Meditation. Sitting, or walking, preferably bare foot on grass or sand.
- Making use of the internet for guided imagery, meditations, recorded nature sounds. (Really useful for town or city life and insufficient time to walk in a park.)
- Deep candlelit baths with favourite bubble bath, oils.
- Visualise a place that feels special, maybe it was – or reminds you of – a childhood haven. Take yourself there whenever you feel the desire to be in touch with the energies that make that place special to you.
- Research and visiting ancient sites connected to deep feminine, ancient roots, e.g. Avebury.
- This is one to explore with a therapist. Find the internal characters, known as sub-personalities, who, as it were, all play an instrument in your internal orchestra, some working in harmony, others less so! I suggest identifying no more than half a dozen main sub-personalities; name them, e.g. the mother, boss, father, the fearful one, the eco-warrior. Draw or paint or make each. Note which characters emerge in certain situations. Which dominate, which appear shy. Notice which you particularly like or dislike. What qualities does each one have? Note how they interact and play out in your everyday life.

A powerful and often revealing experiential exercise when working with the client's image of mother and father 'parent' is to ask the client to stand, eyes closed, and imagine their mother (say) to one side of them a metre plus away. Allowing time for that experience to be as filled out as possible, I'll then ask the client to take a small step towards the mother and to note, silently, how the proximity feels; noting too their thinking, and how their body is experiencing this. Then I'll ask them to take another step closer to this parent figure, again noting but not speaking what the experience is like for them. Then back to where the client was standing before taking these steps, noting how it is to move away. I'll ask the client to physically shake off the experience before repeating the exercise again, this time moving in the other direction, towards the father figure.

A woman I worked with for several years, when asked to move a step towards her mother, instantly felt a heaviness in her body and resistance to move closer. When she did take that step, her energy seeped from her and she experienced a dragging down towards the earth. Her experience in relation to her father was, by contrast, an energising force and was accompanied by the word, 'yes'.

This client's mother had been ill all the client's life, dying in her teenage years. 'In the exercise I felt I was being dragged into the grave too', she said.

The positive experience with her father had surprised her as she'd disliked him for much of her life. However, in the exercise she'd felt a positive surge of energy, ... 'like a yes to life'.

In our work together, it was no surprise that this woman had identified with the masculine in herself and wanted to distance herself from her experience of the feminine.

There is a point in every woman's therapy – and particularly those women who have had insufficient mothering – when it's appropriate to give her an experience, via her imagination (bolstered by a good solid cushion and wall behind that) of all the women in her mother's family who have come before her. She will begin by visualising and feeling her mother's limbs around her, her body behind hers, then her grandmother's behind her mother's, and so on, back and back through the generations. She will feel the solidity of that life line and may marvel at this lineage about which, in all probability, she has never given a thought.

These women have given her life. Through their lives she recognises her own roots, and she'll want to claim them for herself. Clients often ask, how long will this journey take? And, how will I know when I'm there? And, are we nearly there? No! There's nowhere to get to and yet it's a lifetime's journey. Sooner or later, when therapy has accomplished what has been needed for that particular time in a person's life but increased her desire for consciously travelling more of her soul's journey, she will – with her mature wild child at the helm of her little sail boat – notice that the guiding soul star has been with her all along. And she will see how her personality has needed to veer sometimes far in one direction before correcting, or over-correcting. As years roll on, with growing self-knowledge and life's experiences, the tacks she makes will become shorter, more nuanced. She'll work in unison with her soul guide to return to her homeland, where she's always been.

References

Woodman, M. 1993. *Conscious Femininity: Interviews with Marion Woodman (Studies in Jungian Psychology by Jungian Analysts)*. Inter City Books, Toronto Canada.

Woodman, M. & Mellick, J. 2001. *Coming Home to Myself: Reflections for Nurturing a Woman's Body and Soul*. Conari Press, San Francisco.

Chapter 8

A safe haven

Ulrika Ernvik

A safe haven. A harbour protected from storms and danger. Somewhere to put the anchor down and attach the ropes, to repair anything that has been broken, and to replace the stores of nutrition and fuel. A safe haven. A safe person. A safe adult. That is what every child needs. Actually, that is what every person needs. However, a child can't survive without a safe adult present in her life; an attachment person who waits with open arms and glad eyes. Who says: 'My little child. I love you. You are safe here. I will protect you. I will warm you. I will feed you. I will not leave you'. A person with a safe, reassuring, and calm voice who tells the child stories to remind them who they are, and sings songs to them which remind them that they are loved.

If a child is fortunate enough to have such a safe adult person in her life, she will understand that she is precious. She will be aware of her strengths and her value and the weakness that we all have within us will not scare her. When life becomes chaotic and stormy, she will know how to find her way to a safe harbour, and the worries will not eat her up. The child will find ways to navigate through storms, and she will always see the lamp from the lighthouse, through fog and darkness.

A safe adult needs to be very present during the child's first three years. During this time, billions of neurological pathways are developing in the brain of the child as neurons wire together based on the child's experiences. However, the safe adult needs to be there, both physically and emotionally present, throughout childhood. As the child brain will not mature to be an adult brain before the child is around 23 years old, it is not only during the first three years that the child needs the presence of a safe adult brain. During her pre-school years, her school years, her teenage years, and into her young adulthood, the child needs the presence and support of safe adults who love her, see her, and are there for her – physically and emotionally. If the child experiences that there is always a safe haven to sail in to, her brain will learn how to lead her into safety and calm. If she does not get this experience, she will feel lost and impressions and emotions will easily overwhelm her. When she feels lost, it may be hard for the child to navigate safely in life, to set up boundaries, make wise decisions, to repair herself after storms and disasters, to be resilient, and to build in well-being and joy in her life.

DOI: 10.4324/9781003533665-8

As the child receives impressions from around her and within her, her brain needs help to process information and emotions as they arise. The immature child brain cannot do this on its own. When impressions are multiple, new, strong, and/or heightened, they can be overwhelming and frightening. When emotions are strong and intense they can also be overwhelming and intimidating. In these moments, that occur on a daily basis, the child needs to borrow the safe adult brain to regulate what is going on within her. This is what we call co-regulation. A child cannot regulate herself. She needs to do so with a safe adult.

When fear, loneliness, and shame overwhelm us, the three parts of the brain – the thinking brain, the emotional brain, and the reactional brain – disconnect from each other. We are overcome by emotions, but can't process or make sense of our feelings, far less listen to their messages. We just react – which is a beneficial response to danger. But just reacting is not helpful if we continue to be under stress day after day, month after month. A disconnected brain can't learn, can't listen effectively, can't express itself, and can't interact in a healthy way with others. In our emotional brain, the social structures – what is called the social engagement system – are embedded. These systems do not function when our brain is disconnected.

What happens to a child who is left at boarding school? If she received safety and experienced a safe haven before she left home, and if there is an adult that the child feels safe with welcoming her and being there for her, she might do well at boarding school. However, it is hard for an adult to be emotionally present and available to many children at the same time. It is unlikely the child will feel that there is a safe adult there for her when she needs it in a boarding environment.

In addition, a great deal is happening in the child's brain at around the age of nine. Those who are left at boarding school before that age often have a harder time finding safety than those who are left after the age of ten. I went to boarding school as a ten-year-old. It was a small Swedish boarding school in a village in the jungle of Congo. There were only about 15 of us and our dorm parents took good care of us. They sat at our bedside to say goodnight, saw what we needed and protected us. But even though we were such a small group of children, it was still hard for them to be as present for us as we needed. They had many different responsibilities besides being dorm parents, and they could not provide a sense of present safety the whole time. They did not know each one of us well enough to read our faces and understand our needs. They could not protect us from everything.

In our brains we each have an amygdala – actually we have two, one in each hemisphere of the brain. The amygdala has an important job: to spy for danger. The amygdala perceives anything that is new or foreign as dangerous. It reacts if we are lonely, or if the people around us have angry faces, angry voices, or move their bodies in ways that communicate that they don't like us. The amygdala also reacts if something happens unexpectedly, or if there are sudden, loud sounds. When the amygdala reacts it activates our stress response. When our stress response is activated we first try to find safety. We look for a safe place and a safe person – a safe haven. If we can't find safety, the fight or flight response is activated to give us strength in our arms so we can fight, or in our legs so that we can run, and in our jaws so we can scream for help. If we cannot fight, or if we are unable to run and scream, the energy that was built up in our bodies will be stuck. We become frozen or paralysed; we can't move either our bodies or our thoughts. We might feel a great deal, but we can't process our emotions, or we might feel numb. If this state persists we may become traumatised. Shame has filled us and we are lonely; very, very lonely.

In the frozen state, we need the presence of a safe person. A child needs a safe adult. In the presence of such an adult the child's nervous system can move from the freeze state to the fight or flight state, and then to a state of safety and calmness. The interesting thing is that we can't move straight from the freeze state to a state of safety. We need to move our bodies, to use up the energy we received to protect ourselves. During an ordinary day, our nervous system moves back and forth in between the different states. If we, as children with the help of safe adults, found our way back to safety again and again following stressful and scary events, our nervous system will learn to find its way back to a state of safety. We will have internalised that safe adult.

In boarding school we were alone. Most of us did not have a safe adult present with whom we could regulate our nervous systems. We may have become stuck in a fight/flight response or a freeze/paralysis response. Our social engagement systems might have closed down so that it was hard for us to give and receive love and care. However, it is never too late to give ourselves what we did not receive as children. By going back to the memories where we felt lonely and abandoned, shameful and scared, we can open up the memory capsule and weave in to it what we needed at that time. Whatever we imagine, the brain will perceive as real. We do not forget what really happened, but as the presence of a safe person is imagined and woven into the memory, new neurological pathways will be established in our brains, and this will affect how we live, think, and feel in the present. When we feel the presence of safety our bodies, we will start to feel differently. We can feel safe and secure and able to rest.

Memories connected with loneliness, fear, and shame have a tendency to fly around in our minds and they do not come to a place of stillness and peace. They make sure we do not forget them by disturbing us in different ways. When we weave safety into the memories they will calm down. They do not have to disturb us any longer. The capsule where the memory is stored can now be closed, and the memory can find its place on the timeline of our lives.

Stories are a beautiful way to help the memories to find their rightful place. Stories help us to see what has been, what is, and what will come. They remind us about who we are and who we can be. Stories can help us to see that we are connected to others, to ourselves, and to the web of life. In boarding school no one was available to tell us the stories we needed to hear about ourselves. No one reminded us about who we were and who we could be. We need to make up for all those years of lost stories. The stories no one told us then we can now tell ourselves. These stories about the lonely child who made it through, about tears and laughter, bad dreams, and good dreams need to be told. In my professional experience, when the stories about the hard stuff have been told, room is made for the stories about the good stuff.

We can also cultivate acts of triumph. The actions we wanted and needed to do then, but could not, because we were too lonely, too weak, or too small, we can now take. We can fight and run, scream, and shout, protect ourselves and set up healthy boundaries. We can also protect others and tell the perpetrators of hurt the truth. We can laugh and dance, climb up in the highest tree and dive into the deepest water. Our bodies want and need to get their power back; the power we have over ourselves.

There are many experiences that are too hard for children, and that no child should have to experience. Boarding school is one of them – or it can be one of them. However, if there are safe adults present, if the child is not too young, if there are small groups of children and safe adults living together, and if there is an awareness among all adults involved, the boarding school experience does not have to be a hard experience.

So what can we, as adults, do to make sure that the children in our care do have safe adults around them? Here are a few suggestions:

- Consider wisely what schooling option will be the best for your child at different ages.
- Don't send children to boarding school until they are ready for it. How do we know when they are ready? Will they ever be? Well, some children will never be. Some children might be. I strongly believe that it is best for a child to stay with their parents if the parents are safe for the child, if the educational option involved with staying with the parents is good enough, and if there is a community with peers that the child can socialise with.
- If we send children to boarding school we need to identify at least two adults that the child can feel safe with who will make themselves physically and emotionally available to the child. We also need to find good communication and living arrangements that help the child and their parents to stay in touch with each other and to spend time together on a regular basis.
- If the family has another language and culture to that of the boarding school, we need to find out how the child can keep and develop her family language and culture, so that she is able to live well in her passport country as an adult. We need to set up long-term goals that include the ability for the child to thrive as an adult in their passport country because that is the only country we know for sure will receive our children as adults.
- Do what you can to make sure that the boarding school will create a safe experience for your child. Ask the school about their child protection policy. How does the school work to ensure safety in all areas for the child during the school day and in the dormitory or boarding house? Talk with the child before she leaves for boarding school about what she can do if she does not feel safe. Talk about boundaries, and the right to set up boundaries. Decide how you can be in touch with each other on a regular basis. Do what you can to get to know the staff at

the dormitory or boarding house so that you can make informed judgements about your child's safety. Don't hesitate to act if you get any signs of your child not being, or not feeling, safe.

- Practice with the child what she can do if she feels unsafe or lonely. Who can she contact and how?
- Teach your child good life skills such as the importance of sleep, exercise, outdoor time, and limited screen time. Help your child to be aware about the balance she needs between social time and time on her own. Teach her that self-care is the best way to thrive both academically and in life in general. Many hours sitting, and studying late into the night can lead to depression and anxiety.
- We need, as parents, to befriend our own emotions, and to understand what triggers our own stress response and moves us into the fight/flight or freeze response. When we know and understand ourselves, we can guide our children to better understand themselves and develop strategies that help them move into a state of safety and calm.
- We need to learn to tell stories that help our children navigate life. Stories can develop safety and joy. Over a number of years, I have developed an approach called 'SafetyStories' as a way to assist parents and others to help children process what they go through. By asking 'Who do you imagine would come and be with you and help you when you feel lonely and vulnerable?', we can give the child an amazing tool to calm herself and to heal from traumatic events. When we imagine something, the same neurological pathways are activated in the brain as if the experience were real. Imagined safety cannot be a substitute for real safety, but it can be an additional safety in moments of loneliness. By retelling a child's story – what the child experienced that was hard woven together with what she experienced as imagined safety came in – the child is at less risk of becoming stuck in unhelpful reactions.
- We need to remind ourselves that as parents we are the most important adults in our children's lives, and we are responsible for nurturing the relationship with our children. We need to make sure that we continue to be a safe haven for our children under all circumstances. We need to remind ourselves how stressful it can be for children to be away from their parents.
- We need to involve children and teenagers in the decisions we make. We need to be sensitive to how they experience their situation. Let the child know before leaving for boarding school that if she feels that the boarding school is not working, you will, together, find other options.
- Make sure you know what fills your child with a sense of feeling loved, and what stresses her. Fill your child with unconditional love, again and again, both when she is close by and when she is far away in boarding school.

Index

abandonment xiv, 2, 12, 15, 33, 39, 72, 77, 86–87, 89, 91, 104, 112–115, 119, 126, 144, 148–149, 163

abuse xiv, 1, 5, 12, 16–17, 19, 25–27, 47, 50, 61, 74, 80, 86, 92, 119

academic achievement 86, 88, 95, 99–100, 125

ACEs (adverse childhood experiences) 5–6, 12–18, 22, 25–26, 129, 134, 136, 138, 140–141

addiction 2, 43

adult ex-boarders, affect of boarding school on 1, 4, 6–7, 12–13, 16, 18, 31–32, 41, 45, 60, 74, 77, 115–116, 121–122, 124, 126, 128, 137–138

advantages of TCK life 24

amnesia 31, 38, 44, 51, 53–54, 58, 64, 72, 77–78, 81, 93–94, 102, 113, 134

amygdala 162

anima and animus xv, 7, 146, 153

attachment xiv, 1–2, 10–13, 15, 17–19, 26, 145–146, 148–149, 157, 161

authority figures 2, 98, 154, 158

bedwetting 54,65,81,120,153

bereavement 32, 112, 114, 126

Boarding School Action coalition 18

boarding school survivors xiv, 1, 6, 11, 15, 17–18, 30, 77–78, 105, 121, 128

Boarding School Syndrome 1, 6, 10–11, 13, 15–16, 102

body image 3, 124–125, 150–151

brain development 10–11, 140, 145, 161–162, 165

British education system 1, 9, 19, 34, 146

British class system xiii, 2, 12–14, 82, 106, 126, 141, 146

bullying 2, 12, 15, 19, 26, 31, 34, 47, 54, 74, 78–79, 96, 118–119, 123, 128, 137–138, 140–141, 146, 158

captivity 1, 27, 112, 116–120, 126

caregiving role 27, 40, 134, 145

CCK (cross-cultural kid) 31, 128, 141

censorship 30, 40, 73–74, 118, 124

character building xiv, 9–10, 20, 45, 146, 148

class *see* British class system

colonial xiv, 25, 42, 52, 61, 146

control: institutional xiv, 3, 11, 23, 46, 111, 117–119, 122–123, 125, 139; punishment 18, 36, 49, 53, 68, 73, 87, 94, 96, 110, 114, 117–119, 121, 131, 139, 146

co-regulation 10–11, 162–163

courage xiii, 10, 15, 17–18, 20, 91, 147

crying 36–37, 49, 72, 77–78, 87–88, 95, 102–103, 107, 113–114, 117, 147–148

denial 10, 16–19, 114, 116

depression *see* mental health

development, childhood 11, 16, 22, 26, 67, 116, 138, 140

difference 3, 6–7, 14, 31, 52, 68, 119, 140–141, 148

diplomats, children of 24, 84, 140, 146

dissociation 38, 41, 112, 121, 126, 138

distress 1–2, 10–11, 13, 15, 17–19, 30, 48, 57–59, 71, 114–115, 122, 126, 135, 149

dormitory 36–38, 44–46, 48–49, 53–54, 56–58, 65, 69, 72–74, 78, 84, 88, 93–95, 106, 109, 117–118, 125, 131, 137, 148, 151, 153, 162, 164–165

double burden experience 27

double standards 125

For Product Safety Concerns and Information please contact our EU
representative GPSR@taylorandfrancis.com
Taylor & Francis Verlag GmbH, Kaufingerstraße 24, 80331 München, Germany

www.ingramcontent.com/pod-product-compliance
Lightning Source LLC
Chambersburg PA
CBHW062031270326
41929CB00014B/2397